Simple & Direct

# Simple & Direct

## A Rhetoric for Writers

*Revised Edition*

JACQUES BARZUN

*1817*

HARPER & ROW, PUBLISHERS, New York
Cambridge, Philadelphia, San Francisco, London
Mexico City, São Paulo, Singapore, Sydney

Grateful acknowledgment is made for permission to reprint the following:

Exerpts from pp. 128–131 of *Working and Thinking on the Waterfront* by Eric Hoffer. Copyright © 1969 by Eric Hoffer. Reprinted by permission of Harper & Row, Publishers, Inc.

"Aristotle on Detective Fiction" from *Unpopular Opinions* by Dorothy L. Sayers. Copyright © 1947 by Dorothy L. Sayers. Published by Harcourt Brace Jovanovich, Inc. Reprinted by permission of Watkins, Loomis Agency Inc.

"Language Defined" from *Language* by Edward Sapir. Copyright 1921 by Harcourt Brace Jovanovich, Inc.; renewed 1949 by Jean V. Sapir. Reprinted by permission of Harcourt Brace Jovanovich, Inc.

"Hints for Sawing" from *Tools and How to Use Them for Woodworking* by Alfred P. Morgan. Copyright 1948 by Alfred P. Morgan. Reprinted by permission of Crown Publishers, Inc.

Exercepts from the Journal of Fred Dodge from *Under Cover for Wells Fargo* by Carolyn Lake. Copyright © 1969 by Carolyn Lake. Published by Houghton Mifflin Company. Reprinted by permission of Carolyn Lake.

"How to Be Respected at an Inn, Hotel or Pub" by Hilaire Belloc, reprinted by permission of A. D. Peters and Company, Ltd.

"Writing Less—and Better?" by Red Smith, reprinted by permission of *The New York Times.*

Reproduction of photograph of page proof correction from *Eugénie Grandet* by Honoré de Balzac. Reprinted by permission of The Pierpont Morgan Library.

Library of Congress Cataloging in Publication Data

Barzun, Jacques, 1907–
    Simple & Direct.

    Includes index.
    1. English language—Rhetoric.  I. Title.  II. Title:
Simple and direct.
PE1408.B436   1984        808'.042        83-48936
ISBN 0-06-015283-4          85 86 87 88 10 9 8 7 6 5 4 3 2 1
ISBN 0-06-091122-0 (pbk.)   85 86 87 88 10 9 8 7 6 5 4 3 2 1

# Contents

# Preface
## to the Revised Edition

The reception of this little guide by the public has been so warm and widespread (some readers report reading it mainly for pleasure) that the publisher has summoned me to "bring it up to date." The chief points, the good advice, are of course permanent; if sound yesterday, they will be tomorrow. But in writing at any time, new confusions and absurdities are cropping up, and it is these—or some of the worst of them—that I have added two chapters about, numbers VII and VIII. These new pages will serve as a guide through contemporary usage and at the same time supply an informal review of the main principles.

I have in addition tried to assuage one pained complaint—it was too anguished to be a criticism—having to do with the periodic exercises consisting of faulty sentences to set straight: I failed to provide the "correct answers." Quite a few readers evidently remembered with longing their algebra books with answers at the back. They did not believe me when I said that language is *not* an algebra and that there is no single right answer to any given predicament with words. A proof of this truth is that one "solution" is always open—that of starting all over again with a different construction. In algebra you can never say: "This problem baffles me; let me instead multiply $a + b$ by $a + b$, which I know I can manage."

One must add that in language two different constructions or phrasings for the same thought will rarely say exactly the same thing; so in rewriting, one must take care to adjust verbs and modifiers until one's original intention is satisfied.

Despite these truths, I have yielded a little to the demand for "answers." (It is churlish to play deaf to public outcry.) In this revised edition I give hints and leads to possible ways out of some of the bad corners the writers quoted in the exercises worked themselves into.

I have also corrected errors and misprints, tried to improve diction, replaced one of the "refreshers" (extracts from good writers), and added two more for the reader to study and enjoy.

# Preface

My qualifications for putting forward the hints and guidelines in this book are altogether accidental and practical. I have never taught a course in composition. But for over half a century, I have almost continually been engaged in editing the work of students, colleagues, and friends. In dealing with the students, graduate and undergraduate, I have had the special obligation of finding ways to arouse their dormant attention to words, so that they could in the end edit themselves.

These students had of course been exposed to one or another method of teaching grammar and writing, and some even had a touch of author's pride in their essays. But almost in proportion as their minds were bright and strong and full of interest in their chosen topic, they assumed that written expression was a minor matter compared to "the facts" and "the findings of my research." Their previous study of writing they had endured like vaccination—and it had not taken; they did not even suspect that it held any intellectual interest. In the result, the papers they produced suffered variously from obscurity, incoherence, ambiguity, jargon, pedantry, mannerism, or downright illiteracy— to say nothing of haphazard organization and fitfully recognizable spelling and punctuation.

That this writing made dull and hard reading goes without saying, and saying it was a blow to their ego. They were, many of them, adults, married, fathers and mothers of small children, ready to "qualify" as professional people. It was impossible to require or even suggest yet another course in the all-too-familiar rudiments. It was therefore necessary to help each one individually and in such a way as to enable the patient to cure himself as soon as possible.

The root difficulty in all cases was the state of being blind and deaf to words—not seeing the words for the prose. Being adults, they had forgotten what every child understands, which is that giving or taking a meaning is not automatic and inevitable. In reading, the adult merely thinks that such-and-such a writer is "difficult" or "boring," "long-winded" or "involved," as if these were inborn traits of character and not failures of craftsmanship. About their own work, writers of this description are either complacent—*they* can read it all right—or apologetic and resigned, again as if the trouble lay in their genes.

Clearly, this state of affairs is not limited to degree candidates in higher education. Everybody complains of poor writing in business, government, and the professions. Even in the writing trades—publishing, journalism, scholarship, and science—the groaning about prose that is muddled, overlong, "dangerously misleading," is continual; and the complaint, naturally, is always of the other fellow's carelessness or incompetence. How, then, begin to reverse the attitude that allows so much *technological failure* to persist?

For mature minds a new plan was needed; its object: *to resensitize the mind to words.* Not a multitude of rules or topics, but a few large notions under which many kinds of trouble can be grouped. To make the point of each principle stick, continual illustration *and discussion,* so that the habit of analyzing what is said, what you say, what I say, becomes second nature. After that, the "problem of writing" does not of course disappear, but it is met with confidence and skill, in the spirit of the good workman, never scamping the job but doing his best with native talent and acquired technique.

This book, then, is an introduction to the art of becoming self-conscious and analytic about words. A few things follow: nobody is expected to remember all the advice and exhortation given in these pages. Nobody need agree with all of it. Part of the technique of good writing is to have prejudices for or against certain words and expressions. Ambrose Bierce, the great storyteller, once wrote a little handbook called *Write It Right.* Half of what he says is unacceptable to me, but unless he had felt strongly and been led to reason and argue about what is right, he could not have written as well as he did. All artists argue about their ways of performing—the painters about color and composition, the musicians about sounds and form. This is taken for granted, but because writing is at the mercy of the largest number of amateurs—almost the entire population—it seems foolish to "make a fuss" about this phrasing or that.

The reader who comes to this book prepared to make a fuss, that is, discover what he or she thinks and feels about this or that phrasing, will benefit most. But no one should try to take all these suggestions and arguments in one long swallow, or suffocation may ensue. There is a great deal to know about writing one's own tongue, as there is about Russian or mathematics; it cannot be learned in six easy lessons. Read one section at a time, ponder the examples, do the exercises (either on paper or mentally), go back to an earlier passage when a subject comes up again in a new context—in short, use the book like a person to listen to and *argue with*. For as Yeats said, "The correcting of prose is endless, because it has no fixed laws; a poem comes right with a click, like a box." The attentive reader will no doubt find here violations of my own precepts, some intentional, some inadvertent; he should try to tell them apart, since his purpose is to discover error and also to understand why, when there are "no fixed laws," one wording is better than another. Preferring, choosing for good reasons whenever one is facing words is the very practice of self-criticism here advocated, and which alone leads to improved writing.

Words, therefore, as well as things, claim the care of an author. Every man has often found himself deficient in the power of expression, big with ideas which he could not utter, and unable to impress upon his reader the image existing in his own mind.

—Dr. Johnson

I sometimes think that writing is like driving sheep down a road. If there is any gate to the left or right, the readers will most certainly go into it.

—C. S. Lewis

. . . here and there a touch of good grammar for picturesqueness.

—Mark Twain

# Introduction

You want to be a writer, or let us rather say: you want to write. Or again, you do not want to write but are required to. In any of these cases you face Difficulty. The trouble is not "to learn to write," because you already know how to form letters and words and you have written prose for years. But you probably need to write better, or would like to—with less pain each time and with fewer faults and errors. Writing always presents problems, dilemmas, some of which beset all writers, even great ones; but there is no need to be baffled by *all* the difficulties every time you write. The effort to which you are being invited is to learn the usual pitfalls and how they are avoided, while also learning the devices—tricks of the trade—by which writing can be both improved and made easier than it seems to most people. With alertness and practice, writing can in fact become enjoyable, like physical exercise or playing the guitar.

By the same effort, you may also learn to be clear and to afford pleasure to those who read what you write. Bear in mind that the person you address, friend or stranger, is like you in his capacity for being bored by dull writing and irritated by what refuses to make sense. Consider the following exchange of words between persons whom we will call Q. and A.

Q. There was one other you remember
A. There was like I said
Q. And the one you knew I mean the one
A. The one yes that's the one I knew otherwise

1

Q. But not his name just another

A. Yes like I said

Why is the meaning of these few plain words so hard to follow? The dialogue, as you may have guessed, took place in court. You must imagine it as very brisk—a series of mutual interruptions, which the stenotypist took down as so many spoken words and nothing else. Before they could be printed for the report of the trial, punctuation had to be supplied, in order to reproduce the connection or disconnection of ideas. For the intended meaning is not apparent and how to punctuate not obvious. In the first question, for instance, did the attorney say:

"There *was* one other—you remember?" or:

"There was *one* other, you remember?" or:

"There was one other [that] you *remember?*"

In speech the pauses, stresses, rising inflections, and other uses of the voice and facial expression help to make the meaning clear. There is also context, which is that part of the entire situation which explains another part, by ruling out such doubts as are expressed in the three possibilities just cited.

But even with correct underlining and punctuation, which partly make up for the indications of voice and face in speech, the chances of misunderstanding remain great, because the art of writing differs at many points from the practice of speaking words. Even in court it takes a great many questions to work the meaning free and clear of entanglements. If you observe your conversation with friends, you will note the same difficulty. Few people organize their thoughts and words in fully intelligible remarks. It seems easier to use a sort of oral shorthand and rely on the listener to jump to the right conclusion. He often fails. You correct him or he asks you questions to settle his uncertainty.

With a written text there is no opportunity to ask questions. All the reader has is words and punctuation marks. It follows that these must be set down right—right for the purpose and right for the reader. *Rhetoric is the craft of setting down words and marks right;* or again: Rhetoric shows you how to put words together so that the reader not simply may but must grasp your meaning.

Rhetoric in its essence is not concerned with your reason for writing. It is not for "formal writing" or "important writing" or "official writing." Leaving a note on the door for the milkman, or sending news to the family, or translating one's confused feelings of loneliness and longing into a love letter—all these alike make demands on rhetoric. The word *rhetoric* comes from a Greek root meaning *word* or *I say,* and for centuries the term was used for the art of haranguing masses of men in the open air on political or legal subjects. Now the meaning has shifted with changes in civilization and it refers chiefly to the art of making oneself understood in the modern situation of continually having to put words on paper for the perusal of readers known or unknown.

ALL GOOD WRITING IS SELF-TAUGHT

Almost any professional writer will tell you that nobody can teach another person to write. That is true. But all writers admit that they were helped by criticism; somebody showed them the effect of what they had written—the unintended bad effect. In doing so the critic pointed out where the trouble lay and perhaps what its cause was. Since troubles of this kind are not unique to each performer, it is possible to discuss types of faults and suggest how to correct or avoid them. That is all that a handbook of rhetoric does.

The truth remains that the would-be writer, using a book or a critic, must teach himself. He must learn to spot his own errors and work out his own ways of removing them: "This is the bad phrase [sentence, connective, transition]; what do I put in its place, or how do I get around it?" Every writer asks himself this sort of question a hundred or more times in each extended piece of writing. You do not, I hope, imagine that I sat down one day and, beginning with the word *Introduction* on page 1, wrote straight on to the last word on page 275. On the following page is a photocopy of one of the manuscript sheets of this book. It is rather messy, yet does not show all the corrections the first draft required; more were made on two successive typescripts and again in the printed proof.

The first job, then, is to look at what one has spontaneously written and go over it critically. This is not easy. The mind tends

Q.  And the one you knew I mean that one

A.  The one yes. That's the one I knew otherwise too

Q.  But not his name just another

A.  Yes like I said

*is the meaning of*

Why are these few plain words so hard to follow? The dialogue, as you have guessed, took place in court. You must imagine it as a very briskly a series of mutual interruptions, with which the stenotypist took down as so many spoken words & nothing else. When they came to be printed for the trial report of the trial, punctuation had to be supplied, in order to reproduce the emphases, the connection or disconnection of ideas. Even so, the exact meaning is not apparent. In the first question, for instance, did the attorney say:

"That was one other — you remember?" or:

"There was *one* other, you remember?" or:

"There was one other [that] you remember?"

In speech there are only pauses, stresses, rising inflections, & other uses of the voice & facial expression to make the meaning clear. There is also context, which is that part of the entire situation which helps to explain another part by ruling out such doubts as are expressed in the three possibilities just quoted.

But even with correct underlining & punctuation, even with the usual indications of the voice, in speech, the chances of confusion & misunderstanding remain great. That is why in court it takes so many questions on the same point to work the meaning free & clear of entanglements.

to run along the groove of one's *intention* and overlooks the actual *expression*. That is why writers usually put their work aside for some days and go back to revise when the *ideas* have faded from the memory and they can scrutinize the *wording* with a stranger's eye. But this delay has one drawback. If the first draft is not reread on the very day of writing, one or more phrases may later prove incomprehensible, their meaning irrecoverable. Hence the first brushing up while one's intent is fresh in the mind. As you can see on the facsimile page, the so-called first draft is not an entirely uncorrected piece of work.

We are thus led to ask what the writer looks for and how he trains himself to look for it. The answer is: he makes himself habitually aware of words, positively self-conscious about them, careful to follow what they say and not jump to what they might mean. Suppose he finds a headline in the paper which reads: "City Bottleneck Soon to Be Broken." * If he has the slightest humor in him, a concrete image will flash before his mind's eye and he will laugh. *Bottleneck* as a metaphor means *traffic jam, congestion, slow exit.* But as soon as the idea of breaking is joined to this figurative expression, the bottleneck becomes literal again and one hears the tinkle of falling glass. This danger from metaphor everybody has heard about, but it is not the worst. There are hundreds of other pitfalls to be avoided, confusions to be dispelled, common errors to be rooted out of one's verbal habits, before one's prose can be called good. And I mean by good reasonably clear and straightforward. These truths suggest the scope of the task that lies ahead.

THE WRITER'S ATTITUDE: SELF-CRITICISM

In saying that a person who wants to write adequately must put his mind on words to the point of self-consciousness, I was not exaggerating. Words for him must become objects in themselves,

---

* All the sentences and headlines I use as examples in the text or in the exercises were actually written in books, periodicals, or student work. The names of persons and a few other irrelevant details have sometimes been changed or removed. Only in illustrating the use of technical terms have I occasionally made up phrases or short sentences of my own.

as well as automatic signallers of meaning. (Notice *signallers,* which I have just used: have you ever seen it? Is there such a word? Why not *signals?* Explain to yourself the difference between the shorter and the longer form—and why not just *signs?* If questions like these leave you undecided, reach for the dictionary.)

What a fuss over a word! Yes, but let me say it again: the price of learning to use words is the development of an acute self-consciousness. Nor is it enough to pay attention to words only when you face the task of writing—that is like playing the violin only on the night of the concert. You must attend to words when you read, when you speak, when others speak. Words must become ever present in your waking life, an incessant concern, like color and design if the graphic arts matter to you, or pitch and rhythm if it is music, or speed and form if it is athletics. Words, in short, must be *there,* not unseen and unheard, as they probably are and have been up to now. It is proper for the ordinary reader to absorb the meaning of a story or description as if the words were a transparent sheet of glass. But he can do so only because the writer has taken pains to choose and adjust them with care. They were not glass to him, but mere lumps of potential meaning. He had to weigh and assemble and fuse them before his purposed meaning could shine through.

If you will set about mastering this rebellious material, the reward—I can guarantee it—is that you will soon find words interesting. Making them do their proper work will become a hobby. You will catch yourself reading the ads in buses to improve them and injecting sense into the directions on the bottle, because you will recognize the types of mistake the writer fell into.

But ads and printed instructions and your friends' stammerings are not enough. Reading abundantly, in good books, is indispensable. It is only in good writing that you will find how words are best used, what shades of meaning they can be made to carry, and by what devices (or the lack of them) the reader is kept going smoothly or bogged down in confusion. You may think the sense of motion and pleasure depends on the subject matter. That is not so. It depends on tone, rhythm, sentence structure, selection, and organization. The *com-position* of all the elements of writing is what occasions the reader's pleasure while ensuring his comprehension.

The writer, consciously or not, writes for someone. He begins by being his own audience, in the sense of having to act toward himself like a demanding reader. His perpetual question is: do these words, does this paragraph, does the entire piece, suit my present purpose? The purpose at large is always the same: it is to be understood aright. Reader and writer have both wasted their time if mental darkness is the only result of their separate efforts. And—this is the very ethics of writing—the reader's part of the effort must never become a strain. You have no doubt attended speeches or lectures that consisted of a paper read aloud. These are often dull and hard to follow, not because of poor delivery or poor material, but because of a defect in the rhetoric used. The person on the platform is not making a speech, but reading an essay; that is, he has neglected the special needs of listeners. The syntax, rhythm, diction, and other elements of the prose do not suit the occasion.

The adapting of words to needs, this goal of *suitability,* about which the writer continually challenges himself, naturally breaks up into a great many particular questions—is this the suitable term or form? the suitable order of ideas? the suitable length? and so on. At every point there is a choice to be made ("Do I use *signs, signals,* or *signallers?"*) and behind the decision there must be a reason. For to acquire self-consciousness also means finding reasons for what you do with each word and being able to state them. Granted that after a while most of the choices are made by reflex action on seeing what the trouble is, that desirable speed and sureness come only with practice. And practice gets under way only when one has learned to *see a choice wherever there is one.*

Your inner response to what I have been saying may be: "That's all very well, but it's hard enough to make a start on a piece of work and push through to the end without getting into a nervous state over each miserable word." I should not blame you if the prospect I have raised of endless "choices" made you groan. But hold on! You already make choices as you write; only, you are not aware of them, and so probably make them blindly. How do I know? I know because I am a writer myself and because I have watched students writing exams. You do not run on like a streaming fount of words any more than they or I do. You pause and chew your pencil or x out phrases on the typewriter. You hesitate because you feel your thoughts leading you this way or that, and you must choose—or else halt altogether. When you get stuck it is no doubt because you are facing so many possibilities that they cancel each other out. Your mind, you feel, is a blank.

I am not proposing to add to this paralyzing excess, but to suggest ways of sorting it out, of testing the words and forms that crowd your attention—or that refuse to come because of that crowding. Without damage to your intuition of what is good or suitable, you will find yourself developing principles of choice, devices for substitution, heightened powers of awareness about the work in hand. In law, medicine, diplomacy, business administration, scientific research, and other professions where writing is frequent, the subject matter itself often provides the writer with such decisions and devices ready-made. These are the technical terms that come easily to mind and must be used correctly or not at all. The undertaking proposed to you in this book is to acquire the same control over common words that the professional has over the technical—and this for whatever purpose you may wish to use words in future.

# Diction
## or Which Words to Use

I

The choices I have just mentioned as occurring over and over again in the course of writing may be sorted for convenience into six groups. They form the main headings of this book.

The first is naturally the choice of words taken singly. Words are endowed with certain properties—their meaning, their sound, their length, their past (rosy or ugly), their acquired suggestiveness. For example, in the first sentence of this book I wrote: "You want to be a writer"; and I added immediately: "or let us rather say: you want to write." The reason for the afterthought lies in the suggestion carried by the word *writer*. Its bare meaning is: someone who writes, but its implied and predominant meaning is: someone who writes professionally; so that "you want to be a writer" might elicit from a good many of my readers the rejoinder "I do not!"

Fortunately, as in this case, it takes no special effort to recognize a large number of these secondary meanings; every native speaker knows them and avoids misusage without a second thought. But we shall see when we come to speak of Connotation that people with their eyes open—good readers—respond to secondary meanings that unskilled writers do not suspect. The reader at first is puzzled by the intrusion of the irrelevant idea, then shakes his head at the writer's clumsiness.

Another property possessed by words is their ability to combine in some ways but not in others. They have "hooks" reaching out in certain directions only, which enable or forbid two or more words to go together. Right now, for example, I started to write: "which enable or prevent them to go together." But one cannot say *prevent them to go;* one must say *prevent them from going.* And this *from* in turn would rule out the use of the earlier *enable.* Hence *forbid* to replace *prevent.*

That bit of juggling was easy and quick—it did not reach the paper—not because I had run into the same obstacle before, but because this type of choice recurs very frequently: will my two verbs go with the same preposition? Making sure that they will becomes automatic—provided one starts by being sure of each verb and preposition, which is to say, of idiomatic English. The need for complete familiarity with all the words and idioms one wants to use is evident and unarguable.

"ANYTHING GOES"—IS IT TRUE?

You may, to be sure, come across persons and books that do seem to argue against this conclusion. They maintain that in these enlightened days the idea of right and wrong in language has been discarded. The reasoning goes like this: Since language is bound to change and since some of the changes in the past have come from errors gradually accepted, new errors should not be criticized or restrained. This is a fallacy, for it says: "Some regrettable things have been assimilated after a time; therefore all must be accepted at once." Nobody would reason in this way about disease: it is not welcomed, but fought to the very last. The alteration of a language takes place by chance; no one is in charge of it; but writers are in charge of their work; they exercise care, both to simplify their task and out of courtesy to their readers; and this care acts as a restraint upon others' ignorance or carelessness.

It is perhaps the desire to be emancipated from "old-fashioned rules" (which never had much currency outside grammar books) that accounts for the exaggeration of "anything goes." Apart from dialects, which also have rules of their own, such combinations as *we is, she do, they comes,* advertise their wrongness immediately. The foreigner who spoke fluent English and who brought his hostess a box of chocolates on a hot summer day, saying,

"I'm very much afraid they are molten," had to be told that *molten* is a perfectly good word, but wrong as he used it: he must say *melted*.

All of us automatically distinguish the meanings of *struck* and *stricken, wooden* and *wooded, below* and *beneath, aft* and *after,* a *flashlight* and a *flashing light,* and thousands of other close and confusable terms. There is in principle no difference between these obvious possibilities of correct and incorrect use and the subtler ones about which writers take thought. The inattentive may suppose that there is no reason for the recommended choice or the established distinction, but the practiced writer knows that neglect of the fine points catches up with him and ties his hands later on. It is because of neglect that such words as *disinterested, deprecate, cohort, controversial, sensitive,* and others can no longer be used as freely as before. Misuse or overuse has robbed them of strict meaning in various contexts; the natural resources of the language have been depleted by a careless pollution.

Since usage, or the main stream of accepted meanings and forms, is not ascertainable with complete precision—even the biggest dictionary cannot list all the uses and all the variations of sense—every writer must make up his mind about borderline cases between Accepted and Unacceptable. Being highly conscious of words, he decides in the light of his experience, which includes wide reading, what he can tolerate and what he must do without. For example, I do without *contact* as a verb because of its connotation of surfaces touching, and though I read *disinterested* in the sense of *uninterested* if I have to, I stick to its former meaning in my own prose, because no other word supplies it. But I have given up on *restive,* which used to mean *stubborn, refusing to budge,* and is now a (needless) synonym for *restless, uneasy, impatient.*

In the choice of single words one is often advised to consider the level of discourse to which one or another belongs. Some words, it is said, are formal, others informal (or colloquial), and still others slang. The division between the first and the third is also indicated by the words *standard* and *substandard,* the second sharing the characteristics of both. I shall have more to say on this subject in the section on Tone. Here the place of any term in the wide range between breeziness and solemnity will be assumed to be easily felt as soon as one really pays attention to words. No one capable of sympathy would write to a friend: "Sorry to hear your old man kicked the bucket."

A few unfamiliar (or overfamiliar) words may, of course, be mistaken now and then. In a published translation from a Greek classic, I found the expression *give it the go-by,* which is not quite in keeping with the tone of the rest—a slip. Besides judgment, one must also use caution and not throw in a term that sounds attractive but is not clearly known—it may explode into nonsense or worse in the eye of a knowledgeable reader. Thus in a metropolitan newspaper the profile of a newly appointed cabinet officer described him as "wholly unprepossessing." The phrase was clearly beyond the writer's grasp, since it was never put in to be insulting.

The test of what word to use, then, is made up of three questions:

Do I know what this word means *and suggests?*

Do I know what its quality or atmosphere is?

Do I know what its "hooks" are for linking it with other words?

When a writer of fiction chooses to characterize persons or scenes by using dialect, which, as I have said, has its own integrity, he must be thoroughly conversant with all its speechways, or someone will catch him out as incompetent: the same knowledge and the same accuracy of performance are required of the writer of standard speech.

### SIMPLE & DIRECT

Let us now come down to cases. The whole world will tell you, if you care to ask, that your words should be simple & direct. Everybody likes the other fellow's prose *plain.* It has even been said that we should write as we speak. That is absurd, as we know from the courtroom dialogue. Most speaking is not plain or direct, but vague, clumsy, confused, and wordy. This last fault appears in every transcript from taped conversation, which is why we say "*reduce* to writing." What is meant by the advice to write as we speak is to write *as we might* speak if we spoke extremely well. This means that good writing should not sound stuffy, pompous, highfalutin, totally unlike ourselves, but rather, well—"simple & direct."

Now, the simple words in the language tend to be the short ones that we assume all speakers know; and if familiar, they are likely to be direct. I say "tend to be" and "likely" because there are exceptions. For example, *bort,* meaning industrial diamond, is short and direct, but it is not simple in the sense of readily understood. *Emergency* is a long word; it is simple in that same sense of being familiar; but being also abstract, it is not direct like the concrete words for which it stands: *fire, accident,* or *hemorrhage.* (Query: Should the last word be replaced by *bleeding* [*to death*]? It is impossible to tell without knowing the context and the audience.) Our tentative conclusion, then, is:

Prefer the short word to the long; the concrete to the abstract; and the familiar to the unfamiliar. But:

Modify these guidelines in the light of the occasion, the full situation, which includes the likely audience for your words.

The French call *mot juste* the word that exactly fits. Why is that word generally so hard to find? The reasons are many. First, we do not always know what we mean and are too lazy to find out. "The handyman came and put a thing and in a second it was fixed." *Thing* is not the *mot juste.* If we really want to know how the object ("it") was *repaired* or *secured* (not *fixed,* which is ambiguous) we must be told whether the *thing* was a *nail, brad, dowel, rivet, tack, thumbtack, screw, staple, bolt, pin, cotter pin,* or other fastener. Use one of these words (with its proper verb in place of *put*) and the picture raised in our mind is clear—and we gain in addition a sense of confidence in the writer: he knows what he is talking about and he consults our convenience. That is the fundamental courtesy from the writer to the reader, matching the reader's courtesy of close attention to what is said.

Another reason for lack of simple directness is the clutter of vague words and "vogue words" filling our heads—e.g., *dimension, interface, gap* (as in *credibility gap, capability gap, reality gap*), *realistic, processing, replicate, operational,* and many more, usually Latin derivatives three or four syllables long. Such words or phrases are vague from the start or become so by vogue—overuse. They are in our heads because they are in fashion at the time. We hear them continually on television: hence they occur first when it is our turn to talk. In this regard, talk may be said to be the enemy of writing. If you observe yourself when on the point of writing, you will notice that the words rising spontaneously to your mind are not the hard, clear words of a lover of plain speech, but this mush of counterfeits and clichés. Observe further and you will see that most of these do not point to one definite object or idea, and rarely fit what they are paired with. Take three instances of *dimension* from the daily paper:

> It was a night when songs we have hummed and listened to for as long as we can remember took on a new dimension.

> The idea of a divided skirt has taken on new dimensions: it has been adapted for a one-piece dress.

> News of a plot to assassinate [the Mayor] has added a bizarre dimension to Philadelphia's embittered campaign.

The idea of *dimension* proper—measurable extent—is clearly absent from every one of these sentences, the one about the skirt that took on new dimensions being the most alarming. The presence of this vogue word proves that the writer could not be bothered to discover what he meant. He expects us to do this for him, but does not give us much of a clue.

⌘

First Principle: Have a point and make it by means of the best word.

We have only begun to look at words critically, but enough has been suggested to enable you to question the sentences below in the recommended way. Try to guess what the writers intended, and put it in simple-&-direct. After each "translation," find reasons for your choice of the words you substitute. By way of encouragement, examples of the procedure to be followed are supplied at intervals and also on pages 277–282.

1. To allow for the x-variable the values in Table 3 have been adjustmented. (*Adjusted* is enough: why make a verb out of the longer noun when the short form is in common use?)

2. The residence experience could be a revelation to you, too.

3. It is good to read in your news story of Nov. 16 that the Superintendent of Schools is about to make life more viable for members of his staff. (*More agreeable,* even *more livable.* The word *viable* is abstract and absolute. It says that the conditions for living have been met and life is thereby possible. Hence nothing can be made *more* viable. In the sentence under review, "the staff" is already alive, and the only question is whether its working conditions are tolerable. *Livable* in its figurative sense fits the case; *agreeable* goes one step further in the scale of explicitness and may be more than the writer wants to say.)

4. As of right now we don't anticipate any replication of the trouble.

5. The moment of truth in launching a new product is when the housewife does or doesn't give you the benefit of the credibility gap.

6. They said they had sought a meaningful dialogue on their demands which, as they made clear before, are non-negotiable. (*Meaningful* is usually quite meaning*less.* Does the writer mean *productive, fruitful, satisfactory, fair-minded?* It is hard to say; the word *dialogue* itself is too vague to suggest its proper epithet, and taken together with *non-negotiable* it lands the writer in self-contradiction; for what is there to discuss if the issues are not subject to negotiation? The only tenable sense is: "they faced their opponents with an ultimatum." This result is a good example of the way in which the criticism and simplifying of words discloses a hidden thought.)

7. It was a controverted production of *Huckleberry Finn* that came to the High School last night; all its previous notices have been controversial.

8. The attorney in requesting a suspended sentence asked the judge not to engage in genocide of minority groups.

9. Durable press adds a new dimension to wash and wear garments very much as stereo adds a new dimension to Hi-fi. (If we accept *durable press* as a technical term meaning that creases will remain where wanted and will not occur where not wanted, it would seem that this desirable *property, feature,* or *quality* of the garment is what is new about it. No *dimension* is involved. But what of *dimension* applied to stereo [phonic] music?)

10. The governor's office calls the figures conservative; the committee reporting the bill says this is unrealistic. We believe they are both victims of wishful thinking.

11. I have not myself been sending despatches, and therefore I feel a personal disinterest in the matter. Anything I say now is strictly non-operational.

12. Art critics have been positively apostolic in praise of his engravings.

13. Saying Yes to Life can arouse inner forces to help us discover new dimensions.

14. This month the Association will take a quantum jump into the world of tomorrow.

15. Stamps in this book have been gummed with a matte finish adhesive which permits the elimination of the separation tissues [U.S. Postal Service]. (This is really bad from stem to stern. The stamps have not been *gummed,* for that means licked and affixed to the envelope. *Matte adhesive* (versus *shiny adhesive*) is enough; leave out the *finish.* And what this change permits need not be put in so roundabout and puzzling a way, as if everyone for years had been plagued by separation tissues and tried to eliminate them. The simple thought is: "The stamps in this book will not stick together, because of the new adhesive used." The fiercest critic of government can then see for himself that no tissue is needed.)

16. Mint has also achieved great familiarity in the delicious creme de menthe parfait.

17. The pilot's instrument-scanning proficiency probably was degraded because of his lengthy absence from flying.

18. Cunard now has added a new dimension to winter cruising by giving you the option of visiting those faraway places without taking the whole World Cruise.

19. Surgery should only be advised for cancer of the organ in growths of a low degree of malignancy.

20. Critics have already waxed eloquently on the elegancies and efficiencies of the new theater.

THE NOUN PLAGUE

One of our guidelines said: Prefer the concrete word to the abstract. Follow that advice and you will see your prose gain in lucidity and force. Unnecessary abstraction is one of the worst faults of modern writing—the string of nouns held together by prepositions and relying on the passive voice to convey the enfeebled sense:

> The influence exerted by Christianity upon the arts extends to painting and sculpture insofar as their relationship to Christian religious experiences corresponds to that part of this experience which consists of images; and it extends to architecture, both with regard to edifices dedicated to worship and to the settlement of religious communities.

This "noun plague," as it has been called, is a by-product of scientific writing. In trying to remain impersonal and detached, it becomes flabby and obscure, because the lack of agents and of strong verbs deprives the sentence of its due motive power and needed signposts. Try beginning with a forceful subject: *Christianity* . . . has done something or other to . . . *painting* and *sculpture.* These are the two points of interest for the mind—go on from there. To be sure, Christianity is an abstraction, but not in the sense of *The influence exerted by,* which is pure emptiness at the outset. If you wish, increase the concreteness and say *The Christian religion,* or *The Christian church,* or even *Christian believers.* Grasp, in short, an "imageable" subject and then tell us what it does or has done to another of a like kind.

Often, mere recasting of this sort will not work; the fog is too thick, and nothing short of complete rewording—"translation" —will pull out the meaning and show it to the baffled audience. For example:

> If enforcible deprivations are provided for deviational conduct, the mature members of the community are expected to take these possible deprivations into account as potential costs in assessing the balance of indulgence and deprivation attendant upon behavioral alternatives.

Presumably, the meaning is: Knowing that the law punishes crime, mature people will weigh the risks and think twice before they do wrong. The sociologist might answer that he does not want to use words such as *crime* and *wrong,* because he views these acts without the feelings they usually call forth. Crime is only "deviation"; wrongdoing is just "a behavioral alternative," chosen or not on grounds of "potential costs in assessing the balance of indulgence and deprivation." This objection does not carry much weight against the counterobjection that whole paragraphs written in the noun style destroy the power of thinking in both reader and writer, so that neither can test for himself the truth or falsity of what is said. How could the writer just quoted discover those of his statements that do not pass this test? In his sentence, the *taking into account* is actually the same action as the *assessing the balance of . . . deprivation,* so that all we are told in forty woolly words is that mature people will weigh the disadvantages of committing crimes (nine words).

A shorthand term for this sort of writing is *jargon.* Its appeal lies in the desire to appear learned and its use also favors laziness. Analyzing ideas is work, especially when the ideas are one's own; and covering up the confusion under phraseology that sounds technical is a quick way out. Once the mind has fallen into this habit, nothing but abstract nouns seems appropriate. Institutions tend to issue jargon. Thus the newcomer to the Army Medical Service is faced with the duty to "insure unit level medical capability," and he has to work out for himself that this means "be sure there's a doctor in the tent." But as a physician has said, "The writing scientist is responsible for a controlled presentation as well as a controlled experiment. . . . Good writers strive for discrete meanings in words for purely selfish reasons: it makes their job easier."

JARGON IS EVERYWHERE

We have been scanning phrases and sentences so as to make the point more vivid by the enlarged scale of the trouble; but the principle of jargon lies primarily in the single word. Take *motivation.* In almost every use of that word all that is meant could be conveyed by *motive,* which is a shorter, more compact, tougher word; a word, moreover, free of the deadly "shun" syllable (*-tion*), which spoils the sound of prose by its recurrence. Still more important, when we reject *motivation* and reach for *motive,* we may well discover that although adequate, it is in fact not at all the word we wanted. We ought to try *reason, ground, purpose,* and many others, whose existence was concealed from us by the broad shadow of *motivation.* By way of proof, look at this list taken from Roget's *Thesaurus* or *treasury* of words:

MOTIVE

*Reason,* ground, call, principle, mainspring, pro and con, reason why, ulterior motive, intention, etc.

*Inducement,* consideration, attraction, lodestone, magnet, magnetism, temptation, enticement, allurement, lure, glamour, witchery, charm, spell, fascination, blandishment, cajolery, seduction

*Influence,* prompting, dictate(s), instance, impulse, incitement, press(ure), insistence, instigation, inspiration, persuasion, encouragement, exhortation, advice, solicitation, pull (slang)

*Incentive,* stimulus, spur, fillip, whip, goad, provocation, whet

*Bribe,* lure, sop, decoy, bait, bribery and corruption

*Tempter,* prompter, instigator, coaxer, wheedler, siren, firebrand

You see how far the thought of a single word that is solid and not sleazy can take us on the way to the *mot juste.* Which one of these synonyms you finally fix upon depends on your idea and its context. Nor is this offering the end of the possible choices, for I have copied only the nouns. Roget gives 45 verbs, not counting those implied in the nouns, plus 3 adjectives and 10 adverbs with distinct roots—all told, 124 words capable of replacing *motivation,* 124 ways of sharpening a thought.

Now, a writer is entitled to have Roget on his desk and he will not scruple to turn to it when his mind refuses to summon up the right word. But no writer can perform easily and well unless he can by himself, without books, think of a dozen ways of molding or carving his own meaning. He writes only as well as he thinks, and he cannot think if all he has at command is the worn-out locutions of the marketplace.

A subclass under jargon and equally to be avoided is a set of words, good in themselves, that lax or timid writers use indifferently to eke out their thought: *nature, factor, facet, character, aspect, feature, condition* are such words. Typically "empty" uses are: "It looked like a tool of a useful nature" ("a useful tool"). "Those remarks were of a decidedly unpleasant character" ("Those were unpleasant remarks"). "The proposal appeared to have a definitive aspect" ("appeared to be definitive").

This misuse of verbal resources errs not only by what I have called emptiness—the word does no work—but also by redundancy: there are too many words for the idea, and the extra ones do not add dignity, as some may suppose, but rather the opposite. It is waste of eyesight and brain tissue to read: "The time factor will keep him from attending the conference"; "The weather conditions continue adverse to flying." Say *"Lack of time . . .";* *"Bad weather* will prevent . . .*" Time* and *weather* are words of immense power and "coverage"; there is no need to tack on a little trailer as if they needed reinforcements. Simple-&-direct calls for economy. Ideas will best slide into a reader's mind when the word noise is least.

⨯

Principle 2: Weed out the jargon.

Now for an exercise back and forth. The first group of sentences is to be turned into simple-&-direct; the second group is to be turned into sentences plagued by nouns, jargon, and redundancies.

A.   1. His involvement stemmed from a desire to create a network of approaches, a structure of viewpoints, which could be channeled into a coherent social consciousness.

2. Passengers are requested to refrain from conversation with the operator while the vehicle is in motion.

3. One noticed a flaccid quality in his muscles.

4. Progress toward regional integration in the earlier period was the result of the perception of rewards from unity and the absence of divisive factors.

5. [This one may defeat you through no fault of yours.] A personal reorganization then occurs in response to situational interactors which may be recognized as a special symbolic process conceived to cover aspects of motivation, feeling, emotion, and the choice of adjustment alternatives.

6. Theology constituted the fundamental intellectuality of the seventeenth-century *Weltanschauung*.

7. For the last twenty-four hours there had been a pattern forming in his brain, the nimbus of an idea began to emerge.

8. Yes, observers, in growing numbers, consider sunflowers as a hopeful new crop destined to play an exciting role in lessening the protein shortage.

9. The reason inflation is so hard to beat is that it's no longer monolithic.

10. All house-to-house canvassers are equipped beforehand with a profile of the population density of each house in their regime. [The context makes clear that "population density" here means the number of persons living in any one house. Will you condone the use of *density* in that sense?]

B.  1. To be or not to be, that is the question.

2. I hope it will not be irreverent for me to say that if it is probable that God would reveal His will to others on a point so connected with my duty, it might be supposed He would reveal it directly to me; for unless I am more deceived in myself than I often am, it is my earnest desire to know the will of Providence in this matter.

3. Knowledge is of two kinds. We know a subject ourselves, or we know where we can find information upon it.

4. Intellect is community property and can be handed down.

5. Let us cultivate our garden. [Hint: A garden has recently been called "a personalized recreational eco-unit."]

C.  [To conclude, a related exercise.] Draw up a list of 25 words that you consider most harmful to prose, for the reasons discussed above. Those 25 words need not all be nouns; but all of them should have the power of annoying you now (or very soon) wherever you meet them. Accordingly, you will forbid yourself the use of them in writing as well as in conversation. Refer to this list from time to time if you should forget to be annoyed and thus fail to reject one or another of the words.

WORD QUALITIES I: TECHNICAL AND PSEUDO-TECHNICAL

In saying earlier that it is preferable to say *nail, brad,* or *pin* rather than *thing,* we were close to discussing the subject of technical words. Our civilization has required that many such words be taken into the common tongue. One cannot live or speak or write without using them, and presumably one tries to use them with precision, if only to save oneself from receiving a kaleidoscope when wanting to own a kinescope. But this habit and this necessity have brought on a wider application of technical speech, for purposes not of clear designation but of sounding deep or showing off special knowledge.

The misfortune is that very often the so-called knowledge isn't so. For example, a person has the knack of reconciling people of opposed interests; he is a mediator or a skillful diplomat. Many will jump at the chance of calling him a *catalyst*. But chemistry distinguishes many types of catalyst, and their diverse implications have no place in the ordinary business of life. There is thus no need for the technical term in common prose; it had best be left to the chemical journals. If one absolutely insists on using *catalyst,* the term should be reserved for those situations in which some awe-inspiring person sits by and reunites opponents by his mere presence, not entering into the discussion to blend ideas and feelings. And for that limited purpose, it is absurd to use a special word when dozens of ordinary ones will do.

Similarly, *osmosis* is the equalization of liquid pressures on two sides of a porous membrane. The term is therefore inappropriate for describing the effect of associating with professional actors: "She was no longer simple and spontaneous. Her character had been changed by osmosis." Use *by association, contagion, bad example.* A third specimen, of fairly recent origin: *interface* is the common surface that marks the boundary of two portions of matter or space. Turned into a verb by the half literate, it produces: "We've got to find somebody who can interface Paul and Alex on that tax-recovery job." The possible meaning is: *act as go-between, ensure liaison, coordinate the work,* or whatever the function is—we are not told, and the chances of misunderstanding after the remark are as numerous as the people present, including the speaker.

The double conclusion about borrowed technicalities is: there is harm and there is no need. When we can use *repeat* for ordinary purposes, there is no need of *replicate;* and it is harmful to the language to shrink *replicate* to a lesser meaning than its own.

In all cases, regard should be paid to the figure the technical term will cut in the company of non-technical ones. If among workaday words the reader comes upon *zoonoses,* he is entitled to complain. The writer could well afford the space to say: *diseases transmitted from animals to man.*

Let it be added that not all technical words disclose themselves at sight. Some are—or look—quite ordinary, and these present the difficulty of knowing when they should be used with technical precision and when not—assuming one knows the technical sense to begin with. The following, for example, have generally unsuspected technical meanings: *swamp, marsh, stalemate, buttress, verse, maverick, groundswell.* Of the first pair, a *swamp* is fertile, reclaimable land; a *marsh* is not. A *stalemate* in chess is final, not just a deadlock to be broken. A *buttress* is only one kind of support; look it up in an illustrated dictionary. A *verse* is one line, not a group of lines, properly a *stanza.* A *maverick* is unbranded cattle over a year old; and a *groundswell,* far from being the magnificent uplifting that successful politicians want for victory, is a motion of the sea that stirs up the bottom, muddies the water, and throws up debris in all directions.

Such ambiguities only strengthen the writer's resolve to know his words, and to avoid all terms and expressions, old or new, that embody affectation. Why *dual* instead of *double* in *dual zone refrigerators, dual biography, dual* (traffic) *lane?* Why *dialogue* in every context, including negotiations at a distance between whole nations? Why the sign near a private beach: "Beware! Dog is *Carnivorous"?* Why, in the White House, a *cosmic* review of economic policy?

WORD QUALITIES II: MISSHAPEN, PEDANTIC, OVEREFFICIENT

The answers to the foregoing questions—if indeed there are answers—need not be taken up here, except as we are forced to notice our contemporaries' fumbling purpose in the choice and manufacture of words. Nowadays everybody feels free to launch new words, usually mongrels combining parts of other words. A very few are well made or justified by a previous lack, and it is astonishing to observe that in spite of the strong prejudice against Latin and Greek—"those perfectly useless dead languages"—ordinary journalists, professionals, and office holders keep making up vocables out of ancient roots excluded from their all-modern curriculum. The number of *ologies* grows yearly—and heedlessly. We now have two brands of *pedology,* one from *paidos,* the study of children, the other from *pedon,* the science of soils. To this profusion are added hybrids in *-atics* or *-etics,* such as *proximetics,* denoting apparently the "science" of measuring space for people to work in.

Perhaps the chief illiteracy of the kind in recent years is *psychedelic,* attributed to a physician who evidently did not know that the case called for the usual ending in *o* at the end of the first root; we do not say *psychelogy* or *psychepathic* or *psychesomatic.*

The same principle—that of joining only what is joinable—is violated by *aquatennial* (a meaningless echo of *cent-ennial*) and *septuplicate* (where *septem* provides no *u,* but *duplicate* haunted the creator), as well as by Winston Churchill's unlucky invention of *triphibian* to mean an attack by land, sea, and air. He thought of *amphibian,* which describes the double life of frogs and other creatures, first in water, then on land, but forgot that *amphi* (*on both sides*) means nothing if it is split, and is not raised one notch if *tri* replaces *am.*

More recently, a periodical tried to launch *Prosumerism*—"a word that's very new to consumers"—in the belief that putting *pro* in place of *con* would indicate siding with the—what?—well, the *sumer.* And quite lately there has been a wave of hybrids ending in *holics* to signify addiction, *workaholics* being people who love work excessively. One could wish that creators of words would have enough interest in earlier coinages to find out how they were made. *Alcohol* consists of the prefix *al* meaning *the* and *cohol* (same as English *kohl*) meaning *powder;* so that *holics* means just nothing and can bring nothing to *worka,* which is in the same fix.

To avoid foolishness, then, do no compounding on the spur of the moment and use only established compounds—as the doctor does in prescribing medicine. Keep clear especially of those with *-phobia* and *-itis,* in which the first part (sometimes a proper name) is cut off arbitrarily, in perfect ignorance. Roots have their rights too.

Note in passing that *phobia* does not mean *obsession, mania, idée fixe;* it means fear and hatred combined: some people suffer from a phobia in the presence of cats; dogs develop hydrophobia. Again, *-itis* indicates the irritation or inflammation of an organ, as in *appendicitis.* Hence a fervent admiration of the selfsame Churchill is not *Churchillitis;* if the term means anything, it means the opposite of admiration and delight.

Sense is allied to form, and the responsible writer will see to it that in his dealings with Greek and Latin he knows enough to tell a plural from a singular. The occurrence of *phenomena, criteria, strata* with *is* or *was* shows up the careless writer, even though *agenda* (and *data* for some) have achieved the singular number, thanks in part to their collective meaning. When one finds a distinguished academic writing of *bustling metropoli* as if the singular were *metropolus,* one is inclined to ask for total abstinence from imports out of antiquity: *huge bustling cities* is all the occasion called for.

Those who are tempted to fiddle and tinker with words and who thereby lead some users astray might bear in mind that making up words is an art, not merely a trick of combining roots according to rule. It takes genius and at best success is chancy. Sir Thomas Browne in the seventeenth century launched *hallucination, umbrella, medical, antediluvian,* and *literary*—a record performance. The word *typewriter,* a century ago, also succeeded, but that was undeserved luck. At the beginning it was pointed out that the word had no deducible meaning at all. In fact, by a kind of logic, it was then used as often for the typist as for the machine. I once found in an old book a clipping headed: "Typewriter Charges Her Employer with Assault."

Nowadays innovators carelessly stretch meanings as well as coin new words. Scholars are familiar with *disciplinary* in the unnecessary sense of *related to a discipline* (e.g., history). With the older, equally current sense of *carrying out punishment* the new use creates ambiguity. So does *categorical grant,* which ought to mean *definitive, not tentative,* whereas it is designed to mean *belonging to a category. Categorial* would have been better, and better still, *a series grant*—series A, B, C, etc. What is almost sure to destroy sense is the desire to put everything into one all-encompassing word—a childish desire. Consider "The dinner meeting was short-noticed, so very few were able to come." Let us hope that at the end of the dinner those few were not long-speeched by the guest of honor.

It is hardly necessary to add that the same childishness inspires the vogue of naming by initial letters or acronyms. When our minds are already crowded with facts, numbers, and ideas, with the names of devices, movements, and public figures, it is neither courteous nor effective to throw in symbols that conceal the subject being discussed—do you know what OPEC, LOOM, SEATO, NEA, stand for? The last stands for at least three different national organizations. It would be better to write out what we mean and refrain from making up titles that will yield such pseudo-words. A very few exceptions to this caution may be tolerated, beginning with U.S.A. But remember the force of contexts: those same initials also mean Union of South Africa, and in Denver there has been a move to adopt another USA (Urban Service Authority), which will add to the momentary but frequent confusion. In some scientific journals today the summary comes at the head of the article instead of the end. One result is that unfamiliar abbreviations—say *o.g.*—occur before the reader can know what they mean. He must scan three or four paragraphs to discover that the reference is to *oak galls,* which is spelled out only once in the whole article. I give these examples with little hope that they will discourage the use of all monograms that are (*a*) ambiguous through duplication and (*b*) not easily decipherable by the audience addressed. All the more reason for not creating new sets of initials each time you write an essay and introduce a subject which is very likely of greater interest to you than to the reader: "I packed the sandwiches and my watercolor box and the sketching paper in my old rucksack. Half way there the WCB slipped out through an open seam."

By an interesting paradox, the same zeal for efficiency that leads to initialese and neologisms (new words) leads also to diction of an opposite kind. In place of new compounds, Graeco-Latin monsters, and overextensions of quiet vocables, a type of would-be efficient writer will use short, crackling words much too violent for the occasion. Readers of paperback crime or adventure will recognize the style: "The telephone smashed the silence of the room." "The old tub waddled out of the bay." "Then we hit a little burg; the bus shuddered to a halt; the passengers spilled out onto the road." It is tiresome after a few paragraphs. Nor is this "efficient" diction as imaginative as the author believes, for it takes no genius to think: "the ring of the telephone *broke* the silence" and to exaggerate *broke* into *smash;* any fool can do it.

✳

Principle 3: Look for *all* fancy wordings and get rid of them.

The object here is to detect the ill-advised expressions and sort them into classes: Pure Jargon, Technical, Pseudo-technical, Misshapen, Overextended, and Overefficient; after which you should try, when possible, to rewrite the sentence in simple-&-direct. Remember to catch and correct other faults than those chiefly aimed at in this exercise.

    1. After Deposit Plate and Slip have been properly positioned in the imprinter face up, move handle to extremest left.
    2. Statistics show that of all indictments brought up to the city courts during the preceding five years, no fewer than 47% proved to be durable cases.
    3. All major exhibitions are previewed for associates at formal evening receptions.
    4. He is not just an area man, he is a born and bred Kansas citian.
    5. There are S.R.O.'s and S.R.O.'s—which is the new ordinance of the council directed against?
    6. The First International Congress of Mycenaeology will be in care of the Centre of Mycenaean and Aegeo-Anatolian Studies in Rome.
    7. The sky fell and the light waned. Pain shot downward to his feet, loosed his knees. The light continued to wane. Grip—grip!
    8. We shall now leave you to coagulate your thoughts.
    9. None of the passengers thought to inquire the cause of the train's inertion.

10. With the Cervipillo, any other support for comfort in bed is obliviated.

11. He criticized certain relicts of the Judaea-Christian tradition.

12. Unsuspected there is one agency of the U.S. government that is participating in the despoilation of one of our most beautiful regions.

13. The answer he gave surprised even him. It was a cortical reflex.

14. Enclosed are three examples of a unique artistry—the world's finest letter paper made literally by hand, one at a time, and bearing a personal watermark.

15. "Factoids" is a word he coins for "facts which have no existence before appearing in a magazine or newspaper, creations which are not so much lies as a product to manipulate the emotions."

16. We recommend the use of ———'s Corrasable Typewriter Paper. [Unriddle the pseudoword *Corrasable* and then pronounce it.]

17. The new ski speedometer or *Skidometer* . . . [Again, pronounce at first sight.]

18. We labeldate our bread for freshness insurance.

19. The walls are lined with a space-age insulated material (imprisoned air cells) which will keep a fine wine ice cold right at the table.

20. The company, called very simply the Danscompany, is under the direction of ———.

WORD QUALITIES III: CONNOTATION, DIRECTION, MALAPROPS

The connotation of a word is that part of its meaning which has grown by usage around its core meaning, or denotation, and is therefore not discoverable at a glance. We noticed earlier that in "be a writer," *writer* implied *professional writer*. Since connotations come by use and some words are used only or chiefly in writing, it is rash to use such words without paying attention to *how* they are used in print—with favorable or unfavorable or neutral meanings, with general or restricted application. To learn connotations, read widely. Then you will readily find out that (for instance) *verbiage* connotes a foolish or superfluous display of words and not merely an output of words (*wordage*), good or bad.

Sometimes the linking of ordinary, familiar words will create an unexpected connotation, as happened when a proud village put up a sign on the highway: "You are now entering Westwood and are welcome to it." There is no logic in connotations: compare the common elements in *sneak* and *sneaker, sweat* and *sweater, hospital* and *hospitality*. Every word that possesses a marked connotation—not every word does—has to be learned separately. One more example should clinch the point. A newspaper reviewer wrote: "The continuing demand for the book reflects not only on the subject but on the author also." The intention was complimentary, but *reflect on* means to every thoughtful reader the same thing as *throw discredit on*. What happened was that the reviewer started with the idea: the demand for the book *reflects, is a reflection of,* the importance of its subject; but he wanted to bring in the author and skip the importance; so he cast about for a preposition that might suit the purpose and used one that did the opposite.

From the nature of connotation you can perceive that its territory gives access to absurd error on one side and the sharpest precision on the other. Both cover a wide gradation of cases. Error goes from wrong connotation to malapropisms (shortly to be explained), and precision goes from due clarity to superior expressiveness. Compare the journalistic and the precise use of the common word *admit*. Many reporters would write: "Rescued after 36 hours on a raft, Mr. X. admitted that there were moments when he gave up hope." Or again, in a statement given to an investigating committee: "Mr. Y. admitted that he had felt uncomfortable in his interview with the President." In both statements, as the context shows, the featured remark was offered, volunteered. It was therefore not an *admission*. For exact use, *admit* should be restricted to what is said in response to a question, usually with reluctance on the speaker's part. You *declare* or *announce* or *proclaim* or *pretend* that you have seen a ghost; you *admit* it only if you are being quizzed and are trying to keep your belief secret.

At the other end of the range are the malapropisms (*mal-*

*apropos*) just referred to. They get their name from a character in Sheridan's comedy *The Rivals.* Mrs. Malaprop confuses the long words she fancies with others that resemble them in sound. Since her day, the spread of the so-called communication arts has increased everybody's liability to the same error. A person half hears a word that sounds attractive and useful and half sees in print another word that he mistakes for the first. In *Sports Illustrated,* the famous coach of the Houston Oilers was once quoted at length as an expert who made a specialty of malapropisms. "This is the crutch of the problem," he would say; or, "He has a chronicle knee injury"; "We're changing our floormat this week"; and so on. In ordinary talk you will hear: "She went ahead and *flaunted* their instructions" much oftener than *flouted* —which no doubt *floated* somewhere in the neighborhood of the wrong word. Even in a well-written and much-edited journal one reads: "The planned Office of Education Liaison should not *impinge* [infringe] upon the authority of the board." This mistake also brought about the false use of *upon* after *infringe.* The sentence should read: "not infringe the authority of . . ."

Often, the origin of a malapropism in pure echo seems farfetched, but there is in fact no limit to the size or kind of jump that the ear and mind will make, which is one more reason for close reading and conscious hearing. Ponder these examples: "Both operations were performed by the *illusory* [elusive] Dr. B. in California." "I fell for him at once—his looks, his manners: he was the perfect *antithesis* of a gentleman" ("epitome," no doubt). "The suggestion was greeted with *overweening* disapproval" [overwhelming]. Notice especially in the last sentence the desire for novelty. *Overwhelming* is too obviously the right word; let's use one that's not so common. It must mean the same thing since it also begins with *over.*

In some cases, what I have called echo does not so much mislead the ear as fail to suggest the right choice among several words built on the same root. It is a problem in semantics or in connotation, but it comes out as a malaprop. This is what happened to the reviewer who wrote: ". . . a *compulsive* novel built around a police investigation of LSD." Now, psychiatry has set aside the word *compulsive* to denote those acts of a neurotic which he does not will but cannot refrain from doing—e.g., Dr. Johnson's touching all the lampposts along the street. No word could be clearer or more useful: the compulsion is from within. Close to *compulsive* is the much older word *compulsory*, which denotes a compulsion from outside, that of a rule or an enforcing power. Finally, there is the critic's word *compelling*, which is a metaphor suggesting that a work of art makes the beholder yield to its emotional or aesthetic force. Those three compellings are too useful for their distinguishing forms not to be kept clear. Be sure to make yourself aware of important distinctions in *repel* and *repulse; precipitate* and *precipitous; exposé, exposure,* and *exposition; assure* and *insure; alternative* and *alternate; seasonal* and *seasonable; heartburn* and *heartburning; assignation* and *assignment; perspicacious* and *perspicuous; diverse* and *divers; enormousness* and *enormity; relics* and *relicts; militate* and *mitigate.* . . . The list would stretch far, even if limited to such frequent confusions as these. If you do not see the point of some of them, go to a dictionary.

Yet another cause of the misuse of words is ignorance of what might be called their Direction. By this term (which you will probably not find in other books on writing) I mean the ways that words point when linked with other words. A familiar example is: "Every owner was issued with two keys." The very idea of *issuing* is that of *going out,* here of *giving* from hand to hand, so that the mind rebels at the notion of *giving* every owner *with* two keys. The notion of *furnished with* is the deceiving phrase hovering nearby. What then? "Two keys were given to each owner" would be simplest and best, but if one insists on the verb *issue* in the passive voice, then: "Every owner was issued two keys."

In general, the pair of directions to be attended to are the transitive and the intransitive. These two words mean *carrying across* or not doing so. For example: "a career of outlawry that boggles the mind" makes a transitive out of *boggle,* which is contrary to usage. To *boggle* (as horses do) is to start or shy in alarm. Therefore *the mind boggles* and that's all. If the occasion has to be mentioned, the mind *boggles at* something, but the something does not boggle *it.*

An instance of the opposite error, making a transitive intransitive, is this attempt to give a new direction to the verb *foster:* "The second woman, Mrs. B., is the one with whom they have been fostered for the past 30 months." Mrs. B. was the foster mother; she fostered (i.e., fed and cared for) the children; everything in *foster* goes from her to them; they were fostered by her. But they can neither *have been fostered with* her, nor can they *foster with* her, as the writer says later on, in a second try at redirecting the word.

Another common instance: "He never lost his fascination for 'The Miller and His Men.' " Ask yourself what *fascinate* means. It means stare at a person or animal (snake versus rabbit) so as to paralyze the victim. In the common law, witchcraft was often called fascination. Figuratively the word has come to mean the spell, the magic power exerted by a work of art as well as a person. It is therefore the tale about the miller that performs the fascination—that "holds" it—and not the man being fascinated; and if that is so, he cannot lose the fascination, though the story might. Write: " 'The Miller and His Men' never lost its power to fascinate him"; or, "He never ceased being fascinated by . . ."

Here are cases from current writing in which the direction of a noun or verb has been twisted away from the normal one: "He was reported in the past to have had strong *convictions toward* Communism" ("leanings toward"). "It reminds one of travelogues, with lovers *strolling* rainy Paris streets" ("strolling along"). "The tragic occurrence will not *deter its being* rented again" ("deter anybody from renting"). "Times Square is *purported to be* the crossroads of the world ("purports to be"). "I *shop* Allen and Hawkins" ("shop at"; *to shop* followed as here by proper names means to *sack, dismiss, create trouble for*). "Miss X. *Wed by* Cardinal S." ("Married," meaning that the cardinal performed the ceremony; *wed* would mean that he was the groom). This last example should perhaps be classed under technical terms, though when a common word becomes a technicality, there is more excuse for changing its usage and direction. Thus in physics it is usual to write: "A particle plus an antiparticle must be able to annihilate." That is, the final verb has become intransitive, or it implies "each other"; whereas in common speech we want the object fully stated—annihilate *what?*

If you think about transitive and intransitive verbs you will never again mix up the common little words that a teacher once called catchfools: *sit* and *set, lie* and *lay, rise* and *raise.* Their misuse is a sure mark of illiteracy, not because the mistake is in itself more damaging to sense than others, but because the failure to master the differences in direction argues a general inattention to the details that make the conventions of writing almost as important as those of bridge.

It is clear, for instance, that the direction built into a word has a great deal to do with the prepositions that may or may not follow. The principle covers thousands of cases, as we shall see when we come to the subject of Linking. The point to note here is that the direction in the word must not clash with the direction in the preposition—as we saw in the *issued with* example. To avoid such a conflict one must make sure of the connotation of the main word. Consider *delineate.* Its bare meaning is *draw a line,* but connotation dictates that the line drawn be *around* an object or situation to depict it, not *between* two entities to separate them. Hence the request heard in a Massachusetts court: "Can you *delineate between* the checks you deposited at your bank and those you kept at your firm?" violates both the connotation and the direction of the verb.

A similar perversion of sense and speech habits is found stamped on the side of certain grocers' bags: "We are ecology minded. This bag will self-destruct in mother earth." To begin with, the statement is not true; the bag will not commit suicide if buried in the earth, it will *be* destroyed by the moisture and minerals in the ground. More important, there is no verb *destruct* —it is *destroy;* and even if there were, *it will self-destruct* cannot mean *it will destroy itself,* because a transitive requires a direct object to complete its meaning. You do not say *my car will self-start, stunt fliers often self-kill,* and the like. Direction in words is all-important in that it commands the presence or absence of other words.

The converse is also true. You must become aware of the change in connotation that affects one and the same verb when different allowable prepositions are tacked to it, or when the form of the root or main word is modified. One *agrees with* a person or point of view, but *agrees to* a set of conditions, and *upon* a plan of action. Any writer can *compare himself with* Shakespeare and discover how far he falls short; if he *compares himself to* Shakespeare (i.e., puts himself on the same level), then he had better think again. Under the law everybody is *subject to* punishment, but only a small number are *subjected* to it.

⢤

Principle 4: Make sure you know not only the meaning but also the *bearing* of the words you use.

Exercise your wits on connotations, malaprops, and false directions in these sentences and try to correct them in all needed ways. When you have finished, choose ten of the errors and explain by intelligent guesswork how they probably came about.

1. There simply isn't enough income coming in. We'll have to abridge the gap some other way.

2. Though a co-author of the bill, he attacked it in committee as if he belonged to the opposition—a quixotic situation, surely!

3. They remained vast friends for many years.

4. *Moving Day*—it tells you how to dissemble, pack, and carry everything from teapots to grand pianos.

5. The peroration that S. has intoned for molecular biology may seem somewhat premature. The subject is alive and kicking.

6. Was it feasible that this girl, missing for a month, had been in their car two nights ago?

7. A worthy successor to the author's earlier travesties of history in a series unequalled for truth and readability.

8. *To All Tenants:* Extermination Will Come Tuesday Morning.

9. There is more than a twinge of existentialism in Aquinas.

10. The dean said that only a smattering of students had turned up at the special meeting.

11. He debated him from the first point to the last.

12. I want to divert from my usual sermon and put in a word for our friend ———.

13. Europe has to face every summer a growing quantity of tourists.

14. The report notes that there is widespread unfamiliarity about large sums of money.

15. A complete physical exam is compulsive for all new employees.

16. Both farmers were charged with an outbreak of swine fever and failure to notify the disease.

17. The Secretary of State is attributed as writing that the Administration would not oppose an annual ceiling on immigration.

18. You could see that the accusation had often been levied against her.

19. For nearly 70 years these piers have withstood the impact of inestimable tons of ice.

20. That was the year in which the town had been ravished by an earthquake.

21. Our assumption is that the girl was taken when her escort was killed. That doesn't sound very inviting from the parents' point of view.

22. Ground rules covering TV journalism have always rankled radio and TV reporters.

23. The flour was invested with insects and the concern fined $7,500.

24. You would forgive a youth who from a child had been inflicted with a stepmother.

25. There is really no need to belabor the point.

26. The champs cemented their third straight victory with a nifty piece of ledger domain.

27. As experienced trappers and woodsmen they went to work with a certain *éclan*.

28. The idea has long been exploded that the novels of Dickens contain not characters but characatures.

29. Not far away a young policeman was beguiling a young woman.

30. Due to the pending shortages of fuel oil, we have instructed the superintendent to lower the thermostat settings.

WORD QUALITIES IV: EUPHEMISM, SLANG, SYNONYMS; THE USE OF ETYMOLOGY

Among the properties of words to be noted by the conscious writer are the opposite ones of Euphemism and Slang. A euphemism is the substitution of a word or expression for the blunt term that one has reasons for not uttering. Diplomatic language is a set of precise euphemisms: "This Government would accept such an explanation of the act complained of only with the greatest reserve." Translated into "clear," this means: "Don't try to put us off with a silly excuse—we don't trust you one inch." The advantage of euphemism is that it avoids giving offense and maintains the fundamental social virtue of civility. The parties can go on arguing without the interference of strong feelings. Something of the same sort is the reason for euphemism in ordinary conversation. The guest says: "Where is the bathroom?" or: "I'd like to wash my hands." There would be nothing wicked in stating his purpose more definitely, but it would interrupt everybody's current of thought with irrelevant ideas and images. The agreed-upon formula produces the least disturbance of the common mood.

At certain times and places, euphemism has gone so far as to forget its aim. It then conceals reality without any need. Such was the ultimate effect of poetic diction in the neoclassical seventeenth and eighteenth centuries. At first the intention was to create an aura of charm or splendor around common things, but the convention ended by making lifeless and dull an unchanging set of euphemisms: *the finny tribe* for *fish,* or (in French tragedy) the perpetual reference to *flame* for *love.*

This excess, which would logically create two vocabularies for naming things, also occurs from prudery or genteelism. There was a time when underwear (and even trousers) were called *unmentionables* and when the legs of a piano or other furniture were called its *limbs.* To this day, in certain places, people feel compelled to call manure *barn dressing* and refuse to say that someone died: he or she *passed on.* ("He passed on, did he? What did he pass on of?") All good modern prose excludes genteel, prudish, or "poetic" euphemism. That rule is a corollary of simple-&-direct.

In the light of such advice—call a spade a spade—it is easy to understand why the novice at writing believes that if he can catch and set down the colloquialisms and slang of his day in their extensive variety he is bound to write prose that will be vivid and strong—"terrific!" The misreckoning becomes evident when it turns out that much of what he writes under that inspiration was not of the day but of the hour. It does not last; often, it does not carry very far. A region or profession, a circle or clique is the total audience; and if such a group keeps its identity by slang, it will only laugh at its own words of a few months earlier: what was "in" is now "out." For the student or educated reader, nothing is more annoying than to find a sentence made unintelligible by a key word in slang that has faded into oblivion. If Shakespeare had not written thousands of words that are still standard English, no one would bother to find out what he means when he has Hamlet say "Buzz, buzz!" It means *stale news*.

Again, readers of the Sherlock Holmes stories have noticed that when Holmes and Watson first meet and discuss sharing rooms on Baker Street, Dr. Watson lists his drawbacks as a roommate and says, "I keep a bull pup." The curious fact about that dog is that he is never heard of again—and no wonder, for *keep a bull pup* in the 1880s was army slang for *have a bad temper*. The author probably put the phrase in the army doctor's mouth for vivid local color.

To point out these limitations of the colloquial is not to deny the force of slang or the appeal of words made up for super-expressiveness. A writer from the Southwest lingers reminiscently over the two words *antegogglin* and *slaunchwise,* and one may agree that they have charm; but if he had not explained that the first means *disfavored* and the other *out of kilter,* all one would have gained was the charm, devoid of usable sense.

Some slang stays in use and thereby is no longer slang. *Mob, cab, pub, fan, vamp, bunk, wig, bus, flu,* were originally slang shortenings. *Shilly-shally, namby-pamby, helter-skelter, bamboozle, hush money, cotton to, squeal* (to the police), *cold feet, rubberneck, rig(a)marole, mascot, robot, stag party, racketeer, highbrow, hard-boiled, tightwad, double-cross, crank* (lunatic), began as metaphors or compounds of doubtful origin but evident utility. They survived where others equally fresh and strong and useful perished.

The notable fact is that once discarded, the brightest inventions look absurd. How can people ever have had such expressions in their mouths? Who now can interpret *Twenty-three, skiddoo! masher, backfisch?* At the turn of the century, Mark Twain speaks of artists as being *given rats* by their wives: does this suggest anything but a vague idea of disapproval? It is no longer vivid. Two hundred years ago, a *blackjack* was a beer mug made of leather. Only fifty years ago, in a representative novel of college life called *The Plastic Age*, the young men and women say: *isn't it the darb!, that's the bean!, pike along, pash, razz, bughouse, simp, smack for him,* among other mysterious remarks. The very word *plastic* in the title of that book has almost lost its original meaning thanks to the chemical industry.

For a loss of sense now taking place, notice how in stories and articles the slang use of *bird* is becoming ambiguous: it has long meant a male person usually not known to the speaker ("Some bird was looking for you"); now it also denotes, appreciatively, a girl, that is, a "chick." The second usage comes from England, where the first is unknown. The one certainty about slang is that its life and its connotations are unpredictable to a degree not found in the use of the standard vocabulary. Why should the game now known as *bingo* change its name every so often, having been *lotto* and *keno* before? All one can see is why the final *o* is retained.

The line that divides colloquialism from slang is never clearly drawn and is perhaps not worth drawing. It is better simply not to forget that colloquialisms *and* slang should be used sparingly. In the later novels of Henry James one finds many colloquial phrases of the time, not so much in the dialogue as in the description of feelings. These phrases are set off in quotation marks to show that they should not be taken literally. Most of them are easy to grasp, but the effect is less simple and direct than the author hoped for, and the quotation marks, if nothing else, grow wearisome.

For present use, then, bear in mind that expressions such as *be with it, up tight* (death-house slang as far back as the 1920s), *but definitely,* together with all the exaggerations—*awful, great, terrific*—are likely to wear badly. They will look—even to you when you come to reread your work—like ugly blotches on the surface of otherwise fair prose. To think of them in that way is more useful than to suppose them sprightly enliveners or forbidden plums.

Euphemisms and slang would seem to imply, like poetic diction, two words, at least, for each thing. This duplication would be a fact only if one overlooked the color and connotation of each of the paired words. Among the terms usually excluded from polite discourse, for example, it might be thought that the obscene word, the neutral word, and the scientific word all covered the same ground. But the very fact that one will convey contempt or hostility, that another merely labels, and that the third comes from the art of medicine or the science of physiology makes of the apparent equivalents three distinct sets of meanings, that is to say, separate words for three divergent objects of thought.

This generality holds true of so-called synonyms. All carry different loads of information or implication, and skill in writing (once the rudiments are mastered) consists in having at command an array of synonyms, together with a sense of their fitness. Take this roughly acceptable sentence: "The report was written in such a way that it indicated to very few the real nature of the difficulty." Now, *indicate* means to *show, point out,* with the implication of showing *on purpose* (think of an *index* finger pointing). But that report was written so as to *conceal* the difficulty; therefore those who wrote it had no desire to *indicate.* Instead, they wrote it in such a way that it *betrayed to very few,* or it *allowed very few to discover* the difficulty. The rewording, whatever it may be, should embody the writer's awareness that when he put down *indicate* he gave the reader *a wrong signal.*

In an excellent article I come across: "In the sixties, the embattled university had to face attacks from the students, the faculty, the local community, and the general public." I understand what is meant, but am vaguely troubled, because some idea has been insinuated into my mind which I think false, yet I cannot say what it is. Going back, I find it: *embattled* is an aggressive word that applies to the party taking the offensive. It does not mean forced to do battle, but ready for battle. Consequently, I question the picture given of an institution out to commit assault on these four opponents. The sentence should read: "the *beleaguered* university," and as I think this over I wonder whether the writer did not vaguely visualize the *battered* university and by echo produce the misleading word.

Propriety of terms is achieved only through the hard work of acquiring the sort of "absolute pitch" for words that the musician has for notes. By words I mean of course all types of locutions, many of them prepositional compounds. Everybody knows the difference between being *in the market* (to buy) and *on the market* (for sale). But how many distinguish between actions *in behalf* of someone and those *on behalf?* What preposition is called for in: "You should know that I am concerned with the provincial character of our publication"? The writer is concerned *about* the provinciality; it worries him. But what he has said is that he is in charge of supplying it to the publication. English usage is full of important distinctions expressed in small ways. For example, apropos of an historical figure: "But his real interest lay elsewhere than at the court of George II." It turns out on further reading that his real *interest* (singular) did lie at court; it was one of the ladies-in-waiting; but his real *interests* (plural), meaning what would be better for his fortune, lay in his country estate.

If in doubt about the differences among words that are not in everyday use, recourse to etymology will help. It will prevent the kind of miscasting to which we shall return in discussing metaphor; meantime it will teach the making of distinctions. Etymology is a tough discipline, and not for amateurs; but everybody can at least take one step back from a figurative use of the literal idea. Students of words have an advantage; they know a good many literal roots. To exemplify their usefulness, imagine the writer of "Bloodshed flared all over France" asking himself: What is a flare? It is a light, a flame. Does bloodshed (liquid) suggest a flame?

His Latin-taught counterpart will be bothered by a more willful (and increasingly frequent) misconception. He reads: "Russia's pre-emptive strike against China would have to come soon." / "The broadcast on drug abuse will pre-empt 'To Rome with Love' on the same date." / "She answered with a pre-emptory gesture." / "As they came in one by one they saw that the gangsters had pre-empted the bank." (This last, a spoken account, gave the pronunciation *pre-emptied* to the word in dispute.) We now have before us four pieces of nonsense. The word *pre-empt* means only *to buy first;* by extension it may be made to mean *to put in the*

*first claim, forestall* someone else in the possession of a place
(seat), an advantage, or the like.

Clearly, the bandits had not *bought* the bank before the employees arrived, and they *emptied* it after, not *pre-*. The *pre-
emptory* gesture is a gross blunder for *peremptory*. The change of
programs for a given hour is not done by the replacement *pre-
empting* the time; it is just the opposite. The word to use is: B.
will *displace* A. at the same hour. Finally, Russia's *pre-emptive*
strike is surely *preventive* and nothing more. No one who sees
*prae-emptor* in *pre-empt* could venture on all these blunders,
committed by writers no doubt scornful of Latin but "compulsive"
about misusing it.

⌘

Principle 5: Consult your second thoughts about slang, euphemisms, and "what everybody says," so as to make your diction entirely your own choice.

Here, recognition, comparison, explanation, and alteration are
called for as needed. Begin by familiarizing yourself with
Partridge's *Dictionary of Slang and Unconventional English* and
Funk & Wagnalls' *Handbook of Synonyms, Antonyms, and Prepositions*. Then give an account of everything you do to improve
or recast these sentences.

1. The legendary Italian soprano, Mme X., will be presented in a program of operatic arias at the Lyceum tonight.

2. He had for them truly affectionate thoughts, but not deep
friendship.

3. They suffered his vagaries? No! they suffered from his
vagaries.

4. The flood will maximize within 24 hours.

5. The police said that the victim had not been interfered
with. At the hospital the report was that she was still serious.

6. Milton said of poetry that compared to prose it was "more
simple, sensuous, and passionate." [Who said, then, that men and
women, singly and in couples, should be sensuous?]

7. You and your daughter have a mutual interest with all
the other parents and students of the college in its continued
excellence.

8. Those heartrending letters let you see the seamy streak of his life.

9. Frankenstein in this film is given to you in a monstrous new version.

10. The woman's face was a vase suddenly overtaken by centuries of time.

11. Probably, she told herself, he would not be heard of again unless he had something hopeful to say.

12. Do not lean on this wall or the paint will release on you.

13. Don Juan was a gay dog. After three cups he was completely gay. [The philosopher Nietzsche wrote *The Gay Science.* What is it about?]

14. When he lost a leg at sea the King gave him smart money. On Wall Street the smart money goes into the blue chips.

15. The lounge lizard was tickled pink; he thought they were all bully.

16. Report for the city and suburbs: Precipitation Precluded.

17. In his masterful know-how he had the what it takes for a good living.

18. Well, that's an idea; we'll pass it along and see if it orbits.

19. Soft tints that conduce to slumber.

20. Going out on the street and getting mugged sure is counter-productive.

## TIME OUT FOR GOOD READING I

Eric Hoffer was a longshoreman in San Francisco, whose interest in ideas as well as his power of communicating his observations of men and things made him a respected writer and social philosopher. Between June 1958 and May 1959, when he was fifty-six years old, he kept a diary, which he published ten years later. Here are four consecutive entries.

### Working and Thinking on the Waterfront

*February 22*
Nine hours on a Luckenbach ship at Pier 29. I am taking the

place of a steady hook-on man. All day I had the bay before my eyes. The water was light green speckled with white caps. The hills beyond were wrapped in a powder-blue veil through which shimmered the mass of white houses. In the afternoon, over Treasure Island, there was a massing of dark gray and smoky white clouds. One could trace the roots of the white clouds in the gray mass, and the whole thing gave the feeling of a violent reaction out of which something wholly new might emerge.

8:15 P.M. The question of the readiness to work keeps tugging at my mind. My explanation of freedom as an energizer of the masses, and of individual separateness as an irritant which keeps people on the go, is not wholly satisfactory. These are valid causes, but not the main ones. There is, for instance, the fact that there is a greater readiness to work in a society with a high standard of living than in one with a low standard. We are more ready to strive and work for superfluities than for necessities. People who are clear-sighted, undeluded, and sober-minded will not go on working once their reasonable needs are satisfied. A society that refuses to strive for superfluities is likely to end up lacking in necessities. The readiness to work springs from trivial, questionable motives. . . . A vigorous society is a society made up of people who set their hearts on toys, and who would work harder for superfluities than for necessities. The self-righteous moralists decry such a society, yet it is well to keep in mind that both children and artists need luxuries more than they need necessities.


*February 23*

Eight hours on the *Old Colony* at Pier 46B. This was a time-and-a-half day, which gives me a good start for the week. In the back of my mind there is the question why I should go on trying to work four or five days a week. The real job before me is to write the book. But I have become a prisoner of my own routine. Though I have not deposited a penny of waterfront money during this year, I have only about $140 on hand. If I am to take out the Norwegian and the Polish sociologist for supper it will come to at least $30. On the first of the month I have a fixed expense of $62, which includes rent, dues, and the boy's tuition at the nursery. This means that I am earning only about $20 more than I ought to. I could work four instead of five days a week. . . .

### February 26

Eight and a half hours on the Norwegian ship *Besseggen* at Pier 7. It is a paper ship hauling newsprint from Canada for all the bay area newspapers. An easy and fairly pleasant day.

It is an established fact that most of the time on my days off I do not feel like writing anything. I am supposed to rest. It is conceivable that if I laid off long enough I would eventually come around to writing. But up to now all my writing has been done on the run. . . .

### February 27

Four and a half hours on the *Besseggen*. Back in my room at noon.

My brevity is partly the result of a reluctance or inability to write. Delight in the act of writing breeds expansiveness. One shudders at the thought of the innumerable thick volumes which come into existence as the result of the sheer habit of writing. How many people with nothing to say keep writing so many pages a day in order that their body, particularly in old age, should perform its functions.

❖

After one has read a text with pleasure (or distaste), it often adds pleasure (or wisdom) to reflect on its contents, form, and mode of expression. In these daily notes, for instance, what do you think of the opening bit of nature description? Did it ring true, or was the writer just showing he could do the literary thing too? In either case, did he make you *see?*

What of Eric Hoffer's diction? Is it simple? uneducated? or a mixture of simple speech with inappropriate bookish words, or what? And are you entitled to jump to conclusions about a longshoreman's self-education? Your present concern should be the prose he writes, as it stands on the page.

In the fifth paragraph, how do you classify "laid off"—as an error or a technical term? What evidence have you on the point? Finally, how do his views on writing habits square with yours?

# Linking
## or What to Put Next

## II

LINKS ARE WORDS AND IDEAS, BOTH

The idea of linking comes naturally after such a survey as we have made of the powers of single words. For linking is an operation performed by words, phrases, and idioms, as well as by simple placing. Linking is felt in the relation of pronouns to antecedents and of verb tenses in sequence, no less than in the order and aspects of the larger parts of sentences. In short, linking is for the writer a principle of construction. There is not much linking, or not good linking, in the spontaneous expression of the mind when it gropes toward a meaning. For one does not usually think in full sentences or in single words, but in clumps of half-formed ideas that correspond very imperfectly to one's intention. The intention itself changes and grows as one talks or writes.

In the attempt to write well—which is at the same time to think well—these clusters of untrimmed thought must be taken apart and looked at to test their connections and to find the best order of setting them down. A handbook of rhetoric by definition invites to several kinds of analysis, of which the kind called for in linking is a main one. Passing from the choice of words to the manner of their linking is thus practical and logical, as well as natural.

A completed sentence, all agree, is a piece of construction; but we should not think of it as a house made of building blocks. Rather, it resembles a skeleton, in which the joints, the balance, the fit of the parts and their inner solidity combine to make up a well-knit frame. To gauge the effect of a grossly bad joint on such a frame, consider the sentence: "He began a newspaper career that was to last 47 years as a copy boy on the town's one newspaper." The reader must rearrange for the correct meaning, which is: *began as a copy boy* and not: *47 years as a copy boy*.

To link or separate what has been wrongly split or joined is nothing else than to straighten out the syntax. Syntax is usually defined as the arrangement of words in a sentence so as to show their relations; it is a set of instructions for linking and against linking. A further reason for good syntax beyond that of avoiding nonsense is that the writer wants his sentences to give the reader the feeling of forward motion. Movement makes the difference between prose that reads at a pleasant speed and that which is slow and dull. The analogy of sentence and skeleton continues to hold. All parts of a skeleton or a sentence, small and large, must be properly articulated *and balanced*. For as Yeats pointed out in comparing the two forms of utterance, "Poetry needs no balance like prose—it runs on."

We begin, then, with one of the simplest, commonest links imposed by the language. The very phrase "split infinitive" tells us that someone is complaining about a broken link. In English the verb and its handle *to* ought not to be carelessly pulled apart. But the prohibition of the split infinitive is not absolute. An infinitive may be split for good reasons. The best reason is that a necessary modifier of the verb (e.g., an adverb) would be clumsy if put after a verb and would sound stilted if put before the *to*. There being no third place to put it, the infinitive is stretched apart and the adverb popped in between. Examine this pair of sentences: "You were not in a state to consider calmly the consequences" / "I want to encourage as many members as possible to not only attend our Annual Meeting but to actively involve themselves in the programs."

The first sentence sounds awkward, because the normal order in English is to modify verbs and nouns by putting the modifier before. The result is that *calmly* seems to go with *the consequences* and does not properly look back to *consider*. Indeed, to avoid splitting the infinitive, the writer badly splits the verb and its object (*consider / consequences*). Two modes of repair offer themselves: *calmly to consider* and *to calmly consider*. Of these, the first sounds priggish. I should without hesitation split the infinitive and write *to calmly consider.*

In the second sentence the reasons for the double split are null and void. *Not only to attend* is perfectly easy and normal, heralding a *but also* (of which we are given only the *but*), which can precede the verb in the same way. One feels no split between verb and object because *actively* is followed by *in* instead of a direct object. Anyhow, *actively* is unnecessary if *involve* means what it should; or, if *involve* is felt to be weak without an adverb, *to take active part* would do the work with no further trouble.

Most questions of splitting can be resolved in the same way. I need not add that the allowable split of the infinitive is limited to inserting one word, and the shortest possible. Anyone who writes: "They wanted to, in a manner of speaking, eat their cake and have it too" is virtually deaf and blind to language and requires severe clinical treatment.

Note that only the present active infinitive (*to go, to think, to find*) poses the question to split or not to split. Compound forms, perfect and passive (*to have gone, to be thought, to have been found*), all permit the insertion of modifiers between the auxiliary and the main verb without any sense of split: *to have permanently gone, to be unjustly thought, to have invariably been found.* All attempts to avoid an imaginary split in these compounds brand the writer as clumsy from fear and incompetence.

Turn now to the opposite type of linking, that which is done by closeness alone. Unlike the infinitive, which calls for *to,* there are many idioms and phrasings where the insertion of a linking word is redundant and therefore disallowed. The most blatant instance is provided by the recent colloquial use of *like* whenever the speaker halts for an idea. It soon becomes a habit like the *er—um* of a poor lecturer, and it chops up utterance, in disregard of the strongest habit of the language, which is to go straight from the verb to its *direct* object. Hence, "Oh, I'll have, like, a hamburger and a Coke" is detestable even in talk, because of the linguistic norm just mentioned, and also because of its draining all meaning out of *like.* What the speaker wants is a hamburger, not something *like* it, made of plastic.

There is little danger that this bastard *like* will find its way into written prose, despite millions of spoken uses every day, copied in many works of fiction. Usage is strange in its rejections as well as its acceptances. Time and numbers do not govern it. For example, *invite* as a noun has been used in speech for 250 years but never taken into standard use; "Hand me them pliers" for 600 years, and just as far from good form as ever. Nor has the shortening *'em* ("Give 'em the ax") displaced *them*.

INVARIABLES AND INTRUDERS

From *to* and *"like,"* which illustrate dissimilar modes of linking, we can generalize and say that idioms, clichés, verbs formed of two or more words, and original phrases properly made up for a single use must all be handled as organic wholes. Their internal and external links are fixed, except in the idiomatic postponement of the preposition to the end of a sentence. To pull phrases about is not to be bright and creative but to be sloppy and destructive. The reader who comes upon the distortions will stumble over the meaning and be irritated by the smartness. What follows illustrates in various ways this principle of integrity.

The simplest whole is the combination of verb and preposition, which has already been discussed under Diction. Certain verbs take one preposition invariably, others several with different meanings, still others take none. Respect each type of link. Thus in "His second testimony verged even closer to the incredible," the *closer* has insinuated its own *to* in place of the *on* that belongs to *verge*. And that mistake shows up (as so often happens) the shaky idea: to *verge on* something is to be as close to its edge as possible. Therefore *closer* is impossible.

You can often help yourself over an uncertainty by remembering the probability that the wanted preposition goes with the one buried in the word: *con-* (*com-*) mean *with* and call for *with*. In "This project is commensurate in size, scope, and complexity to our international organization" the *com-* rejects *to,* for *com = with.* Write: "commensurate with our organization." What led the writer to use *to?* Very likely the synonym hovering at the back of his mind, *corresponding* . . . *to* (for *corresponds* is a double-header—*to* and *with*). If you spot the hidden synonym you can usually straighten out the prepositions. But bear in mind that when you use two verbs in a row with a single object following, either both verbs must take the same preposition or the first must take none. Some writers are afraid of this second option and neglect it. Yet one can write: "His experience makes him the best person to *tackle* and succeed *in* his difficult task." These details may seem endless in number and difficulty, but they will become easy and obvious if the writer will only make it a habit to read good prose, prose in which correct linking is also habitual.

Verbs that take no preposition (*consider, infringe, commiserate*) are frequently given a needless one by the same hidden influence of a synonym. *Infringe* (your rights) suggests *encroach* (upon) and out comes *infringe upon*. *Consider* suggests *regard*, which needs *as*. If you are tempted to say, "I consider you as a fool," remember that you are applying the epithet to yourself.

That unexpected meaning lodged in *as* and linked with *I* is but another proof of the statement that language is not a set of interchangeable parts. Beware of heedless switching, inspired by some vague thought we happen to be toying with before expressing it. If this strictness seems to you excessive, reflect upon *may* and *can*, which are as close in idea as any pair of words. We say: "It may be that she's lost it," but we do not say: "May it be that she's lost it?" And we say: "Can it be that she's lost it?" and yet would not say: "It can be that she's lost it." This resistance to interchange is what we mean by idiomatic expression—one way, yes; the other, no.

The readiness with which we perceive unidiomatic turns in others is no guarantee of infallibility about our own. A native speaker is not likely to ask a stranger, "Please show to me the way." But he is being just as unidiomatic when he writes: "John would place his arm casually around the shoulders of anyone he was standing next." Hundreds of idioms require a given word and exclude another. Ignorant speakers or ill-read writers mix them up, but the idiom remains: *suffice* it *to say; see* to it *that it is done; hard put* to it *to survive.* It is ignorance to write *No question but what;* the right word is *that.* The choice of idiom is between *I cannot but go* and *I cannot help going;* not the mixture *I cannot help but go.* If you must pair *as a whole* and *in part*, you should

not leap to *in whole or in part,* for you would never say *in whole.*
One way out is *in part or in full.*

After *different* and *prefer,* idiom is a hard-hearted tyrant.
Whereas the illogical *different than* is common in England, it is
still frowned on in the United States, where readers will not even
accept *different to* but expect *from.* Using it leads to the awkward
but necessary: "She found the place very different from what it
used to be"; or, "In its effects, the hurricane of 1954 was no different from that of 1946." The trouble with *prefer* also occurs
with *than,* for the verb insists on *to—*"I prefer marmalade to
jam"—but with comparisons of acts in the infinitive the result is
awkward, indeed impossible: "I prefer to die *to to* submit." You
have to switch: "I prefer dying to submitting" (weak); "I prefer
death to submission"; "I would rather die than submit"; or—note
the useful turn—"I prefer to die rather than to submit."

CLICHÉS AND CAST-IRON PHRASES

Reasons will be offered later on for guarding against clichés. These
ready-linked expressions are not all of one kind; some are less
trite than others; some wrap up a complex situation in a few words
(e.g., *sour grapes*); and their use even when undiscerning implies
a fair amount of retentive reading. Once committed to a cliché,
however, you must not tamper with it. You cannot make it fresh
and new by unlinking and adding or changing words. If you must
say: *more sinned against than sinning,* leave it as you found it.
Your taste will be thought even worse if you write: *than consciously sinning.* The interloper underscores the poor judgment
shown in (*a*) using the cliché and (*b*) fiddling with it.

The same rule, "Keep hands off," applies to the many common
phrases that stand halfway between idioms and clichés: use them
as they are when they first come to mind. The typical one is *at
his (her) best, at its best.* Avoid: "chocolate cake at its tastiest
best"; "Alexander, playing at his unusual best." The added superlative about the cake adds nothing to the meaning, since the best
cake must be the tastiest. The inserted modifier about the tennis
player is actually ambiguous, since it is not clear whether he was
unusually brilliant, not usually brilliant, or even usually good.

In other cases of tampering, affectation and bad logic often go together: "The attorney went on, sparing the listeners not one sordid iota of the evidence." / "Things came to an unpleasant head." The unpleasantness has nothing to do with the head, and what are sordid iotas? The phrase is *not one iota* and it means *not one little bit;* for the Greek letter iota (= i) is a very small mark, without a dot, and it is sometimes written under another letter as a mere trace of itself. *Not an iota* brooks no descriptive supplement whatever. On other occasions writers will try to jam a secondary idea into an ordinary turn that is not so much a set phrase as the only possible sequence of words: "This would not have been true a brief four years before." The writer's first notion was: *not true four years before;* his second was: *and that is not a long time, in the given situation.* This afterthought is not rendered by *brief* where the writer has put it. Two thoughts often need two sentences, or a properly compounded one, not a last-minute squeeze-in.

THE USE AND MISUSE OF "A" AND "THE"

It may seem strange that the two links most chaotically applied in current writing are the two articles, definite (*the*) and indefinite (*a, an*), which link (it would seem) so naturally. The very word *article* means *a little joint,* and the convenient size of *a* and *the,* as well as their frequency in print, show that their function is not negligible or their behavior hidden from view. Why, then, the misuse, particularly the wrong omission of *the?* The main reason is the habit of reading captions and headlines: TRAIN RAMS CAR; PREFERRED STOCK CONVERSION MAY 20. In these typical summaries of fact there are no joints, no links; idiom is flouted for brevity, and sense often depends on the body of the text, which is *forced to repeat* in order to make the facts clear. After the first headline we read: "A freight train on the B & O lines north of town struck a station wagon driven by . . ." And the other caption is amplified so that we may know whether the date refers to this year or last, what the terms of conversion are, and who may or must convert.

The first type of misdeed, then, is to write running prose and suddenly fall into caption style. It is no mere inelegance; it affects meaning, and the contrast of the two manners over a short space can be annoying. "D. University *announces formation* of management and advisory foundation which . . ." / "Having seen their list *dwindle with desertion* of the best names on it, they could wind up supporting a Democrat." The "buried headlines" here are: "University Announces Formation of New Unit" and "List Dwindles with [from? by?] Desertions."

Yet one may doubt whether this offense against idiom would occur so often if another influence were not also at work—the desire for generality, coupled with a sudden wish to link the general with a particular. Here is a case: "Scott had begun the story in 1805 and put it aside on well-meant but poor advice of a friend." Idea no. 1: *put it aside on well-meant advice.* (*Advice* here is general, not attributed to anybody.) Idea no. 2, suddenly grafted on it, particularizes: *the* advice *of* a friend. Second thoughts are always allowed, but then one must go back and see to it that the links hold. The maxim is: *the* is indispensable in all places where later words define; *the* is the definite article; *the* . . . *of* is an undivorceable pair in the circumstances here discussed. Some examples to clinch the point:

"Though brought to the stake to be burnt, they were often shown mercy of strangling." *Often shown mercy* is one (general) idea; *the mercy of strangling* is another (particular); they don't link without *the* ahead.

". . . as important as Veblen's *Theory of Leisure Class.*" Look up Veblen's actual title if you do not know it from memory.

"With selection of the two final courses planned for the Community College . . ." Why *the* two courses when *the* is left out before *selection?* The first omission is arbitrary and jarring.

A letter from the Soviet Academy of Science inviting American scientists to a conference was written in excellent English except for two or three slips, all having to do with *the* and *a*. It showed that idiomatic linking requires close attention, for it is intimately bound up with the forms of thought established in the language. The letter said (1) that the meeting was "under sponsorship of the State Commission for Use of the Atomic Energy" and (2) that "the Organizing Committee has a pleasure to inform you . . ." In Russian *the Atomic Energy* is the normal way of understanding such an entity—the language defines at large what in English we leave indefinite unless we mean to specify, as in "*the* atomic energy of Plant No. 62." Again, in English we say "*the* pleasure of informing you" or "take pleasure in informing you" or "it is a pleasure to inform you," but not the combination (linking) of ideas that the Russians used.

Notice that the English particularizing with *of* expresses a possessive, or *partitive,* meaning. "The bill on meeting educational needs of the state" leaves us without a means of sorting out from all the needs of the state the portion being discussed. In the same editorial column the writer evidently felt the force of this demand, for he wrote: "... commits the nation to *the* suppression of this terrorism." In his earlier mood he might have written *to suppression of,* but idiomatic or logical linking is not a matter of moods.

That the present subject has to do with logic is shown by the different treatment required when the general idea is particularized by means of a preposition that is not partitive: "The patient is doing nicely after emergency surgery *for* the removal of a bullet in his back." No *the* required before *emergency,* but required before *removal.* To repeat, the . . . *of* forms a tight, unbreakable link; an indefinite general thought followed by *for, in, about,* and other prepositions forms a loose, non-partitive specification. We could rewrite our earlier example: "They were often shown mercy *in* their last moments"; the *in* phrase does not define the kind of mercy shown and therefore needs no *the.*

The difficulties with *a* arise most often when it is used instead of *the* in sentences similar to those just reviewed: "Some who read Blake's 'Prophetic Books' believe it a work of a madman." / "She then received a proposal of a commercial traveler." (Write *the work, the proposal* or *a proposal from.*) Usually, *a* . . . *of a* makes nonsense. So (as I think) does the universal use of *a* with a proper name to characterize a person's attitude or emotion: "It was a rueful Janet who met him." / "An angry Tomkins dominated the next round." / "A sarcastic Mephistopheles taunts a bewildered Faust." It is surely *the* Mephistopheles and *the* Faust who are before our minds; and the same goes for any individual named.

Their particularity, their uniqueness, calls for the definite article, formerly always used. The only time when "a sarcastic Mephistopheles" would be in order is when an actor plays a role in a certain manner. The logic of the *a* is then clear: out of all the possible conceptions of Mephistopheles he gives us *a* thus-and-so Mephistopheles. Note that with a general name (not proper or singling out) the use of *a* is clearly right: "It was *a* distraught mother who came to the police station"; but that same mother was "*the* nearly fainting Mrs. Jones."

MISSING LINKS

Two other kinds of unwarranted omission interfere with the well-knit sentence by weakening its parts. The first is an echo of the loosest colloquial speech that has no business in plain writing, and it can be quickly dismissed. "He's just a little stuck on himself, is all." Query: What is the subject of *is* and what are we to understand after *all*—all what? A variation on this shorthand occurs in: "So we got talking about this man used to visit Tarbell occasionally." / "We go out you have to mind the baby." It may be that decades hence *who* (relative) will be dropped idiomatically with certain verbs, as is now done with *that* (conjunction) after verbs of knowing, thinking, and the like. Until then the link stays in. Likewise, in the second example, the implied *if* at the beginning.

Worse, because in better repute, is the tendency to glue nouns, modifiers, verbs, and adverbs together without links, as in Eskimo or German. Here is a thirteen-unit compound with no visible joints: "Two women and 50 men set sail on a *three-to-eight-week three-thousand-mile* Observer *newspaper Transatlantic Solo Yacht Race* to Newport, R.I." Science, business, and education are the worst producers of this kind of writing. It is offensive even when only a few terms are fused, because the relations (and often the denotations) are scamped: what are *vocational skills areas?* Consider with ear and mind the following: "Our need is for a direct data acquisition system for electron diffraction patterns." (Doesn't *direct* go with *acquisition* rather than *data?* And surely the *system* is *for* the acquisition *of* data *about* the patterns. What the sentence mumbles about is a *system for patterns.*) Wrap your mind around this one if you can: "Costs are determined under the aggregate entry age normal frozen initial liability method of funding." While you struggle, let me only point out a second liability in such writing, and one not frozen: it is that the wide separation of the agglutinated terms tends to break idiomatic links: costs are determined *by* a method, usually, not *under* it. But the writer felt the weight of all his aggregate jargon and could only think *under*.

The "Germanic" phrases are most often advertisers' verbiage: "4,000 hard-to-find biographies"; "an easy-to-order form"; "an easy-to-follow, hard-to-put-down volume." These are overextensions of our privilege to write: *a soft-spoken stranger, a puce-colored housecoat, an up-to-date directory*. The privilege is not without limits. *Up-to-date, never-to-be-forgotten, ready-to-wear,* and a few others are tolerated because they are few and because they refer to commonplace facts. They would become intolerable if the way were open to endless manufacture—e.g., bitter-to-drink medicine, hard-to-assimilate information, processed-not-to-tarnish metal, and so on—one strong objection being that the final verb enters into a false relation with the following noun. It is not the *form* that is *easy-to-order;* it is easy to order *on.* Spoken aloud, the phrase *easy-to-read books* does not disclose its hyphens and suggests a statement: "It is easy to read books." The traditional *books easy to read; suits ready to wear,* which are locutions of equal length and greater clarity, are alone articulated—duly linked by thought and word, instead of merely thrown together for the reader to rearrange.

✳

Principle 6: Respect the integrity of set phrases, partitives, clichés, and complex modifiers.

Look over the sentences below, sort out the links that are broken, missing, or intrusive, and rewrite. Note down the principles of your rewriting by discussing implications, false leads, etc., in the manner of the text. (And don't overlook any flaws mentioned in earlier sections.)

1. Certainly the chief attraction of the projected visit would be absence of all previous plan.

2. All craft have been tested in anticipation of end of the strike.

3. Guest valet service is provided on demand of manager.

4. They were lucky enough to find an easy-to-upkeep, no-long-passage apartment.

5. The Council of Supervisory Association College Information Service Line is being operated by advisers from 9 to 5, Monday through Friday.

6. Some think widows ought not remarry.

7. Second by leaping second the copter was gaining height.

8. "What we got now," said O'Malley, "is a jewelry salesman got murdered and robbed. They tell me they got the case as good as solved, but they still put me on it. What good I should go around and ask a lot of questions when they already got the answers?" [This might be a faithful transcript of some other O'Malley's best utterance, but *this* O'Malley is represented as intelligent and educated. What do you think of his affectation?]

9. The best procedure would surely be to dredge thoroughly the pond.

10. The best procedure would surely be thoroughly to dredge the pond.

11. "No quid for no quo" is and always will be my motto.

12. Though elderly people, they courageously took a course to learn to defensively drive on the highways.

13. Demonstrators sometimes have and sometimes not interfered with rights of others.

14. His claim for the American reporter—"at his very good best the most active and persistent of his breed"—seems a trifle hyperbolic.

15. The editor said yesterday that the title of the book would be "The Death of a President." However, the magazine is calling its series of excerpts "Death of a President." There was no immediate explanation of the change. [Query: When is *a* President *the* President? And what do you think of *immediate* as used here?]

16. The challenge of these difficult to describe shifts in attitudes lies not only in describing them but also in putting them into a form that can be used to provide direction for the School.

17. Bewildered Speck Arraigned For Murder.

18. So far bodies of eight of the twenty victims have been recovered in the open sea.

19. Donation of urgently needed life-saving kidneys could

be increased through money incentives, a sociologist has proposed. [Watch out, in this example, for the easy solution that won't work and for the misleading modifier a little farther on.]
20. The visitor will want to view the only Puvis de Chavannes mural paintings outside of France.

LINKING NEXT-TO-NEXT WITHOUT AMBIGUITY

The English language having dropped most of its inflections (endings that show the function of a word), it depends on *placing* to show functions. The difference in meaning between *Dog bites man* and *Man bites dog* is entirely shown by placing. As a result, the connection between ideas in a sentence often depends on the order in which they come, the reader always assuming that what he is reading at the moment relates to what he read immediately before. In "There was discussion about having breakfast inside the swing door before they all stepped out of the building," the reader is told to visualize having breakfast inside the swing door before stepping out, whereas what took place inside the door [behind it?] was discussion, not breakfast. The most ludicrous blunders of this sort usually disclose themselves in revision, but not always. A first-class newspaper printed: "The Congressman sat informally on the carpet and discussed food prices and the cost of living with several women."

More likely to pass uncorrected are lesser scrambles, such as: "Earrings are available for pierced ears on request," where the proper linking is inevitably broken twice, since the first break (*earrings/for*) causes its counterpart later (*available/on*). The way to restore the sequence is to ask what the subject is. Obviously, *earrings for pierced ears;* then the predicate, *are available on request,* flows of itself. The next example is so twisted as to defy comprehension on first reading: "He hummed the song till the squall coming round the corner stung what of his face he could not bury like small shot." Here the final phrase, *like small shot,* invites us to look for the item it modifies, which turns out to be *stung.* Write *stung like small shot* and the meaning before and after the central idea is at least discoverable, though the sentence may still be ailing from other causes.

If you should harbor doubts about the ambiguity and other damage to meaning that false linking by juxtaposition can cause, ponder these sentences, the first of which is from a bank circular offering loans: "We have given help to people with money since 1792." / "The Army's investigation turned slipshod minutes after the fragmentation grenade killing of two officers when a sergeant emotionally named Private Smith as the probable killer because of his personality." / "The Courts and lawmakers united to put owners of animals which might stray in a state of absolute confusion as to what their liability might be." / "Federal officers entered a cabin where three men were hiding to execute an arrest warrant on one of them." The false linking occurs at: people with money / a sergeant named / stray in a state of confusion / hiding to execute a warrant. Knowing this, you can rearrange the rest, noting along the way that inserting commas is not possible except after *two officers* in the second sentence—feeble help at best. In reading, nothing is more annoying than to have to backtrack and reread after a false linkage of the sort here discussed. And simply rearranging will not always answer. For example, in an otherwise excellent novel one comes upon: "*Early morning bears* with it a sense of pressure." The trouble here needs *brings* instead of *bears,* and the absurd link thereby disappears.

LINKING BY USING CERTAIN SMALL WORDS

Of all English words, *like* and *with* are the linking words par excellence. The one makes a direct comparison; the other states a direct connection. Both need more careful use than they receive. Having spoken earlier of the unnecessary *like* in modern slang, which links nothing but the speaker's disjointed wits and which means just the opposite of *like,* we may go on to (*a*) the confusion of *like* with *as* and (*b*) the self-contradictory *like.*

It used to be that educated English and American speakers, without any special effort, marked a difference between *like* and *as.* The former was used for comparisons directed at nouns or their equivalents: "She looks like her cousin." / "The summons sounded like a Stand-and-Deliver." The latter, *as,* had a monopoly of comparisons introduced by verbs: "Do as I say, not as I do." / "The situation was just as you described." Under various influences, especially strong in England, the use of *as* with verbs declined, so that many educated people now say *like I do* and *like you described.* Were Shakespeare alive now he might entitle his play *Like You Like It.*

Certain writers who have discussed the change have recommended yielding to it without further fight. This acceptance might in time be tolerable, if the old usage and teaching had not tainted the new and brought about a chaotic state of affairs in the use of *like* and *as* with nouns. People vaguely remember that "there is something wrong" with *like* and they substitute *as* in places where it makes nonsense. Here, for example, are two consecutive sentences from a novel: "They were as two small boys taking a train ride in the zoo. Like a sardine in the middle of the tin, Bony managed to . . ." Clearly, the situations are identical: they were *like* two small boys and Bony was *like* a sardine. The variation is pointless.

But (you may say) what's the harm? Use *like* or *as* just as (like) you please. That, again, might be endured if *as* with nouns did not have to carry a meaning other than *like:* "He went to several banks and borrowed money *as* his brother." This strictly means impersonation and false pretenses, whereas *like* his brother would mean that they both went about raising the wind. That the confusion is not an imaginary danger can be seen in: "He threatened that if I interfered I would suffer. I now know what he meant. He had signed the blackmail letters as me." Here *as* tells us that forgery has been done, and this indication will disappear if *like* is used interchangeably with *as.* The temptation to merge them must be strong, when we find a well-known scholar and essayist garbling Keats's famous line and giving us: "The very word is as a knell."

I don't suppose we shall go as far as replacing "That's a good likeness" with "That's a good asness," but the idea of likeness, resemblance, things looking or behaving alike, is dented and diminished when we read: "She was surprised to find us sitting on the bench together relaxed and talking as old friends." The irony of the situation is that one senses under this blunder the pull of the former usage: *relaxed and talking as old friends talk,* in the very place where the same writer would probably insist on: *like old friends talk.* The mess is a prime demonstration of the truth that the neglect of old distinctions takes its toll in false fears, ridiculous confusions, and reduced verbal power.

Before going on to the troubles arising from *with,* a word must be added about the need to keep on an even keel comparisons using *like.* It will not do to liken the *quality* of A. with plain B.: "You may find religious mysticism in Whitman, but it is never witty like Donne." Religious mysticism cannot = Donne. Write: *like Donne's; like that found in Donne; as in Donne*— or substitute *"he* is never witty. . . ." Both ways compare comparable things. Again, watch *like* after negatives; they are always ambiguous: "Copperheads are poisonous snakes that give no warning, like rattlesnakes." Does this say that rattlesnakes give no warning either? For the truth you have two choices: "give no warning, as rattlesnakes do"; or, "snakes that, *un*like rattlesnakes, give no warning."

The nonsense that springs from *with* is due in part to its secondary or figurative uses and in part to its wrong attachments. The plain *with* in *Come with me* offers no chance to go wrong. It is when we write the figurative *with* in sentences such as "With her relatives gone, she could start on the housework" that error becomes possible. In that acceptable sentence *with* does not mean *with* at all; in fact, it means *without* (her relatives). What it links is the unexpressed idea of a necessary condition (people out of the way) with the equally unexpressed idea of purpose. You might call it an abstract parallel of the concrete statement "With this hammer, I can drive a nail."

You need not go through this sort of analysis every time you write an abstract *with,* but you must develop the habit of querying the *withness of the with.* Try: "Most are young with ages ranging from 16 to 21." What is *with* what? Nothing. It is unidiomatic to say "I am old with seventy-five years" or anything resembling it. The writer should have made a second sentence: "Their ages range . . ." Similarly, in: "The text had to be redone, with new copies arriving only yesterday." The text was not "redone with the new copies . . ." but rather *"and* the new copies arrived"— two distinct statements that refuse to be more closely linked.

Quite often the *with* is contrary to fact, as in: "G. was about forty, married with three oldish children and a wife who preferred his absences" ("married to a wife . . . and father of . . ."). "He was respected and well liked, *with* no one having any grievance against him" ("and no one had . . ."). *Married with a child* is frequent on book-jacket descriptions of authors, but it is not made reasonable by repetition. All such misuses betray the writer who will not think a moment to find the right link.

*With* is likewise the easy, sleazy mode of escape when the writer is ignorant of the right preposition accompanying a verb or the direction in which it faces: "They were cleared with [of] causing a public scandal, but sentenced for an offense against public order." / "Pearl was not a name she was often bestowed with by her friends" ("her friends often bestowed on her"). "Radiant sunbursts of 14-carat gold are centered with balls of dark green jade" ("have as centers").

The ambiguities that follow combine wrong placement and inattention to the force of *with:* "My habit of sandwiching holidays between jobs with my married sister . . ." The writer was a headlong linker who wanted *holidays between jobs* and *holidays with my married sister.* He could not have both and wound up having *jobs with my married sister*—the very opposite of the truth. Put *between jobs* after *sandwiching.* A similar case: "A car was seen standing close to the bungalow with its lights out." Query: Which is without lights? Yet another—and a peculiar—mislinking occurs in this orthopedic remark: "Doctors recommend the application of a narrow elastic bandage with sufficient force and for a sufficiently long time to give the sprained tendon a chance to recover." The context makes it clear that it is *a bandage with sufficient force* which is recommended. But the parallel form *for a sufficiently long time* can only modify *application.* The result is that the reader also attaches *with sufficient force* to *application,* which is nonsense.

MORE LINKS BY PLACEMENT: MODIFIERS AND DANGLERS

The prevailing lesson from our examples so far is that, in linking, closeness governs the effect, whether intended or not. (If in the previous sentence the comma after *linking* were left out, the reader would fuse the two words into one idea; he would think: *in linking closeness* [*with . . . ?*] and be left hanging. Note how he would have altered the function of the words: *Linking* would have changed from a noun to a participle and *closeness* would have changed from a subject to an object.) Experience suggests the maxim: The words we use as modifiers are best put close to the words they are to modify. "We are pleased to offer you a cup of complimentary coffee" violates the principle with no visible gain. It is the cup-of-coffee that is complimentary. "The man referred to by the Commissioner and his invariable assistant . . ." doubly disturbs our logical sense: are two men involved or only one? Again, no assistant is "invariable"; the meaning is *invariably his assistant;* the modifier was wrong for its place or the place wrong for it. Readers' responsiveness to nuances of placing differs, of course, but it is the power of feeling such distinctions that makes writing an art. It is this same feeling that makes piled-up modifiers always a little silly: in *The Portable Fireside Book of Horror Stories,* is the fireside as portable as the book?

There is a frequent need to link an adverb with a compound verb ("I *have always been*"), and the regular place for the modifier is shown in the example. The advantage of not departing from it in ordinary sentences is that a shift supplies a strong emphasis: "I *always* have been." Accordingly, the subtle writer who hopes to inform a subtle reader will mark a difference between "But it certainly cannot be shown" (regular placing) and "But it cannot be certainly shown."

Having said this, I must now deal with the wayward *only,* which does not follow the rule. One cause of its irregularity is idiom, custom, the habits of English-speaking peoples from Chaucer's time to yesterday. Pedants have tried to make us say "He died only last week," but what we continue to hear is "He only died last week." No confusion results. The phrasing is on a par with "God only knows," which no pedant could possibly alter into "Only God knows," if for no other reason than that there is a shade of difference between the meanings of the two remarks.

None of this implies that the fanatical campaign about *only* has had no results. They are widespread and usually bad. In a short story by a distinguished writer one finds: "She was in only under-wear." Again: "In the cipher the letters he had spelled only non-sense syllables." The sentence would be much clearer if it ran: "the letters that he had could only spell . . ." Can you imagine Ben Jonson's famous song beginning: "Drink to me with only thine eyes"? The fact is that most spontaneous uses of *only* are sound. Vigilance is required only (note the order of these two words) when a sentence contains two or more elements that could be restricted by *only*. It is then imperative to decide which it is and not allow *only* to occur vaguely at the head of the series. "If Bonaparte had sat on Louis XVI's throne, the difference would only have been seen in the longer time that it took for war to be declared." In that amateurish sentence ambiguity reigns from *only* onward. The writer's intention was surely not *only have been seen* (so as to exclude other means of judging), or *have been seen only* IN (excluding other signs of difference). What he probably meant was: The only difference would have been that war would have come later. And that is what he succeeded in not saying. A kindred mismanagement of *only* that might prove dangerous occurs in: "The chemical dissolves fairly readily and only a small dose can be fatal"—i.e., a large dose *cannot* be fatal. Get rid of *only* altogether.

The impulse on detecting this type of ambiguity is to substitute *alone* for *only*. Unfortunately, the placing of *alone* is also diffi-cult, owing to its several meanings. Does "Legislation alone will not right wrongs" mean legislation by itself or legislation, of all other remedies, will not? You will find writers denying you the chance to ascertain the answer. To be unmistakable, write: "will not, alone, right" or "alone among the means proposed . . ." From such examples the valuable lesson emerges that ambiguity is not due to a word's having two meanings, but to the liability of those meanings to be confused.

The so-called danglers that everybody jumps on are modifiers, often several words long and introduced by a present participle, which are not linked to the proper subject: "Quickly summoning an ambulance, the corpse was carried to the mortuary." "Stand-ing on the bank of the river, the first steamboat could be seen sailing majestically up the Hudson." This error in logic by which the corpse summons an ambulance or the steamboat stands on the bank is the bane of grammarians. It is familiar to all from repeated warnings and corrections. Do not neglect them.

But one difficulty remains, that of distinguishing between introductory phrases that can stand by themselves (*generally speaking, all things considered, owing to*) and those that require a logical and grammatical link with the words that follow. A good many writers still decline to use *due to* in the absolute sense of *because;* they insist on a preceding subject: "Her pneumonia was due to prolonged exposure," and not: "Due to prolonged exposure she contracted pneumonia." Yet it is noticeable that *due to* is going the way of *owing to,* whereas *based on* has won no such rights. Those who say "Based on a first survey, the prospects look bad" are still thought slovenly by most readers and writers, and for a very good reason. What is *based* in this typical sentence is not the prospects but the statement about them. "Based on my experience you probably have jaundice." / "Based on the forecasts he could not carry the state." All such basings are illogical and often contrary to fact. To be unable to carry the state means having no base at all: the forecasts and the voters both say No!

Danglers that consist of unattached participles or qualifying phrases need no further illustration or reproof here. Their avoidance may be made easier and simpler by seeing it as a matter of linking: what goes with what—in fact, in logic, and hence in grammar? Make sure of the right connection by testing it, so to speak, visually, and you are bound to be right. Note also that danglers, or more properly unattached fragments of thought and speech, can occur without a participle and in any part of the sentence: "The patience of all the founders of the Society was at last exhausted, except me and Roebuck." (From John Stuart Mill's *Autobiography.*)

⌘

Principle 7: Ideas connected in reality require words similarly linked, by nearness or by suitable linking words.

In this group of sentences, exercise your sense of fitness by going beyond the requirements of linking or unlinking: make better, shorter, tighter sentences.

1. The speed, vigor, and precision of the girls as they pitched, batted, and fielded was fascinating to watch, with never a moment when the ball seemed at rest.

2. She never produced the same impression of being a brilliant conversationalist as Virginia Woolf.

3. The title of the organization is: The Foundation for Aging Research.

4. A camera was already in position taking photographs from all angles of the undisturbed body.

5. The theatre was already full with a long line outside.

6. The complete notes of his lectures were published after his death in eight parts.

7. He is married with one child who is two.

8. Being December, we have very properly laid in a new almanac.

9. He would have liked a girl able to cook and bake and dress herself as his mother.

10. The drug could cause addiction at dosage levels not much above recommended.

11. I asked if he wanted some brandy and he said no, thank you, he thought he mustn't start drinking at his age—after knifing a man with a gun!

12. It is a work not easily found like his later ones.

13. Dr. ——— was shot to death yesterday afternoon in his office in what the police called a robbery.

14. The American dream to own a Cadillac, a Lincoln, or an Imperial may give way to a horse.

15. The Canadian leader won only seven of the 68 seats in the House of Commons, including none at all from the province of Alberta.

16. Deposits are being urged on all drink containers.

17. When the meter is working the driver is entitled to from 43 to 49 per cent of the fare.

18. No return of unacceptable articles due to lack of space.

19. One day, said Mr. W——— during the interview, I took some seeds with me and when the train passed some barren ground I threw the seed out of the window. It grew into a habit, and by the time I finished there was a solid mile of flowers.

20. Do the repairing yourself with professional invisible results.

## LINKING AS AN ELEMENT OF STYLE

Style can mean a great many things. In one sense, everything urged in this handbook is assumed to make for a good style. In another sense, which will come up under Tone, a mode or pitch of expression will be called a (plain, high, arrogant, low, facetious) style. Still a third and a most important conception of style is that which has in view the particular mixture of words, constructions, rhythms, and forms of expression characteristic of a writer, and which makes his work recognizable even when unsigned. Style so understood is a natural outgrowth of the person's mind and not something put together by an act of will.

But there is a fourth and narrow use of the word *style,* which is our concern at this point. A writer will say that he makes a choice between acceptable means of expression *for stylistic reasons;* that is, not grammar or syntax, clarity or logic requires the choice, but some other virtue that belongs to good style. The quality may be elusive or at least hard to name. Smoothness, elegance, force, even harshness, may be wanted in a given passage. Some of these "stylistic" considerations come to mind when linking is in question.

Many writers, for example (myself included), tend to avoid the "broken link" required by a pair of verbs with different prepositions: "I am fond of, and devoted to my mother-in-law." If you disallow this phrasing, find a pair of verbs that both go with one preposition (with none is still better) or link differently: "I am fond of my mother-in-law and devoted to her." Writers who make a habit of the broken link may fairly be suspected of showing off their misplaced accuracy at the expense of style.

In numerous works on grammar you will find a rule which appeals to those who like their guidance cut-and-dried. The rule says that the relative pronoun which introduces a defining (restrictive) clause must always be *that;* the pronoun for non-defining clauses is *which.* I have broken this rule in the previous sentence, where the rule-ridden would insist on: *the relative pronoun* that *introduces* . . . for what follows my *which* is a defining clause: it defines (limits, restricts, identifies) *pronoun* and is not a mere comment upon it. A comment (in this sense) occurs in: "The cutter 'Alicia,' *which* disappeared in a patch of mist, was bound for Valparaiso." Take out the *which* clause and the rest holds up, as is not true with a defining clause. The reason I broke the supposed rule is stylistic: I do not like to put close together two *that*'s of different meaning, the one a conjunction before a subordinate clause, the other a relative pronoun before another clause, nor do I favor the repeated sound.

Other reasons exist for retaining the flexibility I advocate: it has been kept by all the great writers of English; it is kept by writers in England and the Commonwealth to this day; it rarely interferes with clear meaning. In most passages the "defining" is lost even on highly educated readers and writers, who may never have heard of the rule; finally, it seems a bit cranky to limit the demarcation to *that* and *which:* why not also *that* and *who,* a pair similarly employed? Again, the defining sequence *that which* is unshakable ("An atom is that which cannot be further divided"), though the rule would call for *an atom is that that . . .*

Nor will the strict scheme work well where *which* and *and which* or *for which* are needed in pairs. In conclusion, I recommend using *that* with defining clauses, except when stylistic reasons interpose. Quite often, not a mere pair of *that*'s but a threesome or foursome, including the demonstrative *that,* will come in the same sentence and justify *which* to all writers with an ear. Test the suggestion for yourself with the aid of a sentence *that* gives rise not only to a stylistic consideration but also to one of immediate clarity: "It is understood by government agencies that award grants that applications must not cite as referees members of the panels by which the case is to be judged."

Another kind of feeling for style is required to detect awkwardness when, at first sight and even on reflection, no improved linking by placement suggests itself: "Two clerks testified today that they had altered some grades of students trying to enter college." The way to a decent sentence here is to dismantle the structure and recast the parts: They altered what? *Some students' grades* (and not *some grades of students*). What students? *Students trying to enter college.* Those two pieces refuse to be linked in one chain, because one is about students, the other about grades. The clerks, then, "altered the grades of some students who were trying to enter college."

Next is a typical situation which a practiced writer corrects "for style" virtually by reflex action: "He had ordered seasoned lumber of a superior quality to that formerly used." The sentence is clear and solid enough, but it is smoother and neater if one transposes: *of a quality superior to that.* (But remember to pair comparable things; do not make the *quality* superior to *a piece of lumber.* There may be need of rewording when the elements compared are not of a kind.)

It is elementary caution in comparisons that use *as . . . as* not to throw in a third *as* of a different sort: "They raised the height of the pile on deck, the ship sinking lower as gradually as long as the light lasted." For the same reason, it is better to start a concessive clause without a first *as.* Write: "Foolish as it seems, I answer questionnaires," and do not help revive the very old-fashioned form "As foolish as it seems . . .". All needless repetition is to be deprecated.

In your reading you will come across the titles of books used or cited, and you may notice that your author regularly includes *A* and *The* at the beginning of the titles, no matter what precedes. This now widespread habit would have struck our recent forebears as strange indeed. While it is only proper to write: "Gibbon wrote *The Decline and Fall of the Roman Empire,*" it seems to me and some others that it is as absurd to write "Gibbon's *The Decline*" or "his *The Decline*" as it would be to write "Gibbon's the hat" or "his the hat." It is *his hat* and *Gibbon's hat* for the simple reason that the definite article records the independence of the object named from any possession or attribution expressed by any adjectives.

Now, one is free to follow the modern practice, which looks scholarly and seems to show one is taking pains. But there are ways of satisfying both fashion and common sense, and making sure at the same time that the link follows good style. One way is to omit *his* (or *her*) when you are discussing an author and his works—no need to repeat that the successive books he wrote are his. Just say: "In 1884 Mark Twain published *The Adventures of*

*Huckleberry Finn."* A second way, if a possessive or epithet is absolutely required, is to interpose a noun, the title being in apposition: "Then came his first Sherlock Holmes story, *A Study in Scarlet";* or, "the unfinished novel, *The Brothers Karamazov."* (Turn over in your mind and roll on your tongue the horror of "the unfinished *The Brothers K."*)

A general suggestion about the words to be preferred for linking: they should be the shortest, commonest, and hence the least obtrusive you can find. They tie ideas together like a hidden stitch. In the Watergate investigation, viewers and readers were struck by the tiresome repetition of the phrases *at this point in time, at that point in time.* The English for that spinach is *now* and *then.* The superfluous *as of* belongs to the same class of useless terms. "Candidates must be under 35 years of age *as of* the deadline for applications." *As of* here equals *at* or *by.* " 'As of now I have nothing to report,' said Sheriff Martin" is identical with: " 'I have nothing to report.' " We could allow the sheriff a *now* at the end of the remark, or even an emphatic *right now* at the beginning, but his preliminary clucking incites only to asking: "As of when will you have something to say?" *As of* has one legitimate and restricted use: "You will graduate in June, but your diploma will be *as of* the February graduation list."

A hundred temptations exist in print and on the air to divert us from writing simply *in, on, at, now, then,* and the rest of the short, precise signs of time and place. Look out for such lures to vagueness and a pretentious style. *"Within the parameters of* my district I have done pretty well *in terms of sales"* means: "I have made a good many sales in my district." Nobody needs or wants to hear more than that to form a true impression of your abilities and your self-satisfaction.

⋇

Principle 8: For a plain style, avoid everything that can be called roundabout—in idea, in linking, or in expression.

A short exercise on those few aspects of linking (syntax, construction) that we have so far discussed, followed by an example of repetition to be judged and dealt with as it deserves.

A.   1. Tom was the last person to leave on the night crew, so that when Bert, discovered changing into dry clothes, offered them both a drink, Tom accepted.

2. Couples that don't have good communication with each other and can't talk about money are more likely than others to become "credaholics"—people who fall behind in credit payments.

3. We have shamelessly appropriated the idea to give an, shall we say, impressionistic picture of a publishing house.

4. I remember all the films he played in and I think he appeared in a "The Hound of the Baskervilles" that I never saw but was made around 1930.

5. Our impression was that the program was too traditional and that the students were not encouraged to elect the special courses that the college committee that had prepared the 1970 report were recommending.

6. We are both speaking from different frames of reference and it is not surprising that we are far apart in terms of agreement.

7. In a case of mistaken identity, a social service guard was critically wounded while on duty early yesterday by a policeman.

8. He was waiting to note an action that he might follow the influence causing it to its source.

9. I *am* willing to contribute to a birthday present for him, but I don't think we ought to express it bicyclewise.

10. They spent a delightful summer that they would long remember and that even without that windfall from Uncle Ben they could have made perfect.

11. She was sitting, the hostess, on the davenport of her long narrow parlor on one of New York's East Seventieth streets.

12. In the first place, I doubt if we can find a properly haunted house in a pleasant locality, that is for rent.

13. A buys a bureau from B at a sale with money in a secret drawer, of the existence of which neither A nor B is aware —what are the rights of A and B?

14. J.B. referred recently to W. H. Auden as the "greatest living poet in English." On a news broadcast this was paraphrased as: "The greatest living English language poet, alive." [Who was right?]

15. A fourteen-year-old boy was slashed to death early yesterday by one of two men he and two teen-aged companions are accused of having tried to rob.

16. There is no use saying that that boat that I bought was so thoroughly reconditioned that any skipper that sailed her would have wanted to take her away from me all that much.

B. 1. In addition to his lies concerning the company, Mr. ———— has also concealed some of his bank accounts from the Committee of Investigation. When called upon to list bank accounts he has held in the last three years, Mr. ———— concealed some of his bank accounts. Our independent investigation of his financial dealings has uncovered bank accounts he concealed from the Committee of Investigation. [From the committee findings as reported in the press.]

FORMS OF LINKING FOR WHOEVER WANTS TO SOUND NATIVE

The term *native,* as used above, is only shorthand for speaking *like* a native. Birthplace as such does not matter; it does not dictate speech. But we think of native speech as naturally idiomatic. Our earlier example, *Please show to me the way,* is clear; it is *"in English,"* but it is not native English. Neither is "I do exactly my best," as a recent golf champion from Taiwan said to an interviewer. Natives feel no need to learn most idiomatic turns, or indeed any part of the language for daily use. But when there is need or wish to increase the scope of self-expression, learning must be resorted to; and in this conscious effort, "native" comes to mean the best native speech, found to be so by the trial and error of reading and thinking about forms of discourse. The odd thing is that different portions of the one common tongue are differently dealt with by the careful native and the careless.

For example, apart from dialect variations, what is known in grammar as agreement is observed by everybody without thinking. *"They're* off," says the crowd at a horse race, and the same people refer to themselves individually by saying *I am—*not *I are* or *I is.* Plural and singular subject are simple ideas, and each usually (though not necessarily) takes a different form of the verb. But the careless writer will set down: "He is one of those golf players who is always giving excuses for his bad shots." He writes in effect: *golf players who is,* which he is quite incapable of saying in cold blood.

This error is no infrequent event. You will find it in thousands of articles and books, and you will hear it in every other conversation and broadcast. A world-renowned book reviewer permits himself that selfsame blunder: "Alan Paton is one of those lone *voices which,* in a tragic situation such as has arisen in South Africa, *manages* to keep calm." You may say that this defiance of agreement is basically the concern of grammar, not rhetoric. True, but a fault of such high frequency becomes the concern of rhetoric also, by reason of its implications for style. The stylist's warning is: if you must link your ideas in the form *one of those who,* remember the forms of your native speech.

A similar failure of agreement in number plagues those who do not take care of the linking after *no one, nobody, anybody, everybody, somebody* (all singular), and after collective nouns that admit of singular or plural use indifferently. With these last, whichever you choose, stick to. The logic lies on the face of it. If you start: "The public has been dragged in by *its* heels," it should not be hard to avoid what the writer stumbled into by adding: "not of *their* own choice." The public is one or many, not both in the same sentence. As for those other words *everybody, anybody,* etc., the argument that they may be linked with *their* quite logically if we think of them as collective would be sound if anybody had ever been heard to say: "Look, everybody *have* got a bit sunburned!" If *everybody* demands *has* close to it, the pronoun later on should not be *they, their,* or *them. No one* is clearly singular; *none* may be singular or plural, but may not wobble from one to the other.

As for couplings of words that are traditional (such as *wear and tear*), or not usual but close in thought (such as *the point and purpose*), it is either required or permissible to attach them to a singular verb: "The wear and tear is enormous" / "*Cox and Box* is a silly farce" / "The pomp and circumstance was overwhelming" / "Public relations is an instrument of politics" — and this last word reminds us that names of sciences ending in *-ics* vary in their demands on the verb: some take either singular or plural, others show a preference. Only attentive reading will instruct you, unless you live among those who continually use these words, and pick up the usage by ear.

Agreement as to person likewise shows the writer who knows his business. "S. P. & C. Company wishes to announce our new location." The *wishes* implies that the company is referring to itself in the third person; so the *our* should be *its*. But notice two possibilities, with different meanings, when you use *one* as a subject. Sense dictates whether *he* (*his*) or *one* (*one's*) is to follow. Read at a normal pace: "Under an oriental despot one must guess that his ideas of justice will agree with those for the time being of the judge or magistrate when he passes upon the matter." Rereading is needed here to discover that the first *his* does not refer to the despot, but to *one's* ideas; and that false *his* then creates confusion with the next *he,* who is a third character, the magistrate. Most uses of the impersonal *one* require *one* or *one's* linked with it, not *he* or *his,* because the *one* referred to is the same first and last.

A like continuity must be observed in linking the subject with a verb by means of a pronoun. There is an understandable tendency to think that whatever one is talking about is a subject in the third person, even if the subject is I. "I who not occasionally but invariably believes in equality" should be *I who . . . believe* = *I believe*. "It is you, my dear, who forbids me, no one else" (*you who forbid* = *you forbid*).

Questions of person naturally lead to errors of case—witness the extremely common misuse of *I* after a somewhat distant preposition. This blunder has been the result of a well-meant but foolish conspiracy to root out the use of *it's me*. The wrongheaded war against that quite idiomatic, informal locution created a bugbear in the minds of the ignorant or timid, which drives them to saying *I* whenever they have a chance. The upshot is the illiterate *between you and I; she gave it to Dick and I; including Captain L., Major A., and I; they all turned against Betty and I,* where *me* is manifestly the only legitimate word: no one so far has said or heard *they were against I; including I; she walked behind I* or anything like it. But as a letter writer to *The New York Times* remarked, the "carefully prepared and much-edited scripts for TV and radio will contain barbarisms such as 'they called he and I' and even 'with he and she . . .' "

The correlatives *either . . . or, neither . . . nor* would need no special mention (except for the occasional slip *neither . . . or*) if it were not for the spreading attempt to reinforce *nor* with *and* or *but* at the head of a sentence. *"And nor* was he in the least afraid." / *"But nor* did she mind his leaving her for weeks at a time." That is the opposite of simple-&-direct. *Nor* by itself has always done the work of *and* and *but* combined: it links and is adversative, both.

## PRONOUNS: THE SLIGHTEST SLIP IS FATAL

We now enter the dangerous wilderness of Pronouns. It is the duty of pronouns to be not wild but tamed, that is, tied down; yet their natural tendency is toward the jungle. At the same time, no decent prose is possible without the solid links afforded by pronouns with the right connections. Here is a short letter to the editor from a newspaper reader: "In your editorial of . . . , you write: 'It would be ironic if Mr. Johnson's expression of confidence in General Ky contributed to his downfall.' Whose downfall?" A fair question. Every pronoun necessarily has an antecedent. Which person or thing *in the sentence* that antecedent is must be immediately clear to the reader.

So much everybody presumably knows. But in framing and in revising sentences for right linking, you must make sure that no doubt can arise: *find* the antecedent, being acutely aware that (*a*) what *you* clearly see as the only possible link will not automatically possess the reader's mind; other links may seem just as plausible; (*b*) the last-named object or idea is not necessarily the antecedent; (*c*) an idea implied but not stated in the sentence can never be an antecedent; (*d*) you must at all costs avoid, by suitable rewording, the evasion *his (George's) motorbike; loved her (Sarah) for herself,* and so on.

When you have given sufficient attention to this, the greatest difficulty in the writing of English prose, you will know that *which* is the pronoun most likely to go wild: "Nowhere could he find any evidence of the message having been sent, or written, or even thought of, which is nevertheless what the opposition continued to allege." What exactly did the opposition say? That is the thing the reader wants to know, and nothing in the sentence tells him. Even if the writer had stopped at *having been sent,* there would be no anchorage for *which* to be tied to; with those two afterthoughts the link is fouled even worse. We need a positive "that the message was sent" for "the opposition alleged" to mean anything. And, of course, personal pronouns must be held by the same strong ties to an existing antecedent, as fails to happen in "It might yet be written that *mankind,* ignoring the warnings of scientists, continued to brutalize *his* environment and so brought upon *himself* a new Ice Age."

About the doubleheaders *which . . . and which, who . . . and who,* a full discussion would take us far into questions of style. Here let it be said only that the absolute prohibition "No *and which* without a preceding *which"* is wrong. The first may be absent when the parallel relation obtains in that earlier part of the sentence, though not marked by a *which* or *who.* Nobody would say "the girl I love who loves me," but "the girl I love *and who* loves me." No earlier *who* is in sight, yet the sentence is correct, because *whom I love* is so evidently the (hidden) form of the main thought. *Which* and *and which* follow the same logic.

But no logic at all seems nowadays to govern the choice between *who* and *whom,* which are among the most frequent connectives in the language. One finds in reputable print: "The Board changed signals yesterday and offered a job to Mr. G. who it fired as law librarian last week." / "He asked for Dr. Schiller, who he knew, and got him." / "Mr. Konrad, our president, who we had come to meet . . ." In despair, the desirability of dropping *whom* altogether has been canvassed; and on being asked my opinion, I agreed. It does seem as if *whom* had disappeared like other inflections in English—people no longer want to be bothered. But the supposition is in fact wrong, because the same prints, the same writers, fill their prose with: "I would hire only those whom I felt would stay with the job." / "Was this the couple whom he believed had been ahead of him on the mountain?" / "Incredible to her that she could be the woman whom it was thought had set her nets to catch the earl." In these last three sentences *who,* not *whom,* is required, because it is the subject of the verb in the clause introduced by the pronoun. Nobody says or writes: *whom would stay, whom had been, whom had set.* Clearly, there is no great popular resolve to make *whom* vanish from the earth; it flourishes in the wrong place while its rival, *who,* is ignored when its presence is called for. In this confusion caused by the anti-snob snobs, a little empirical advice is all that can be given:

1. Make it *who* whenever the verb form that follows could be wrapped in parentheses without changing the sentence: "who (he believed) had been up the mountain."

2. Make it *whom* when, as direct object, you would write *him* and *her* and *them* in place of *who(m).* "Who he knew" goes against the grain when the same relation would be expressed by *he knew him,* not *he knew he.*

3. If a preposition governs the *who,* current educated usage tends to drop the *m* when the two words are separated by others: "Who do you wish to speak to?" But "To whom do you wish to speak?" The first sentence of this pair seems influenced by "Who is it that . . .?"

4. Finally, there is the idiomatic but irregular *than whom,* which is as deeply embedded in our ears as *it's me* and will not soon be uprooted.

If these guidelines do not help you to choose, try training your ear. "For who is this package?" sounds barbarous; remember *For Whom the Bell Tolls.* Avoid the jingle *who you know*—though unfortunately one cannot avoid *you who.* Finally, make a difference between your writing and your speech, if you feel embarrassed when asking a friend who went to the movies, "With whom?" Say "Who with?" and write "With whom?"

The proper linking of pronouns with antecedent nouns includes one commandment that may seem superfluous because it is difficult to remember: there can be no logical link between a proper name in the possessive case and a personal pronoun. "Wellington's victory at Waterloo made him the greatest name in Europe" is all askew, because there is in fact no person named for the *him* to refer to. *Wellington's* is not a noun but an adjective; it corresponds to "the *Wellingtonian* (victory)" and the only subject word is that same *victory,* with which *him* obviously doesn't go. Since many sentences follow this pattern of possessive + noun + pronoun, watch the connections and take care either to free the person from the possessive or to change the pronoun and make it refer to what is actually named.

As for referring to antecedent ideas—sentences or statements taken as a whole—only the closest attention will prevent ambiguity or blunders. The most frequent linking words are *which* (placed at the end of a completed thought) and *this* (used as the opening word of the next sentence). "He was not only handsome and rather stupid, which didn't do much for his future." The meaning here is altogether obscured by the combined action of the *not only* left up in the air and the *which* clause that is linked to nothing in particular. The same dispersion of thought occurs in: "They hunted high and low, they stripped to the skin, they accused each other in hostile glances—the rare coin was not to be found. This left a mark on all those present that time would not efface." Was it the search, the hostility, or the failure to recover the coin that is meant by *this?* Ask the question and use the answer in your sentence: *this predicament, occasion, unhappy event, unforgettable evening,* etc. Make sure the connection is simple and unambiguous; a demonstrative that points nowhere in particular will not link.

✳

Principle 9: Agreement is as pleasant in prose as it is in personal relations, and no more difficult to work for.

Remember to be conscious and critical of all faults, including clumsiness and bad logic.

1. It is I, please remember, who is on the spot.
2. Conan Doyle is one of those authors who was also a man of action.
3. It is one thing to expose as often as one can the enemy's cruel treatment of prisoners (with which I have no quarrel) but it is another to make reckless statements to which no credence can be given.
4. No one has any business to interfere with anyone else's opinion, even if they are married.
5. He took the mike and in his deepest voice said: "This is thy father, who art in heaven!"
6. The distinguished-looking pair entered the box and sat down; she took off one glove, looked around, and asked of nobody in particular "Whom is singing tonight?"

7. In tracing the thief to that lodge I enlisted the help of one or two of the tenants whom I think were certain to be on the side of justice.

8. The appointment was made by telephone between his confidential executive secretary and I in person.

9. One always thinks the grass is greener on the other side of the fence, until he steps over and finds it's not.

10. Unless somebody has found it since we looked this morning and they have turned it in, I'm afraid it's lost for good.

11. The afternoon was one of those rare perfect days, neither too hot nor too cold (and nor too bright either) which is likely to occur only in June.

12. Hank would not give his consent to his (Arthur's) selling the old clock.

13. I was born on November 29 in the early hours of the morning, while my father was away preaching in a neighboring town. This only happened twelve times a year.

14. Is a point never reached when the aggregate tally on a leader and his chosen associates and their principles be admitted a gross disgrace to the nation?

15. I have rarely seen a finer woman than my mother, never than my father.

16. Come on, tie loose with whatever you know!

17. On the littered table there were a gas bill and an electric bill.

18. He had a disadvantage in his colleagues' view of a private income.

19. [Sign on a scaffolding in a terminal] We are working for the installation of a new escalator.

20. [From a school story of a century ago] "Mr. Smith presents his compliments to Mr. Jones and says he has a cap which isn't mine, so if he has one that isn't yours, no doubt they are the ones."

LINKING WITH AND WITHOUT "APOSTROPHE S"

Some writers still make it a point of elegance to avoid the so-called fused participle—"Do you mind Ethel going with you?" (instead of *Ethel's*), although it is eighty years since Oscar Wilde wrote in *The Importance of Being Earnest:* "I don't think there is much likelihood of you and Miss Fairfax being united"—*Fairfax's* being clearly impossible. How, then, do we link—with or without *'s* (and its equivalent possessive forms: *my, his, their,* etc.)? The case for always dropping the possessive is strong when adding an *'s* is out of the question. "I doubt this being said at such a time and place" seems both natural and neat, and it allows no room for *'s.*

A great many other words also forbid the *'s,* either by their sound or by their meaning: "He was certain of his reticence being favorably regarded." Here a foolish hissing would be set up by adding *'s,* at the same time as the idea of ascribing possession to neutral, abstract, or inanimate subjects repels, as for example in, "They rejoiced at the news of their investments being saved." In his lines "To a Child," the poet Hopkins has: "Margaret, are you grieving / Over Goldengrove unleaving," where *Goldengrove's* would offend neither ear nor sense. We may therefore follow our judgment in linking with or without *'s,* this judgment being guided by the rule that false meanings, even if temporary, should be avoided: "Do you approve of women having equality" creates a momentary confusion just before *having.* The traditional *'s* after *women* is simple and logical and makes it clear that the approval relates to the possession of equality.

CONNECTING TENSE WITH SENSE

When compared with other languages, English is restricted in its power to indicate nuances by the sole use of tenses in combination. It would therefore be sensible to turn conservationist about such few nuances as remain. Yet like the wasters of other natural resources, we are doing just the opposite. Here is a distinction produced by the sequence of tenses alone: "He knew that you and I never met" / "He knew that you and I had never met." The first means: we were acquainted but no longer used to meet; the second: we were never acquainted.

With *yet* and *since,* the perfect tense (verb with *have*) is compulsory: "I haven't yet washed my face"; "I haven't seen him since his promotion." The use of *didn't wash, didn't see* is barbarous; as is, in a lesser degree, the combining of *do* or *did* with a previous verb in a form hostile to linking. "His children knew a lot of youngsters he didn't" implies as the full form: *didn't knew.* Many of us speak in this careless fashion, but ought not to tolerate the same slipshod incoherence in our writing.

The perfect tenses allow distinctions to be marked in the relations between indicated times in the past, and it is not hard to make use of the several meanings thus available. Take *I should have liked to go* and *I should have liked to have gone:* many speakers use these indiscriminately to express regret. But the first says that at some time in the past, usually specified in the context, my wish was to go. The second says that in the past, my wish was *to have gone* at a still earlier time. This contrast gives the clue to yet another form of regret: *I should like* (now) *to have gone* (then, earlier)—three thoughts where only one grew before.

The familiar linkage that expresses condition or hypothesis—*if I could have, I would have*—leads to some miscalculations when the meaning of *would have* is not firmly grasped and the two conditionals are reversed: "If my brother would have been my sister, I could have gone to college sooner." The sentence as written means "if my brother *had been willing to be."* The symptom of error is the *if I would have;* it is almost always a false rendering of *if I had.* What encourages the use of the wrong and clumsy form is the colloquial pronunciation *if I would of.* The same caution applies to *will* in the same illicit hybrid: "If I will go, I'll be sure to win." When the idea of willing is involved, then the *will* has point: "If I will go, they will pay all my expenses." In short, there is a *would* and a *will* that mean desire, determination, and a similar pair that serve as auxiliaries without such a meaning. The former are rarely used and they lead to trouble when not intended.

A developed sense of what is past from the point of view of the present and from the point of view of the past is a desirable skill for the writer who indulges in psychological, social, and historical speculation. Consider: "He was an honest man suddenly seeing where his prejudices may have led him." The *may* here is on the same level of present time as *seeing* and is therefore exactly descriptive. Not so with the following: "Mr. H. told the police he thought his wife may have fallen"; *might* is needed, because of the doubly indirect discourse. His thought was: "Heavens, she may have fallen!" He told the police: "My thought was: She may have fallen"—all plain sailing so far. But the reporter's "He told . . . that he thought . . ." throws the linked verb into the past *might.*

The neglect of these connections of time, actual or commanded by indirect discourse, leads rapidly to a haphazard or arbitrary mixture of past and present. It is a noticeable blight on the prose now coming out of England; and what happens there undermines us here, as is evidenced by the examples that follow. They concern the form required after verbs of thinking, knowing, suggesting, requesting, and the like, which are frequent in all writing. The mood needed for clarity is the subjunctive; it can be shown that the indicative, past or present, is an evasion that fosters ambiguity and generates nonsense. "Was it C.'s idea that you *spent* the evening with me?" This simple question actually means: Did C. think *you had done so?* Whereas the intended meaning is: You are spending the evening with me; was it C.'s idea *that you do so?* The wording must therefore be: "Was it C.'s idea that you *spend* the evening . . ." Again: "But he had insisted that we were his guests." This literally means: He reminded us *that we* already *were* his guests. The context shows that the author tried to say: "insisted *that we be* [that we *become,* from that moment on] his guests." Not: You *are* my guests, but: You *must be* my guests.

These two errors came about through avoiding a plain duty by using the wrong tense and mood, the past indicative. The next examples fly off, for the same wrongheaded purpose, to an equally bad present indicative: "The demand of the American people that the NATO powers are strong enough to carry on . . ." The NATO powers are strong or they are not; no one can demand *that they are,* but only that they *be.* If the plain subjunctive sticks in the throat of the bashful, it is always possible to write *that they should be.* "I suggested to the manager that he provides a new series of morning-hour shows." If he *provides* it, he needs no suggestion. Write *that he (should) provide.* Still more glaringly absurd: "It's a matter of considerable importance that he knows I'm here." *That he knows* asserts the fact of his knowing; but the point of the message is: he doesn't know and it is important *that he (should) know.*

The subjunctive, like the past tense with *as if,* shortly to be illustrated, keeps the present indicative for its sufficiently burdensome duty of indicating matters of fact, realities that *are* and (occasionally) that will be. Notice the muddle in: "As she refused probation, X. said 'It would be the height of dishonesty if I accept.' " Since *I accept* is the opposite of the speaker's action and state of mind, it must signify a future state, and in that case the earlier verb must also be future: "It *will be* dishonesty *if I accept."* That supplies a sound meaning, but it is still not what the speaker means, for she is not for a moment considering acceptance; she is affirming a condition contrary to fact: "It *would be* dishonesty *if I accept*ED—but I am not going to accept." All ideas introduced by *as if* are similarly contrary to fact: "Don't be silly—as if I thought you would steal change off my dresser!" Substitute the present *I think,* as careless writers do, and you stultify your own meaning. "Crowther's the one who walks *as if he has* two wooden legs." Obviously he hasn't, or the comparison would be pointless.

We have done with Linking; not that all conceivable types of connection have been considered—they are inexhaustible. But enough situations have been dealt with to make you conscious of the need to look fore and aft in order to see what ought or ought not to be joined and in what manner. The linking of larger units —sentences and paragraphs—requires attention to other parts of discourse and will occupy us later under the heading of Composition.

⌘

Principle 10: Cling to your meaning. The tense or mood of a verb in a linked pair can destroy it.

As usual, please, a full discussion of the issues raised by your corrections.

1. If only that fire had not occurred, Sergeant, I may have been able to prove to you what I say.

2. It was clear that he would have preferred to have seen every man-jack of them slain by tribesmen.

3. A good scholar but vain, T. will repeat a newly acquired piece of information as if he knows it all along.

4. I suggest with all due respect that I am named executor under the will. [Tricky: be careful!]

5. He liked lazing about on the river in a canoe. He seldom took a skiff. Perhaps he would have been safer if he did.

6. Mother detested me being so friendly with Richard.

7. There was evidence that the young man may have committed suicide with poison. [Tricky: weigh alternatives.]

8. The estate was bequeathed on condition that he lived there.

9. If only I would have proposed she would of been mine right now.

10. Washington was dead against the United States's entering what he called entangling alliances.

11. After a few minutes of awkward silence, he expressed a wish that they went to the park, where the band will be playing.

12. Imagine the nerve! He asks that I am relieved of duty.

13. I don't picture me being tattooed, ever.

14. Don't say "I may," dear—it sounds so unlikely. Say "I might" and make me happy.

15. Since he didn't come yet, the only way to get the check cashed is to ask his wife to endorse it as she did for Edward several times before.

16. There had been fear in his face and for a moment it had been as if I was looking at a person I have never seen before.

17. The manager then required that she plays both roles the same evening.

18. I haven't enough to travel on and you do.

19. If only it would of occurred to him that he goes and tries for the job on a gamble like his brother did and was lucky.

20. Waiting in the other room he wondered while the fans scrubbed away any dust he may have imported.

## TIME OUT FOR GOOD READING II

Dorothy L. Sayers (1893–1957) was a great scholar, a writer on social and religious topics, and the author of twelve detective novels that connoisseurs regard as masterpieces of the genre. She frequently discussed in print the principles on which such tales are to be created and judged. The extract below is from a popular lecture she delivered at the University of Oxford in 1935.

### Aristotle on Detective Fiction

Some twenty-five years ago, it was rather the fashion among commentators to deplore that Aristotle should have so much inclined to admire a kind of tragedy that was not, in their opinion, "the best." All this stress laid upon the plot, all this hankering after melodrama and surprise—was it not rather unbecoming—rather inartistic? Psychology for its own sake was just then coming to the fore, and it seemed almost blasphemous to assert that "they do not act in order to portray the characters; they include the characters for the sake of the action." Indeed, we are not yet free from the influence of that school of thought for which the best kind of play or story is that in which nothing particular happens from beginning to end.

Now, to anyone who reads the *Poetics* with an unbiased mind, it is evident that Aristotle was not so much a student of his own literature as a prophet of the future. He criticised the contemporary Greek theatre because it was, at that time, the most readily available, widespread and democratic form of popular entertainment presented for his attention. But what, in his heart of hearts, he desired was a good detective story; and it was not his fault, poor man, that he lived some twenty centuries too early to revel in the Peripeties of *Trent's Last Case* or the Discoveries of *The Hound of the Baskervilles*. He had a stout appetite for the gruesome. "Though the objects themselves may be painful," says he, "we delight to view the most realistic representations of them in art, the forms, for example, of the lowest animals and of dead bodies." The crawling horror of *The Speckled Band* would, we infer, have pleased him no less than *The Corpse in the Car, The Corpse in*

*Cold Storage* or *The Body in the Silo.* Yet he was no *thriller* fan. "Of simple plots and actions," he rightly observes, "the episodic are the worst. I call a plot episodic when there is neither probability nor necessity in the sequence of the episodes." He would not have approved of a certain recent book which includes among its incidents a machine-gun attack in Park Lane, an aeroplane dropping bombs on Barnes Common, a gas attack by the C.I.D. on a West-End flat and a pitched battle with assorted artillery on a yacht in the Solent. He maintained that dreadful and alarming events produced their best effect when they occurred, "unexpectedly," indeed, but also "in consequence of one another." In one phrase he sums up the whole essence of the detective story proper. Speaking of the denouement of the work, he says: "It is also possible to discover whether some one has done or not done something." Yes, indeed.

Now, it is well known that a man of transcendent genius, though working under difficulties and with inadequate tools, will do more useful and inspiring work than a man of mediocre intellect with all the resources of the laboratory at his disposal. Thus Aristotle, with no better mysteries for his study than the sordid complications of the Agamemnon family, no more scientific murder-methods than the poisoned arrow of Philoctetes or the somewhat improbable medical properties of Medea's cauldron; above all, with detective heroes so painfully stereotyped and unsympathetic as the inhuman array of gods from the machine, yet contrived to hammer out from these unpromising elements a theory of detective fiction so shrewd, all-embracing and practical that the *Poetics* remains the finest guide to the writing of such fiction that could be put, at this day, into the hands of an aspiring author.

❖

There are some unfamiliar words and names in these light-hearted remarks—*Peripeties, Philoctetes, gods from the machine;* what, if anything, justifies their presence in a popular lecture, that is, one not addressed to a class of specializing students? At the same time, how does the lecturer let us know that although we are not to take her words literally, she is not indulging in pure fantasy, either?

Did you notice the distinction between a detective story, which Aristotle would approve, and a thriller, which he explicitly condemns? If you did, can you reword the difference for yourself and think of an example of each?

Who wrote *Trent's Last Case, The Hound of the Baskervilles,* and "The Speckled Band"? Have you any desire to find out? If not, why not? These are obviously classics of crime fiction, which a student of writing might find it profitable to read, and enjoyable besides.

# Tone and Tune
## or What Impression Will It Make?

## III

### TONE RESULTS FROM DICTION AND ATTITUDE

What the reader calls pleasant or dull, what he remembers easily and returns to with eagerness, what he wishes more of in the form of new essays or stories or polemics, or warns his friends to keep away from, is largely a function of Tone. With rare exceptions, the subject matter of writing is common property to hundreds of authors. It is the treatment that makes the subject more or less acceptable. To be sure, the response to any work varies with each reader, but it is possible to describe and classify tones so that the intending writer comes to notice in his own reading not the effect created as a whole—that is virtually automatic—but the features that make it what it is. Only by so doing can he learn to avoid the bad and adopt the good.

Read, then, for Tone as well as for Diction and Linking. Try, for a start, to catch your first spontaneous impression as you read: "When you're busted for drugs over there, you're in for the hassle of your life." Do you enjoy being addressed in that tone? Do you tend to feel that the warning assumes you are a drug-taker? Are you surprised to learn that the words come from the U.S. Department of Health, *Education* and Welfare? You may on second thoughts conclude that the tone is just right for those who need the caution; it wasn't intended for you. But should not an official government notice be couched in language suited to everybody without exception? If it is designed only for some, then perhaps the tone is not right either. One can imagine tougher and hotter words, which would be still less intelligible to those not concerned. And while we are on words, isn't *hassle* a feeble description of the threatened trouble?

Your answers to these questions are your own affair. What matters is that you have been considering tone. Obviously tone is generated by words, so we shall now be discussing words again, as in Section I. Both tone and words are the manifestation of an attitude. Whether put on or unstudied or (in most cases) half conscious, the attitude inspires the choice of words, affects the length and rhythm of the sentences, and produces an impression that the reader *always* takes as deliberately aimed at him. He responds to the atmosphere, and from it pictures the personality of the writer, or at least his professional type. That is why tones can be characterized by such terms as: journalistic, novelistic, legalistic, pedantic, patronizing, arrogant, smart-aleck, shuffling—and as many others as the writing itself puts into our minds.

Dickens's great creation Mr. Micawber had a characteristic tone: "My eldest daughter attends at five every morning in a neighboring establishment, to acquire the process—if process it may be called—of milking cows." That is of course the pompous tone, but it is redeemed into humor by the speaker's evident awareness that he is putting on airs. He gives himself away in "if process it may be called" and in the abrupt fall on "milking cows," instead of some roundabout description of "the process." Today, as we shall see, people who write pure Micawber, modern style, show no sign that they hear themselves, and tedium, not humor, is the result.

Yet in their heavy-footed way those moderns at least attain consistency, which is the prerequisite of tone. Tone need not always be uniform but it can be harshly broken by the occurrence of an ill-assorted word or phrase. The aptest words, if not sustained by good linking, good sense, and good rhythm, will lack unity of tone. The impression given will be incoherent, and the atmosphere—possibly well established and pleasurable at the start—will dissipate.

Any ironic sentence makes it clear that tone is only partly determined by diction: "Some of us can get to work without having to hear the whistle blow first." The remark may be friendly joshing or resentful sarcasm, depending on the speaker's tone of voice. When the voice is absent, we meet again the difficulty of doing its work by other means. Context and comment are two such means, but comment is open only to a narrator; a writer of exposition or argument cannot stop to say "This is a joke"; he must rely on context and, more generally, on the tone he has maintained from the beginning of the piece.

Before discussing a number of tones encountered in the prose of today, I want to lay it down as an axiom that the best tone is the tone called plain, unaffected, unadorned. It does not talk down or jazz up; it assumes the equality of all readers likely to approach the given subject; it informs or argues without apologizing for its task; it does not try to dazzle or cajole the indifferent; it takes no posture of coziness or sophistication. It is the most difficult of all tones, and also the most adaptable. When you can write plain you can trust yourself in special effects. The plain tone is that of Lincoln always, that of Thoreau, Emerson, William James, Mark Twain, "Mr. Dooley," Fitzgerald, and Hemingway at their best. It is the tone Whitman urged on his contemporaries: "The art of art, the glory of expression . . . is simplicity. Nothing is better than simplicity . . . nothing can make up for excess or for the lack of definiteness." Bear in mind this subtle notion that nothing can *make up for* affectation or vagueness.

THE PREVAILING TONE: PSEUDO-TECHNICAL

The attitude that produces the pseudo-technical tone is made up of a desire to dignify the subject and the writer, coupled with the belief that important matters require a special vocabulary. Since most matters neither have nor need one, the vocabulary is made up of nouns and verbs used metaphorically. They come and go with fashion inside professional and business circles, then spread outside by chance imitation. Here is a scientist declining membership on a committee: "I am sorry not to be able to accept the experience of more intensive interaction with your group and its constituency." This is what I have called Micawber, modern style. *Experience, intensive interaction, constituency* are the pseudo-technical words, brought forth by the attitude of a writer who is unwilling to say plainly: "I am sorry I cannot join the committee; I should have enjoyed working with its members."

Here is a young man trying to rise in his profession: "I am now seeking sharper challenge in my preferred sphere." The tone is meant to suggest the knitted brow of ambition and ability combined. And one must acknowledge that it may have impressed others, who also think plush instead of prose. The applicant might have been passed over if he had written: "I want more responsibilities in my work, which is . . ." whatever it was. The educationist is often the worst offender on all counts: "It is hoped that this report will be helpful in the considerations educators are giving to the inclusions of aviation curriculum." *Be helpful* for *help* is a dead giveaway; *considerations* in the plural blurs the sense; *giving to the inclusions* is gibberish, and *aviation curriculum* without *the* in front of it (note the odd *the* before *inclusions*) completes an effect of mixed stuffiness and shuffling which is deplorable.

Certain signs in your own writing will tell you when you have fallen into the pseudo-technical: (*a*) an excess of nouns ending in *-tion* (remember to shun "-shun"!); (*b*) the use of verbs ending in *-ize* suggestive of *process* ("if process it may be called"); (*c*) the presence of terms drawn from technology and other ologies, where they may or may not have a truly technical meaning; finally, (*d*) the clustering of words without links, to define classes of objects and often preceded by *non-:* "non-violent and non-age-discrepancy sex offences."

Symptom *c* may be illustrated by: "Substantive rights and rules should be removed from the *focal point* of legal discussion, in favor of the *area of contact* between judicial (or official) *behavior* and the *behavior* of laymen." The italics are in the original, as if the author had known he was obscuring his meaning with pseudo-technicalities. Symptoms *a, b,* and *d* occur together in: "Three classifications of nominations are processed out of this office and are finalized for payroll name entry action out of the Controller's office." *Classifications* are nothing but *classes* or, better, *kinds. Handled in this office* is preferable to what stands written. *Finalized* should be *completed,* and in any case *by,* not *for.*

The whole story might boil down to this. "Three kinds of nomination [singular] are handled in this office. They are completed when the Controller enters the names on the payroll."

A strong impulse noticeable in the attitude behind the pseudo-technical is the urge we noted earlier, to "cover" all possible details by means of general abstract words, rather than sharpen the sense of action by means of simple concrete ones. In the sentence last reviewed, some writers would feel uncomfortable at the substitution of *the Controller* for *out of the Controller's office*. They would be afraid that someone might think the controller in person entered the names, with a quill pen. Such fears are groundless and reflect on the reader's intelligence. In the long run that intelligence is blunted and baffled by the very use of such covering words. Judge for yourself how cloudiness comes in:

"We suggest that the term 'garbage and rubbish' is not broad enough; the term garbage and refuse is redundant since garbage is refuse; and both tend to emphasize garbage as a major part of the problem, which is no longer factual [a fact?]. . . . We have standardized on describing [help!] the material processed as 'Solid Wastes' and the system as a 'Solid Waste Disposal System.' . . . The entire industry is now known as the 'Solid Waste Disposal Industry.' "

### THE COUNTERACTING EFFORT: RAT-TAT-TAT

The attitude exactly opposite to the pseudo-technical tries to create an impression of headlong speed punctuated by frequent shocks. The reader is to feel that he is being "told" with the utmost efficiency and liveliness—not a dull moment. The tone is emphatic and aims at the senses; eye and ear are bombarded with image-raising and sound-suggestive words. See and listen to this: "Night had deepened with a whoop and a roar. Sleet whistled across open decks and stung the glass of enclosed spaces as the steamer westbound for New York shouldered down against the battering of the Atlantic in January. Yet it was not very heavy weather. . . ." If it *had* been very heavy weather, what verbs would have been left to cope with it? *Whoop, roar, whistle, sting, batter,* and the somewhat obscure *shoulder down* would seem to exhaust the terms of exaggeration that can be packed into four lines. Notice also how the faked noise conceals poor linking: it is not the deepening of the night that whoops and roars; it is a storm that coincided with it. If *shouldering down* compares a ship plunging into the waves to a man hunching his shoulders as he walks against wind and sleet, then the comparison is one-sided, because the ship also goes *bounding up* as it is borne on the crest of the next wave. And after we have shivered and been deafened and stung and battered, we are told that the gale was only of medium strength. The fact is that coming after Kipling and Hemingway, who inaugurated the features of this tone, their imitators now produce it automatically, unaware (perhaps) that its novelty—and hence part of its effectiveness—have long since worn off. Tens of thousands of crime stories have made common-place what was originally a reaction against gentility and ineffec-tual a manner suited only to violent subjects.

While examining such devices we become conscious of the fact that a manner has a sound—a tune. The pseudo-technical gives off a monotonous rumbling. The "efficient," when it is coupled with the four-word sentence (often including the four-letter word), has the sound of gunfire. A student of mine once wrote a parody of Hemingway in the form of a short story five lines long, which he entitled "Rat-tat-tat." Here it is: "I saw her first. She was tall, blond. She looked good. She smiled. I went up to her. I kissed her. She felt good. She smiled. I stepped back. She came up close. She smelled good. She put her arms around me. I kissed her. She raised an eyebrow. I nodded. We were engaged."

Since much of what has to be reported in life refuses to fit into this undersized mold, and yet the rhythm of rat-tat-tat per-sists in the writer's head, his compromise is to start writing in non-sentences, which he scatters over white paper in pseudo-paragraphs:

After that, nothing.
Blank.
Zero.
Blackout.
A shutout.

A row of goose eggs, all circular and empty.
And mocking. Every single one of them. A real Schneider.

It may be said of certain tunes that they cause weariness before the end is reached. Of this staccato incoherence it must be said that it is tiresome from the beginning. Obviously, it saves work first and last, for having no structure, it defies revision; one might cross out *Blackout* or *A shutout* or insert *Knockout* between them and be unable to give a reason for or against. Why *"A* shutout" and not just "Shutout"? Rhythm and progression nowhere seem deliberate. One would think, for example, that *Zero* would be the last of the descending series, before the *goose eggs* come on the imaginary screen. How long, moreover, is *a Schneider* going to be understood? But it is foolish to look for any artistic intention in the passage—the attempt to find one is a fruitless exercise in self-consciousness about words.

THE COLLOQUIAL MOODS: PSEUDO-SPEECH

In the efficient and staccato tones, whether combined or separate, the desire is strong to "write the way people talk," to use the vernacular, to be colloquial, not stilted. This aim is old and respectable; the only trouble with it is that there no longer is a single way in which the plain man speaks. Listen to television and you find that the spoken word ranges from the sophisticated lingo of the advertiser to the modish patter of the master of ceremonies. In between, the common man who is interviewed delivers as many popularized technicalities as the news analyst or other expert delivers vogue phrases and conciliatory slang. In these conditions, any written prose that claims the merit of being in the vernacular—colloquial—can only be a carefully composed work of art. It is not a purified echo of street talk, but a contrived pseudo-speech requiring much ingenuity and a good ear.

What *passes* for the colloquial is a mixture of tones, in which one or another attitude may give the main coloring—the up-to-date fashionable or underworld, the ponderous academic, the coy and cozy, and perhaps others. In all of them what sticks out is the false, affected, put-on personality of the writer: "Shucks, you just missed Paul Scofield, who won all the awards in sight for the title role, but his sub is Emlyn Williams, and that ain't hay." That may be theater-columnist talk, but it is not human speech anywhere or at any time. One guesses the desire to sound intimate, what I have called cozy and conciliatory.

The up-to-date has a myriad forms; it is often disclosed by a purposeful mismating of ideas: "Electronic music for children is not Tomorrow, it's Today." / "This style is without question very now." These are extensions of the tedious *is splice:* "Happiness is a storewide sale." "General Motors is people." / "How a House Happens: This house begins when two big people and two little find themselves in a too-small apartment, where the hamsters are underfoot . . ." Intolerable coyness often infects the up-to-date, as in the last example, or in the fashionable: "The broiling of a steak in the kitchenette makes like a London fog." The advertiser aims at what he hopes is a larger, because lower, group: "It [a new cigarette] sits neat in your hand like it was made for it and fits your face like it found a home." Thought and phrasing here are about as natural as a wooden leg. Dislocation—in grammar, logic, or appropriateness of terms—is used, even at the risk of offensiveness, to signal to the reader that he is not getting a common or garden sort of message, further proof that "up-to-date" is not truly colloquial.

THE SOPHISTICATED TONE: WHO IS BEING FOOLED?

But is there not a reason, if not an excuse, for these contortions? The advertiser, the journalist, the daily or weekly critic, and all but the most original novelists make use of artificial tones, because their professional duty is to catch and hold the reader's attention in the midst of many competing noises. No doubt, but then the efforts cancel each other out. In his description of objects the advertiser tends to roll off sonorous phrases which are mere noise devoid of sense: "To their body-comforming ability, wrinkle resistance, and press-retaining *accomplishments,* knit suits now offer the feel and look of traditional woven fabrics." The suits apparently "offer" one half of their qualities to the other half, and it is not clear whether the clothes look "traditional" or new. Archness is just as vague: "It's still named after James Thomas

Brudenell, 7th Earl of Cardigan, but times have changed m'lord. This crossover cardigan by our artisans swings like late next year." And so is the fake-serious: "There are limits to just how far a man will allow modern technology to encroach upon his lifestyle. Some things remain sacred. With us, it's neckties."

Journalese (which does *not* include the excellent prose of straight reporting) attempts to spice up the commonplace with breathless modifiers (*briefly, swiftly, starkly,* etc.) and with clever imports from other realms. You will often find this tone in the editor's tempting summaries at the head of magazine articles; for example, "California is *not* the future-that-was, nor is it some dream sequence in a Nathanael West novella. This essay reports on the gaping malocclusion between the Golden State of legend and the California of everyday life." (Malocclusion, by the way, cannot be diagnosed while the patient is gaping.)

The same tone in book reviewing yields phrases like these, close together: "A book of gargantuan propensities . . . incalculable in impact . . . There are brilliant passages . . . compulsively readable." Except for the third phrase, which rather lets down the opening ecstasies, the miscast words convey little but the tone of knowingness. (Ponder *propensities* and keep away from books that display Gargantua's.) Since contributors to the leading newspapers and magazines in the country evidently reach out for words they do not fully understand in order to secure impressiveness, one thing more must be said about the futility of the practice: there are still a great many readers of good judgment and they despise such writers as conceited fools.

⌘

Principle 11: Do not borrow plumes.

Tone shows itself more clearly in paragraphs than in single sentences, so that this exercise may magnify an occasional slip into a fault of tone. Still, it is good to be alert to the smallest sign of deviation from plainness. Classify and characterize such signs.

1. It wasn't laughable, it wasn't silly, it wasn't funny at all. It was goose flesh and shudders and you could go mad or your heart could stop beating like the snap of a thumb against a forefinger.

2. It was totally silent in the cavernous parking lot, two levels below the street. The trip in from Long Island had been unreal, a mechanical maneuvering of the car along the Expressway, the sudden realization that he was hitting nearly seventy, the jamming on of the brakes, the anger of some indignant housewife, her hair flapping wildly in her convertible behind him as she simultaneously braked and honked to keep herself from racking up on him.

3. Happiness is a diamond solitaire for Christmas. / Happiness is parking when you want to. / Happiness is a hick town. / A diamond is forever. [If equals equal each other, shouldn't it follow that "A diamond is a hick town where you can park forever?" To answer this question and test the logic of these voguish phrasings, draw a good-sized circle and mark it "Happiness"; then within it draw a smaller circle labeled "Parking" or any of the other "is" counterparts. The area remaining vacant in the big circle will show that happiness is *not* the same as parking when you want to.]

4. Everybody in today's schoolworld admits that tests are bad news—unfair, repressive, elitist. But that don't mean a teacher can't use spot quizzes, written questions, and such as *mere performance indicators,* conscious that human individual diversity must remain viable—and will.

5. A resurgence of interest in the bell-bottomed slacks worn with a color-contrast top is definitely *au courant.* With two tops to each pair of slacks you're fully accessorized.

6. Traditionally we have always had a fairly good turnout for our annual dinners, which is as it should be. On the other hand, our monthly luncheon attendance recently has been—well, spotty. That's understandable. We're all busy, and we don't do much at lunch but friendlyize. And the folks at the office don't really understand why we bring in our coonskin coats and pennants that day.

7. The most plenary thing you can say about Las Vegas is that there is no other resort like it.

8. His friends say that he is abhorrent of untidiness.

9. He stood there as if stunned, then walked away down the road, his arms swinging like pendula.

10. He felt his frown corrugating his brow. His words curled back against his teeth.

11. X. is a practiced escapologist. This is the third time he has circumvented the penitentiary.

12. X-oco gasolines are localized for you at the corner of Logan and Market streets under the aegis of Al and Jerry.

13. Telephone company policy is we don't do wiretapping for anyone under any circumstances.

14. With a community of his apprentices, Dr. S. is beginning construction of his first "arcology"—his word for a combination of architecture and ecology.

15. He is somewhat disoriented by the Islamic mind, several points on which he is totally at sea.

16. Love is caring enough to do something. [Careful! This may be a trap.]

17. Made from space-age chrome molybdenum steel . . . it never needs sharpening.

18. This is a cheese of unhurried excellence.

19. You can't taste or see this wine being poured, but I assure you it's crystal clear as a vintage Stradivarius.

20. The familiar handsome shape of this handbag dictates imagination for its use.

### FIGHTING AFFECTATION ON ITS OWN GROUND

From the various affectations we have sampled, one may conclude that to achieve the plain, even tone recommended by Whitman and Mark Twain, the first requisite is sincerity; the second is a distinct thought. If you are confused in mind or embarrassed in feeling, what comes out betrays your divided self. Nowadays, when public relations is an instrument of social existence, it takes practice to be sincere; that is, to find out: What do I really feel? Am I being genuine? and at the same time make certain of one's meaning. Intellectual honesty is the product of that double and conscious clearing up.

For the writer it should become habitual. One detects the habit in a simple statement such as: "I hope we don't simply react to a defeat. A lot of good can be distilled from this experience. The base of the party has been broadened, involving groups who have never really been involved before." Compare those straightforward words with the bumblings of a chairman whose feelings and ideas alike were at sixes and sevens. The taped record shows his inner chaos: "As to the questions, I regret and to a certain extent apologize for having neglected—not neglected, not really, but passed over—eight or ten which were—it seemed to me, and I hope I've not made a mistake—different formulations of questions that were—had been—taken up—er—answered already."

Sincerity is not enough, for it can be tongue-tied from lack of control over the processes of thought, at which point it may in despair borrow the trappings of some alien tone. Hence the advantage of recognizing the false attitudes currently embodied in words and classes of words. The first and least harmful of these is the cliché. A cliché is a phrase made up, usually, by an original writer, and which has become common currency because it fits or sums up an aspect of life. *More in sorrow than in anger* is a cliché that describes how one kind of rebuke is administered. Shakespeare was so successful a phrasemaker that his works have been described as a mass of clichés. And so they are; but by the alchemy of context, the most battered phrases of his regain their luster when we hear them where they belong.

The use of clichés is spoken of with horror by many writers on style, but the practice shows at least a literary urge, some reading of books, and some regard for what was once well said. The trouble with relying on clichés is that they make prose sound stale. The reader has seen those words before, again and again, and often in places where their fitness is doubtful. One might call the resulting tone the Mechanical, or the Absent-Minded, for the phrases seem to spin themselves out by an automatism that is the reverse of sincerity and distinct thought. Here is a mild case of the affliction: "Such a life, coupled with an economic depression when people who are willing and anxious to work are milling around in circles, wondering where their next meal is coming from, tends to make a man a little bitter toward 'civilization.' " The passage contains three clichés, one of them slightly tampered with. To an exacting mind there is also a touch of the cliché in the use of *bitter,* a word greatly overworked, considering the thirty or forty other adjectives that could in most of its uses replace it.

A writer on style, summarizing a valuable essay by the novelist George Orwell, tells the aspiring author never to use a cliché but always to "invent his own turn of phrase." The advice is good for training or retraining purposes. But it is not wholly practicable; it is an exaggeration: the adviser himself did not invent *turn of phrase*. He found the locution ready-made, and although it is not precisely a cliché, it is an old metaphor and quite indispensable. No, the chief danger to guard against is the inevitable echo: you have occasion to refer to *a dim light* and your uncritical memory supplies *a dim religious light* for no reason in meaning and a bad reason in tone.

An impòrtant subclass of clichés consists of what an English rhetorician has called "adverbial dressing gowns": *seriously consider, utterly reject, thoroughly examine, be absolutely right, make perfectly clear, sound definitely interested.* All these are clichés and the adverb is the dressing gown: the writer thinks the verb or adjective would not seem decent if left bare. The truth is that the meaning is strengthened by the removal of the automatically remembered adverb. Nothing is easier than to strike it out when it crops up unbidden in your prose. Reread yourself and you will feel how much more firm the tone and final the thought of "I reject the accusation" than the spluttering: "I utterly reject the accusation."

NEW INVENTIONS, MOSTLY BAD

The desire for novelty can coexist with an addiction to clichés. Indeed, making up new words and catchy phrases can seem to the maker the spice that renders trite ideas palatable; actually, both habits stem from the same lack of judgment. New words are rarely needed outside trade and technology; rarely, that is, in proportion to the number launched by the citizenry in its yearning to be creative. Can anyone but the inventor feel merit in *scientifiction, fanzines* (fan magazines), *Realtyst,* or *aromarama* (perfumed air in a movie house)? Most such hybrids have a short life, but the urge to beget persists, while the workmanship deteriorates. The tone produced by all the compounds with *-rama* and *-teria, -tron* and *-omat,* and all the mongrels that couple at random any two parts of existing words is the Cheap-and-Tawdry tone.

Before you manufacture compounds, reflect a little on those you know. How are they formed and how do they come to mean what they mean—if they mean anything? The conclusion we reached when considering words under Diction was: leave Greek and Latin alone unless you are conversant with them. I would now add: even if you are, leave them alone. Think how much plainer and finer, less obtruding and conceited the tone of prose would be if from the beginning we had said *speed meter* and not *speedometer*, *laundry shop* and not *laundromat*, *moving stairs*, *icebox*, and *lift*, instead of *elevator*, *escalator* and *refrigerator*. The true democratic spirit is found in the making of *gas station*, *scotch tape*, *dishwasher*, and *jet lag* when these terms were needed, and not in foisting on the public *discotheque*, *polyester*, *infrastructure*, and *paraprofessional*. Even to those who do not linger over etymology, there is something ridiculous and embarrassing in discussing and buying a *slumberpedic* mattress. The analytic are further annoyed by knowing that the *pedic* part means child, although the article is not a child's mattress; it is one supposedly good for the spine. *Orthopedics* ill understood has gone into this wholly nonsignifying coinage.

In contrast with this, *hovercraft* is excellent in tone. Why? Both words are English, their union is descriptive, and the sound blends well with the idea and with other common words. After that, pronounce *aromarama* and frame a sentence around it. Yet sticking to English roots is not an all-sufficient guide. For a while in journalism and advertising people referred to "a for-instance." The neologism is cute and superfluous. So are the new, home-made compounds with *-wise* and *-wide; -conscious*, *-happy*, and *-oriented;* the appositions with *type;* the improvised verbs in *-ize* and comparable "back formations" (*iiaise* as a verb from *liaison*). (Remember in this connection that *burgle* and *sculpt* [with a *t*] are not bona-fide words, though *laze* is as old—and as good—as *lazy*.) When, however, newspapermen had to find a short, expressive term for raising a craft in space, they borrowed the verb *loft* from sports usage and produced an excellent self-explanatory innovation: it is connected with *lift*, and its Germanic root (*Luft*) means *air* or *heaven*. But take care, in sticking to native words for the sake of tone, to avoid foreseeable confusion. "Microfilm by the year 2000 can become so important that readers may be commonplace in the home." *Readers* here means machines, not men. The term *viewers,* also in use, is a little less ambiguous, but since we start with *micro*(film), the word *enlargers* (*film loupe?*) should have been thought of first.

A more complex form of confusion has lately been initiated in the hope that tampering with the language might further equality between the sexes. I have in mind the effort to eliminate the syllable *man* in *chairman, doorman, spokesman,* and the like, the replacement being *person.* The scheme rests on a misconception, which is that the root *man* means *male.* It means in fact *human being, person,* as in *woman,* originally *wife-man,* that is to say *wife-person,* and not *wife-male,* as the *man*-haters must suppose. *Mankind* means the entire human race. Unfortunately, English lacks the free and frequent usage of a common-gender pronoun like *on* in French, *man* in German, that might promote the tone of impartial courtesy.

In matters other than sex and race relations, the tone of courtesy, ever important, is often destroyed by usages copied from snappy journalism. The worst of these is the turning of descriptions into titles or tags, which are then stuck on to proper names. Thus it is widely believed that to write "Author Hemingway" is as legitimate as to write "Bishop Butler"; but that is not true. Certain names of occupations have become titles because the public duties attached affect society at large and must command certain kinds of response—hence *Doctor, Bishop, General, Senator,* etc. But most employments do not carry such implications and it is uncivil to reduce a private person to what he may happen to be doing for a living: "Assistant Town Clerk Mary Jones was married yesterday at noon to piccolo-player L. C. Robinson." This is the tone of bureaucratic regimentation, whether intended or not. If designations are needed, let them qualify the name, not box in the person: "Mary Jones, the attractive chief assistant to the Town Clerk, and L. C. Robinson, the well-loved piccolo player in the town band, were married yesterday . . ." This gives her a chance to study medicine and him to take up the guitar.

The same feeling of what is due human dignity should rule out the formula by which a man is made the apparent chattel of a group or institution—"Yale's Barnaby Rudge" / "California's Robert Elsmere." This practice has grown out of the false relation in thought and speech which produces "Florida's governor" / "the nation's capital." These phrases do not in fact mean "the governor of Florida" or "the capital of the nation" (or the national capital). The possessive *of* in the first set differs from the descriptive *of* in the second. The distinction is what keeps us from turning *a block of wood* into *a wood's block,* and we ought to treat persons as gently as we do wood. If we wish to cut down the use of *of,* think of *the Queen of the May,* which yields, not *the May's Queen,* but *the May Queen;* hence: "Mr. X., the Florida governor . . ." Tone resides in trifles.

⋇

Principle 12: To be plain and straightforward, resist equally the appeal of old finery and the temptation of smart novelties.

This exercise should not prove difficult—the faults exhibited are obvious. Record your distaste and rewrite.

1. Designed to carry either passengers or cargo, the Terrastar gets its name from its star-shaped wheels.

2. The endless macaroni of depressing news coiled itself round the tentacles of his personal disappointments to form an unorthodox political creed.

3. Caught up in the crowd's surging emotion, he looked at his mother with shining eyes and whispered, "When I grow up, can I be one of them?"

4. Almost everywhere—with the exception of fringe or "groupuscule" minority factions—Communism is no longer working as a violent revolutionary force.

5. Instant knowledgeflo is what our machines will afford.

6. It involves Local ———— and four other affiliated plants nationwide.

7. But I am thinking of the 2500 persons totally employed by the corporation.

8. There are times when all Nature seems to smile, yet when to the sensitive mind it will be faintly brought that the possi-

bilities are quite tremendously otherwise if one will consider them pro and con.

9. Toward elimination of delays in serving patrons this Seatomaticket is provided to insure them of an orderly sequel at the evening meal.

10. His answer came: "Nothing, repeat, nothing—and that's the story, period."

11. He was a nervous type guy yet wasn't afraid to go sporting those shoes made of snakeskin type plastic.

12. Why don't you jot down the ideas as they occur to you and then folderize your notes?

13. L.H. lived in a pretty but sadly smelly house in Edwardes Square.

14. The affections of youth never die. They live sometimes to lift the drooping head, and help chase sorrow from the heart of the oppressed. If fostered unduly they gradually prove to be more closely interwoven than if retained through honesty alone, and fight the battle of union with cannon strength until gained for good or evil.

15. He was the undeniable head of his profession, the great tragic actor of his time.

16. Have you ever heard of the expression "Life is a Two Way Street"? This expression is very simple and means cooperation between two parties. It means nothing more than that.

17. In short, the organization would provide a new dimension to our foreign assistance effort, would enable us to focus some of our finest national resources on the critical bottleneck problems of development.

18. Her delicate instrumentation of Line and Color will lead her on her own tracks.

19. To all Gentlepersons: Please accept our most puissant invitation to attend our fantasy.

20. Progressive squeeze-and-talk. Present policies plus an orchestration of communications with Hanoi and a crescendo of additional military moves against infiltration targets . . . The scenario would be designed to give the U.S. the option at any point.

MODIFIERS: MEANING AND TONE

If your nouns are simple, your verbs active (for reasons soon to be seen), and your pronouns in good order, then you owe it to your reader and yourself to be strict with your modifiers. We have seen why nouns should carry no heaped-up nouns on their backs and why verbs should be stripped of their dressing-gown adverbs; what thought should be taken about adjectives? The first is to make sure they are needed: "Of late he had been spending much of his time in a mountain cabin on the pine-clad slope of a rugged range near a brawling stream." Nobody can deny that each of the four epithets is well chosen. But are all four justified?

To begin with, a series of sentences in this vein would quickly become ridiculous, then irritating. The reader can take in only so much commentary on the objects proposed to his imagination. He is soon bored by the tag-and-label tone and turns to some other book. The writer can prevent this disaster by pruning. If we have *a pine-clad slope,* do we need a *mountain* cabin? And of the other two, which is the more valuable? Doesn't a *brawling stream* imply or suggest a *rugged range?* Notice finally that the writer has paid no attention to the rhythm—and consequently the tune—of his sentence. All his epithets have two syllables and are accented on the first and all his nouns except *cabin* are monosyllables. With the attached prepositions and starting at *much of his time,* the rhythm goes: ′——′——′—′———′—′——′——′—′, like a childish singsong mocking the meaning.

Once you have decided the degree of need for a given modifier, you must make sure that its form and meaning do not go against the tone you wish to sustain. Meaning is involved in tone, because every modifier suggests the possibility of its opposite. Consider the ubiquitous *frankly* with which people season their talk and writing. When it comes it logically raises the question: So you've been lying up to this point? Again: "When the driver and his mate came out of the tavern, the horse and van had completely disappeared." Could they have done so *in*completely? What we have here is an unnecessary modifier which is silly besides.

The love of long adverbs is akin to the taste for "covering words" described earlier. *Additionally, initially, reportedly,* and their kind foster the falsely scientific tone. *In addition, at first, it is said,* are their good old equivalents in plain tone. In a would-be dramatic scene one reads: "Fractionally the round eyes narrowed." I grant that "He squinted a little" would not be sufficiently momentous, but there remains the simple fact demanding expression: "His eyes narrowed a little."

To modify with accuracy, a writer must know the force of the words he uses, their proper placing, and their idiomatic habits. For example, *certainly* and *surely* may seem interchangeable and they sometimes are; but when used to modify an assertion, the force of *certainly* is concessive (= I admit) and that of *surely* is pleading (= you will admit). Force must be graduated to the occasion too. If you thank a friend by saying, "This is amazingly good of you, John," you imply that a good turn from him is astonishing; or the favor must be such as one could hardly expect even from a friend. It is the same sort of left-handed compliment when a reviewer characterizes a book as *literate*. As for *meaningful*, give it a hard look and you will see that it is almost always meaning*less*.

In English, adverbs and adjectives generally precede what they modify. We have already noted the awkwardness of putting an adverb after the verb to avoid splitting an infinitive: the adverb then appears to be clumsily trying to modify the words that follow. But a little observation of good prose will show that it is often better to put the adverb or adjective *after*. Read aloud: "He kept his gaze upon distant peaks, and the soles of his feet unpleasantly tingled." Sense and sound require *tingled unpleasantly*. The long adverb gives no clue to the unpleasantness; we want the verb first. And *tingled* is too short to bear the weight of four syllables on top of it. Compare "They reviewed quietly the events of the day" (just as good as "they quietly reviewed") with "They reviewed quietly the day," which is impossible in rhythm though satisfactory in sense.

Adjectives may also come after the noun when they are doubled or tripled: "It is a beauteous evening, calm and free." Wordsworth's line could pass as prose and may be analyzed as if it were. The division of the epithets is justified by our feeling that *a beautiful evening* is virtually a single entity, marked in this case by two other attributes. Try jamming all three ahead of *evening* and see what happens. The tone turns incoherent and *free* changes its meaning by the suggestion of "no engagements" or even of "no admission charged." Such are the subtleties of language.

Now comes the question: When has the English adverb the same form as the corresponding adjective, without -*ly?* And when the two forms exist side by side, how does the choice of either affect tone? Idiomatic writers know the answers without thinking, but those who are confused can work it out without difficulty. Start with words not capable of adding -*ly,* such as *fast.* One *drives fast,* not *fastly.* Then one also drives *slow,* as the road signs tell you to do; it is not a mistake. One can *drive slowly* too, but, in general, if the mode or manner signified by the adverb can be attributed to the result of the action as well as to the process, the shorter form is the more idiomatic. Thus one *stands high* on the list, *drinks deep* from the stream, *flies low* over the trees, and so on. Swift, in *A Tale of a Tub,* uses the form "write correct," though today it would probably suggest a rural and uneducated tone. It none the less illustrates the principle we follow in *talk proud, sound eerie, work hard, pull steady, sleep sound.* Some of these will also take the -*ly* form when the writer has in mind the action rather than the outcome; e.g., *pull steadily.* What is out of tone is to seek a fancied correctness and write *I feel dully.* Clearly, the verb *feel* is not the modifier's target, and the *I* is. A similar affectation has brought in *overly,* when the forms *overanxious, oversupplied, overpraised,* indicate the plain way to link *over* with an adjective.

STILL ANOTHER TONE: THE GENTEEL

Two other kinds of attempted elegance must be spoken of here: genteelism and false inversion. You will remember Mr. Micawber with his highfalutin style and what was said under Diction about euphemisms—"softenings." Some of these, it was pointed out, express a courteous intent. When instead the aim is to avoid plainness because you are too good for it, what results in Genteelism. On a card of invitation to a public dinner one reads: "Remuneration at the door," meaning *payment.* The sponsors evidently thought that the right word was too coarse for their membership and they used a ridiculous substitute. *Remuneration* is payment to a person for services rendered, not money exchanged for objects of consumption.

Dickens introduces Mr. Micawber by saying: "He had a certain indescribable air of doing something genteel." The professional manipulator confesses: "Frankly, our major objection to the usage of the terms incinerator and garbage is a matter of public relations. . . . [They] are very difficult to 'sell.' " Modern feelings are swayed by both gentility and the desire to "sell," in the sense of securing easy acceptance. The upshot is a collection of offensive genteelisms: *the disadvantaged* (the poor); *senior citizens* (the old or elderly); *developing countries* (*pre-industrial? modernizing?*); *disturbed* (unbalanced mentally). The point is not that persons and places in these categories should have their disabilities harshly thrust at them; the point is that the very concealment does the thrusting: no one is fooled and the denotation of words is damaged. *Mentally unbalanced* is already a courteous euphemism; to say *disturbed* robs the language of the word's other useful meanings—*interrupted, upset, worried,* all from external causes. And here again, in these insincere words, the analytical mind raises the question of implied opposites: are not the old industrial countries also developing? If so, the line of demarcation disappears. An apartment house advertises two-bedroom apartments, one-bedroom apartments, and *efficiencies.* Are the larger suites inefficient? Large shops refer to the pilfering of goods by the employees as *shrinkages.* Does that make stealing less odious?

The argument against genteelism extends to what has been called "elegant variation," that is, the avoidance of repetition by recourse to synonyms. The trick is transparent and gives the whole sentence an air of foolish fraud: "A coped rather effortlessly with the tenor part, but B's baritone contributions were always firm and characterful." There was no need to say anything but *tenor part* and *baritone part,* with the comment appropriate to each. Note as an incident of the evasive mood the hedging in *rather effortlessly.* What is effortless must be entirely so: the writer's tone can only be called shuffling.

The other false elegance referred to can be reproved briefly: do not invert the normal order of words in hopes of sounding more genteel, elegant, or forceful: "Owen would deny having seen her, for Bony, the witness, was an intruder from whom must be kept family skeletons." The plain way invariably is: "from whom family skeletons must be kept." A writer quoted earlier thought his indignation would be enhanced if he said: "Is never a point reached . . . ?" He was wrong. The silliness of this finger-curling effort may be gauged in: "Elsa was as independent as, thanks to the canny marriage of his grandmother, was he himself."

From these examples the truth to be inferred is that smoothness is an element of the plain tone. The slightest bump or awkwardness or jingle or unintended joke or negligent repetition derails the thought; the reader is brought up short and starts looking at words when he should be following ideas. For example, in the stage direction "G. rises from desk and goes to bed in alcove," we know quite well that G. does not *go to bed* but *to the bed* or *toward bed,* but no matter what we know, we have stopped, grinned, and mentally revised the writer's words for him.

Readers vary in their awareness of bumps, but smoothness is so glasslike a property that the smallest flaw spoils it. The writer with an ear will change: "who *was, as* we have seen" to "who, *as* we have seen, *was*" in order to eliminate the *wozzaz* that he perceived. He notes this particular collision, too, as one likely to recur, just as he watches out for the frequent coming together of such sounds as *say* and *way:* "Well, I must say, it's always the way, isn't it?" / "And what was to ensure that they would come through single *file* and fall one by one in a neat *pile?*" / "He thought the taxi fare hike would ignite a riders' strike." / "Before registr*ation* students on prob*ation* must obtain authoriz*ation* from an officer of administr*ation.*"

One other component of Tune and Tone is alliteration (yet another *-tion!*), one or more consonants recurring in successive words, usually the first sound of each. It is a powerful means of drawing attention and impressing the memory, as in the famous old slogan "Pink Pills for Pale People," which has dozens of counterparts today. Nor is alliteration to be excluded from ordinary prose, but like everything else in good writing, it must not be accidental. The impulse that brings it on must be tested by ear in the result. When in a playlet Shaw puts Shakespeare and Queen Elizabeth on the stage together, he has her say to the poet: "Season your admiration for a while," an actual line from Shakespeare which we are to believe he took from her spontaneous talk.

And Shakespeare is shown not getting it right when he first jots it down. He says: "Suspend your admiration for a space," to which the queen says: "a vile jingle of *s*'s." Very true: *s* hisses and *p, t, d,* and *k* each makes an unpleasant racket when repeated, especially at the head of a word.

A less noticeable fault is that of assonance, the repetition of a vowel sound, as in the sentence about the taxi-fare hike, where *hike* and *strike* are further echoed by *ri*ders and ig*nite*. Usually, unwanted assonance is less blatant—did you catch any trace of it in the last five words?

TONE FROM TUNE: RHYTHM AND ACTION

Judgment about when to vary and when to repeat must naturally extend to the rhythm set up by the succession of words. Passing reference has been made to this question, from the rat-tat-tat example onward. In the honorific sense, rhythm is altogether personal and, as such, it is a fundamental constituent of great prose. All that the ordinary stuff of good quality can hope for is to avoid the humdrum, which spells monotony—the plonk-plonk sameness of accent, length of words, and cut of sentences, the sameness of forms of thought: *And ... And ... And, There is, There was, It is a fact, It is the ... which, It is the ... that, As we saw, Now we see, But we must turn, What is clear, What is important,* and all the other worn bearings in the old gearbox. Those phrases necessarily have the same constructions trailing after them and they kill interest. I shall have more to say about these devices under Composition, but do not forget their connection with Tone and Tune.

In the nature of things, no advice can be given about constructing good prose rhythms. The mind's ear is the only guide, and its action mainly negative. But if you will "listen" to what you read with these few suggestions in mind, you will readily see how the sounds of words, their lengths and accents, make for *motion,* the prime virtue of prose. Knowing the value of movement, some writers fall into the present tense to narrate events in the past. The trick is sometimes useful, but it has its dangers, the first being the difficulty of sliding out of it and back into the normal past tense.

The reader is almost always jolted and disoriented by the shift, which was smooth enough at the beginning of the passage.

But there is worse still. The "historical present," as it is called, encourages various modes of slovenliness, no doubt from a feeling that the vivid present justifies colloquial turns. We looked at some of these earlier from the point of view of linking, and found that they usually produced false leads, requiring a halt in thought and and a second try at reading by regrouping the words: "I then tell him I think he'd say I don't know the answer a better man could've given." The difficulty might disappear if the words were spoken, but a writer should not forget that he is writing, and that the phrasing (rhythm and meter) of his utterance must disclose itself without research. Telegraphese is by no means down-to-earth; it is but another affectation, particularly when it is not really stripped bare, but mixed and mannered: "It sure was he nervously brought up the question." / "Which, by the way, that was a good piece of work!"

With this last example the writer is on the verge of attempting the so-called stream of consciousness, which is often supposed to represent the actual pulse and rhythm of spontaneous thought. It can in fact never be an actual stream; it is always artificial—selective and doctored; and as such it is hard for any but a fine crafts-man to handle. Here is Virginia Woolf, a specialist and a master, doing it:

> . . . but all the more, she thought, taking up the pad, must one repay in daily life to servants, yes, to dogs and canaries, above all to Richard her husband, who was the foundation of it—of the gay sounds, of the green lights, of the cook even whistling, for Mrs. Walker was Irish and whistled all day long—one must pay back from this secret deposit of exquisite moments, she thought, lifting the pad. . . .

The skill consists in interweaving thought and act intelligibly in a flow of images; it is their continuity despite mutual interruptions that conveys the impression of a mental stream. And here is a short and clumsy attempt at this effect: "She wondered absently who had named the dog Algernon and put the tube of suntan oil in her handbag and wandered up the path." We are told here that a person, unknown, named a dog, put a tube in a handbag, and wandered up a path; whereas it is "she" who performs the latter two actions while in a daydream about the dog. The images are confused, the syntax dull, and the rhythm flat.

The great carrier of tone, as we saw before, is the verb; it is also the source of motion. It must therefore be chosen with preciseness; that is, chosen to fit the action and the actors. This attention to *doing* and to the agents of doing compels the writer to summon up verbs endowed with strength. A verb strong in this sense is, to begin with, a verb other than *is, are, has,* or *have.* These are at best copulas, mere signs of blank identity or unspecified relatedness. So true is this that when we want to affirm such a simple thing as being, we cannot say: "I am sure a fifth gospel *is*"; we must say *exists.* It takes the infinitive ("To be or not to be") or a device of emphasis ("Let there be light") before that all-purpose verb reacquires a strong meaning. The same will be found true of *have* and generally also of *seem, appear, lie,* and other verbs denoting mere presence. They are static, not moving.

It follows that no good prose can tolerate *there is* or *he has* in large numbers. Therefore, not *"he has* a plan to open a shop," but "he plans"; not *"there is* a stranger now in the old Thomson house," but "a stranger moved into the house this afternoon." The depth of weakness is reached in the barbarous infinitive locution "supposing *there to have been* a crime . . ." ("Suppose a crime was committed . . ."). To avoid *has, have* in denoting ownership, see if you cannot use *possess, own, control, claim, belong to, govern, hold,* and the like, shifting nouns and rearranging subject and object to give the central role to a strong verb. The demand on vocabulary may at first cause a sense of strain, but if you keep it up you will discover that you have habitually overlooked many simple strong verbs in favor of flabby phrases based on weak, "omnibus" words—*go, get, put, keep,* etc. Turn to your Roget's *Thesaurus* and look up *Go:* the index gives upward of a dozen meanings radiating from the core, each with a dozen synonyms, from which treasury you may pick the one enabling you to write a more stirring sentence than: "The thing kept on going." This example does not mean that *go* is not a strong verb when well placed. It is weak when it is not chosen but stumbled on, from failure to think of *revolve, buzz, whir, spin,* etc.

These strong verbs of your choosing you must use in the active voice whenever possible. The subject of your thought *acts* upon other subjects and objects. Naturally, no suggestion of this sort can be carried out against the resistance of the material itself, which is your thought. But if you bear in mind the preferability of *agents acting on their surroundings* to the surroundings being acted on by the agents (passive voice of the verb), you will reduce the "noun plague" we discussed under Diction and you will gain the invaluable power of movement that comes from the recital of actions. What is more, visual and rhythmic variety increases as each verb strikes its particular note. But do not in your zeal forget the fault of overefficiency, which we saw producing exaggeration and clatter through verbs essentially inappropriate and violent. A well-tuned motor does not backfire.

We have done with Tone and its ingredients. The only word I would add may be an unnecessary caution. It is to the effect that the plain-and-even tone does not mean the platitudinous, patronizing, or simple-minded. No writer wants to talk down to his audience and give the impression of feeding small mouthfuls to an infant. One cannot help explaining matters that some readers already know, but one need not do it like the editorial in *The Times* of London for July 25, 1815, announcing that the defeated Napoleon had arrived in England: "He is, therefore, what we may call, here."

⋇

Principle 13: The mark of a plain tone is combined lucidity and force.

In these sentences you will detect various kinds of misjudgment as to what ought to be said and as to what certain words mean, or imply, or sound like. Describe the creative frenzy—or drowsy trance—in which the error was born, and correct it.

1. The rest of us were going to depart but he waved us to stay put. So we were part of the audience after all.
2. No industry can afford to spend time and money in training persons who will separate after a few months.

3. It was she decided to run for Congress.

4. The Commissioner made the usual graceful, intelligent and appropriately forgettable speech.

5. There must be a close continuing and meaningful inter-action between management and the task force.

6. In the winter all measures are designed to keep heat *inside,* while in the summer the idea is to keep heat *outside.*

7. Lawyers, jurists, and heads of law schools dominated the list. Diversity was given by the presence of Lady R——, who is an economist.

8. For your added comfort and convenience please lock your door and adjust the chain before retiring.

9. In our restaurant you can count on: Hearty breakfasts, Wholesome lunches, and Satisfying dinners.

10. Books are meaningful personalized gifts.

11. The state of the science was at this impasse, when Professor V——, in a lucid moment, suggested the idea that resolved all the contradictions.

12. I make two phone calls the next day. Both of them are important and necessary. But neither of them accomplished very much.

13. Mrs. O. was a small woman; small and round without being fat. She looked about a careful 42 or 43 years old. Her hair was held stiffly from her face and was coal black against the some-what pale skin. She had small, sharp, brown eyes, a small nose, and irregular lips.

14. One fireman broke into the basement and found the owner sitting incoherently on the floor.

15. One thing that as a practicing lawyer I would say it did *not* mean was that the board should act as a reviewing tribunal and retry the case as a court would.

16. The patient complained of no pain.

17. When the poet died, I wrote an epitaph on her, at the end of which I said: "The loss to literature is inestimable."

18. They reported some visibility degradation from blowing dust, but it was not in the framework of a serious problem.

19. An exciting and rewarding era of your musical life lies just ahead for you—a period of new fascination with the whole rich universe of music creation and performance.

20. Although there is no express rule that a prisoner who wishes to have a friend or lawyer present while he is making

a statement is to be allowed to have him, it is clear that a request of that sort would have to be granted; for if the prisoner were to say that he was prepared to make a statement only on those terms, any pressure upon him to make it otherwise would be equivalent to pressing him to make a statement after he had refused to do so.

## TIME OUT FOR GOOD READING III

Edward Sapir (1884–1939) was German born and came to the United States at the age of five. He made himself an expert on the American Indian languages and taught at Yale and the University of Chicago, pursuing his studies in the relations between language and culture. Besides a large number of learned articles and some poetry, he published one book, *Language* (1921), which is still in print, having almost at once been recognized as a classic.

### Language Defined

The process of acquiring speech is, in sober fact, an utterly different sort of thing from the process of learning to walk. In the case of the latter function, culture, in other words, the traditional body of social usage, is not seriously brought into play. The child is individually equipped, by the complex set of factors that we term biological heredity, to make all the needed muscular and nervous adjustments that result in walking. Indeed, the very conformation of these muscles and of the appropriate parts of the nervous system may be said to be primarily adapted to the movements made in walking and in similar activities. In a very real sense the normal human being is predestined to walk, not because his elders will assist him to learn the art, but because his organism is prepared from birth, or even from the moment of conception, to take on all those expenditures of nervous energy and all those muscular adaptations that result in walking. To put it concisely, walking is an inherent, biological function of man.

Not so language. It is of course true that in a certain sense the individual is predestined to talk, but that is due entirely to the circumstance that he is born not merely in nature, but in the lap of a society that is certain, reasonably certain, to lead him to its traditions. Eliminate society and there is every reason to believe that he will learn to walk, if, indeed, he survives at all. But it is just as certain that he will never learn to talk, that is, to communicate ideas according to the traditional system of a particular society. Or, again, remove the new-born individual from the social environment into which he has come and transplant him to an utterly alien one. He will develop the art of walking in his new environment very much as he would have developed it in the old. But his speech will be completely at variance with the speech of his native environment. Walking, then, is a general human activity that varies only within circumscribed limits as we pass from individual to individual. Its variability is involuntary and purposeless. Speech is a human activity that varies without assignable limit as we pass from social group to social group, because it is a purely historical heritage of the group, the product of long-continued social usage. It varies as all creative effort varies—not as consciously, perhaps, but none the less as truly as do the religions, the beliefs, the customs, and the arts of different peoples. Walking is an organic, an instinctive, function (not, of course, itself an instinct); speech is a non-instinctive, acquired, "cultural" function.

There is one fact that has frequently tended to prevent the recognition of language as a merely conventional system of sound symbols, that has seduced the popular mind into attributing to it an instinctive basis that it does not really possess. This is the well-known observation that under the stress of emotion, say of a sudden twinge of pain or of unbridled joy, we do involuntarily give utterance to sounds that the hearer interprets as indicative of the emotion itself. But there is all the difference in the world between such involuntary expression of feeling and the normal type of communication of ideas that is speech. The former kind of utterance is indeed instinctive, but it is non-symbolic; in other words, the sound of pain or the sound of joy does not, as such, indicate the emotion, it does not stand aloof, as it were, and announce that such and such an emotion is being felt. What it does is to serve as a more or less automatic overflow to the emotional energy; in a sense, it is part and parcel of the emotion itself. Moreover, such instinctive cries hardly constitute communication in any strict sense. They are not addressed to any one, they are merely overheard, if heard at all, as the bark of a dog, the sound of approaching footsteps, or the rustling of the wind is heard. If they convey certain ideas to the hearer, it is only in the very general sense in which any and every sound or even any phenomenon in our environment may be said to convey an idea to the perceiving mind. If the involuntary cry of pain which is conventionally represented by "Oh!" be looked upon as a true speech symbol equivalent to some such idea as "I am in great pain," it is just as allowable to interpret the appearance of clouds as an equivalent symbol that carries the definite message "It is likely to rain." A definition of language, however, that is so extended as to cover every type of inference becomes utterly meaningless.

❖

Could you tell from this passage that the writer's native tongue was not English? Has this question any bearing on what he says? What sort of English would you say he writes?

Are the opening words of the second paragraph a sentence? Argue the question for and against, as if it made a difference. If it makes a difference, in what realm does it do so?

Though Sapir's argument is entirely clear and consecutive, it is abstractly put. Do you think you could rephrase the sentences beginning with "Walking, then, is a general human activity" (middle of paragraph 2) down to the end of the paragraph, using fewer words like *variability, assignable, organic, non-instinctive?* Try it and then see whether the sense is as clear and the statement as exact.

# Meaning
## or What Do I Want to Say?

IV

### THE ROLE OF LOGIC—LARGE BUT NOT EXCLUSIVE

It may seem odd that about halfway through this book the heading of a new section should propose a discussion of Meaning. What else has been discussed since page 1? The observation is sound but incomplete. Meaning is the goal of writing in all its parts and we have discussed it in connection with each; but each part was singled out for features that led or contributed to meaning rather than were the thing itself. In the present section we shall concentrate on *thought* as the prerequisite to meaning. As a great French stylist has said: "The fundamental rule of style is to keep solely in view the thought one wants to convey." And he added ironically: "One must therefore have a thought to start with." We shall once again take up words and phrases, modes of linking, flawed sentences and other familiar units, but our effort to be fully conscious of them will be made from the point of view of thought, or as some would say, logic.

In so doing we shall find that the act of writing is itself an exercise of thought. Many writers have said that they do not fully grasp their own meaning until they have carved it like a statue, using words as material. The reason is plain. One starts writing, not with a well-shaped thought, trimmed and polished, but with an *intent*—perhaps with several, overlapping and conflicting. You see a scene in your mind's eye or know the tendency of a complex argument, but do not know which part of the scene or argument is to come first—what, anyhow, is a *part* of something you sense as an undivided whole? Thinking, and nothing but thinking, will answer these questions; nor will the answer be satisfactory until the words are down on paper that represent the first finished piece of description or argument.

As the pieces (sentences) are added, one by one, they will so clearly show up gaps, inconsistencies, confusions in the *sequence* of thoughts—all quite hidden before you wrote—that you will inevitably come to see how writing is an instrument of thought. For lack of space, we limit ourselves here to short passages that show these defects; the critical, self-conscious process is the same in the short and the long run.

By thought is meant, naturally, good thought, good sense, intelligible meaning; which is why some writers invoke *logic*. The term is suitable if one takes it broadly to denote reasonableness; in the narrow sense of deductive or scientific logic the name does not apply, for language is much more flexible, suggestive, and rich than the propositions and forms to which logic restricts itself. When we say *logical* and *illogical* in referring to a passage of prose, we mean conforming or contrary to the reasonable view of the words and the facts involved.

A last point on logic: one often hears it said that language, "and English especially," is "a mass of illogicalities." And illustrations follow from spelling, pronunciation, verb forms, and idioms. This thought-cliché is foolish. Irregularities are not the same thing as illogicalities, and even when the irregularities in any language are totted up, they prove to be far fewer than the perfectly regular, "logical," ways of expressing like meanings in like situations. What is left over is a number of familiar idioms that deceive no one as to their meaning and an indefinite collection of accepted terms that record a past indifference to the "logic" of a situation. Thus we say *cross a bridge* when in fact we *cross the river* or the road. We say *AC* and *DC current,* when the *C* already stands for *current.* The abbreviation for *member of parliament* is *MP* and we make the plural *MP's,* whereas "in logic" it ought to be *MsP.* We must say before*hand* and after*ward.* Anyone who is bothered by such inconsistencies is indulging a taste for pedantry.

Pedantry is a misplaced attention to trifles which then prides itself on its poor judgment. The editors who would have everyone write *a Frankenstein's monster* instead of *a Frankenstein* are pedants who, if they were logical, would require *a Derrick's crane, a Hansom's cab,* and *a McAdam's road surface.* Positive errors consecrated by time have to be accepted—e.g., the *spiral staircase,* which is not a spiral, since that geometrical figure is flat; only a pedant would write *a helical staircase.* And what shall we say of the *Trojan Horse,* who was Greek and not Trojan? Are we to stop referring to the Marquis de Sade, because he was *Comte* and not *Marquis?* You will probably find that people who stickle over such points are likely to stay blind to the significant ones. The art is to know where and when significance is concerned. Obviously a book about De Sade will use his correct title and an essay on the Trojan War will not ascribe the "horse" to the wrong army. And there an end.

Illogicality of another kind, which requires correction at times and not at others, will occupy us when we come to metaphors. Here a pair of illustrations will show in what way we ought to be alive to meanings even when we understand and find no reason to object. The colloquial phrase: "I'll put you in the picture" really stands for: "I'll put the picture into you." A man recovering slowly from a back injury wrote to a friend: "What I want most is to get my mind off my back." He then reflected that if he had said: "I want to get my back off my mind," he would have said the same thing—or nearly.

The point of these examples is that language is not an algebra; that is, the symbols do not stay put, nor can they be carried from place to place with any assurance that their value will not change. If language were like algebra there could be no poetry or other fiction, no diplomacy or intimate correspondence, no persuasion or religious literature. If language were like algebra, *uncomfortable* would mean *not able to be comforted,* and a myriad nuances of human feeling would have to remain unrecorded and unsharable.

REASONING: IMPLICATION, SELF-CONTRADICTION, DISCONNECTION, DEFINITION, TAUTOLOGY

Errors of logic, or more simply nonsense, most often occur when the writer starts with one thought and allows it to change into another during the act of writing: "It is not anticipated that these occasional papers will be overfrequent." First thought: I do not expect to publish frequently; second: I am certainly not going to publish too often. The two thoughts are related, but their fusion into one sentence is fatal. The postman delivered a letter several months late, with an official notice saying: "This item was found in empty equipment." The word *empty* clearly implies that the bag (down with *equipment!*) had nothing in it, not even the one letter; and implications must be respected. Respect them also in: "Offenbach's widow, to whom he was married in 1844, died in 1887." Offenbach was never married to his widow.

You may say: "Be a sport! You understood; let the poor fellow off." The trouble is that unless this kind of criticism is generally exercised, it is likely not to be exercised by the writers themselves, and the gross national product of nonsense will increase. *The New Yorker* picked up the remark: "Few of his compositions are extant but he keeps working at them and storing them away" and added: "Spooky, that's what it is." While we are concerned with art, what do you make of this: "Dante's *Commedia* is still above all a poem, which is its greatest glory and in some ways its greatest handicap." There appears to be a plausible statement in those words; actually there is none: analyze if you can the meaning of *still* in relation to the rest.

A good way to practice reasoning about words is to frame definitions, without, of course, using the childish *is when* or *is where* ("A home run is where the batter runs around all the bases and . . ."). To define properly, one begins by finding the name of the class to which the object to be defined belongs: "A home run is *a scoring play* in baseball, which . . ."; "A predicament is *a situation* which . . ."; "An alligator is *a reptile* of the group . . ." and so on.

Defining also puts one on guard against tautology, for if *water-dowser* is to be defined, anybody can see that no satisfaction is given by *one who dowses for water*. In ordinary writing tautology is not so apparent, but it still consists in giving as new information what has just been said or needs no saying by reason of its being contained in a previous word (e.g. *sharp and trenchant, visible to the eye, disqualified for ineligibility*). The fault, in short, is another form of only seeming to mean. "My opinion is that he would recover from any injury that was not inevitably fatal"— that is, he would recover unless unable to. The opposite of tautology is self-contradiction: "A simpler arrangement could not be imagined; anyone could devise it." Well, could it or could it not be imagined (devised)? The trouble lies in the *simple(r)*, which is *not* the arrangement (*it*) referred to in the last four words. This form of error draws our attention again to thoughtlessness in linking, either expressed or implied: "They took his loose change, his wristwatch, his cigarettes, his cigarette lighter (he had smoked the prisoner's during his five visits)." / "Moore suffered from varicose veins and was unable to make ends meet."

The logic of situation enters into a good many judgments about the logic of phrasing. For example, certain metaphors, proverbs, and clichés do not permit the suggestion of more or less: "He went off with *a bit of a flea* in his ear." / "Necessity is only *to a certain extent the mother* of invention." When we read: "One of the best witnesses for the prosecution ought to be a man named Gilchrist, if we can only get him," we are at once aware that the logic is the other way about; it is the Gilchrist already known who ought to be a witness and not merely a person of that name. A choice of terms may depend on an intuitive perception of nuances and visualizing of scenes: "She tucked her arm affectionately in his." The tucking of an arm is best done by the party in whose elbow the other's hand is placed; "*slipped* her arm in his" gives the truer sense of the scene.

THOUGHT AND LOGIC IN SINGLE SMALL WORDS

It may surprise that the commonest words—*but, and, if, not, too, some, between, because,* and a few others—require careful handling lest nonsense result. Earlier, our consideration of *with* showed how easy it was to use the word when *withness* was the opposite of the desired meaning. Similarly, we saw that when *like* and *as* are interchanged, absurdities are set down in place of sense. The word *and* is on the face of it plain, and provided the elements joined by it are of a kind—matching parts (see below)—it offers few opportunities for misuse. It is when it is *not* used and should be that its idea is violated.

To see how this happens we must take note of the logical difference between *and* and *but.* The first pursues and adds to the thought just preceding; the second takes away from it a part of its force or truth, modifies it by reduction: "He was penniless, *but* he still had his violin and his grim determination to succeed." I have chosen on purpose a *but* sentence that seems to add rather than subtract, in order to show that the seeming addition actually reduces the scope or effect of the pennilessness. Consequently, *but* is illogical whenever a true addition is made to an idea, even and especially an idea stated in the negative: "The picked guard had never surrendered or so much as retreated, but had always carried the war into the enemy's territory." The *but* must be *and*, because the facts about the guard form a straight addition: no surrender, no retreat, and *what is more,* carrying the war to the enemy. The temptation to use the illogical *but* comes from the frequency with which a negative sentence is followed by a true *reductive* idea. Go back to the man with the violin, changing *penniless* to *he had no money left,* and see how naturally the still correct *but* increases your certainty that it is right. We are always saying *No, but,* whence the too hasty *but* after negative wordings that are being amplified, not reduced.

Negation is a fundamental law of thought—a thing either is or is not, cannot both be and not be at the same time—and much that a writer puts on paper is affirmation or denial. He is usually clear about each until he ventures, purposely or by accident, on the denial of a denial. Then he must reason his way with care or he risks confusion, like the doctor who remarked: "There's no reason I can't say he isn't like anybody else." This was after a successful operation and the intended meaning was: "X is now in as good shape as anybody else." The usual test of piled-up negatives is to pair them and consider each pair equal to an affirmative. If one negative remains unpaired, the sense is negative. If the negatives cancel out, one may ask whether a simple affirmative would not be better: "He would not deny that he had said nothing uncomplimentary" = a tacit admission of courtesy extended. But this algebraic converting of two minuses into a plus is not always reliable. A man once gave his wife a hat for her birthday, which was to be celebrated by dining out. The weather turned bad and the wife said: "I'm not not wearing my new hat because I don't like it." If you apply "algebra" to the negatives you get: "I am wearing my new hat because I don't like it," which is contrary to the facts and absurd in motive. In short, you must follow the meaning of the phrases as such in order to detect a gap between your thought and the wording.

Indeed, you must scan the meaning not only of phrases but of single words. Not all words that have *in-* or *un-* in front of a quality negate its meaning. The famous case is that of *inflammable,* which had to be changed to *flammable* for the sake of industrial and domestic users who thought the *in-* meant *not* and were badly burned in consequence. Other words, such as *invaluable,* are positive in a special way; the meaning is: *so precious that no value can be set upon it.* Even when no unusual connotation of this kind has overtaken a word, ordinary usage may have differentiated *in-* from *not.* A headline once read: "U.S. Concedes Figures Inexact." The body of the story said: "The count is an estimate, not an exact figure." *Inexact* means *erroneous,* not *approximate.*

As a general rule, if you must negate, do it close to the proper matter for negation, do it only once in a sentence, and do not hedge in the *not un-* manner except rarely and for good cause. "She found him not unworthy of her regard" is fair enough if she held him in quite ordinary esteem; it is silly if it is supposed to indicate high regard; for the meiosis (what a word!) is now trite and, when repeated, tedious. This advice applies to the use of similar forms such as: *less than satisfactory;* the absurd *more than accidental;* and the frequent *almost* serving as a mild detergent: *almost providential.* Test your strength of reasoning on the public announcement made after the chairman of the board was found hanging in the closet of the board room: " 'The situation,' said the vice-chairman, 'was almost unprecedented in the history of the company.' "

In writing that means to be colloquial, negation can easily defeat itself: "You can't pour a better drink than Quench-O" (a made-up name). The cynical view of this utterance is: there *is* a better drink but you can't pour it—it's in the solid state. Under the suggestion to keep the *not* close to its object, comes the repeated ambiguity *All do not* instead of the crystal-clear *Not all do.* How does one interpret the timetable that says: "All buses do not stop at the

John Street stop after 6 P.M." or the airport sign that courts defiance with "No Exit For All Persons"?

From these simple traps we pass on to the illogical *not* coupled with *too* and *if.* "This exhaustive survey of men's and women's clothing of the past 5000 years does not go too deeply into the philosophy or psychology of fashion." The meaning is: "does not go as deeply as it might or should." This widespread illiteracy ("I don't know too much about math") may come from Beach-la-Mar, a pidgin English of the South Pacific, in which *very* is rendered by *too much.* Its destruction of the simple idea *too* produces ambiguity and contradiction: "This anthology of modern poetry cannot be too highly praised"—does the reviewer think it very good or just passable? "The flames kept the ground crew from getting too close to the plane." They *wanted* to get close: the flames were not a protective barrier but an obstacle. In these slovenly phrasings, *too* is used as if devoid of force.

In the usual "We didn't get to the station too soon," meaning *just in time,* the appropriate wording is: "We got there *none* too soon"; or, "We didn't get there *any* too soon." The *none* and *any* indicate the measure by which the excess (*too*) is to be gauged.

The illogical *if* has its uses, but they are fewer than its heedless employment would suggest. *If* normally introduces a condition: "If you go, I will pay your way." What is the condition in: "That was a great if terrible event" / "If the sales territory was large, the town itself was too small for Maguire"? In the former sentence there is no thought of implying that the event was *not* great if it was not also terrible. The thought is rather: "It was great and I regret to say it was terrible." In the latter, the idea is: *"Although* the territory was large, the town at the center was too small." It is better to use this *although* when the *if* entails the absurdity of saying that *if* one place is large, another is too small. The same *though* will repair the earlier thought. When is *if* tolerable despite illogicality? When the shadow of a condition is perceivable behind the literal sense: "It is hard, if indeed possible, to take these cases as typical." This amounts to short-cutting: "Even if it can be done it is still hard."

In the negative the trouble is ambiguity. "A surprising if not unmerited award" means equally: "deserved but surprising nevertheless" and "surprising and perhaps not deserved at all." That is, the *not* can be interpreted as modifying what precedes or what follows. When a genuine condition is expressed by *if any* stuck like an afterthought in the middle of a sentence, it must, to be clear, *follow* the noun to which it applies. There is an awkward hurdle to jump over in: "... holding the party to token, *if any,* gains in Congress" ("token gains, if any ...).

Other trifling impediments to thought arise when *both* is used for *either,* when *vice versa* stands among three elements instead of two, when the words *undue, unnecessary,* are hooked to a fact or idea no one could rationally desire. For example: "Naturally the family doesn't want any *unnecessary* scandal." (Necessary scandal they would simply love.) "The group was criticized for *unduly* disturbing the performance." (Twenty minutes' disturbance instead of forty would have been delightful.) An occasional misuse of *unduly* seems to be a wild extension of the misused *too:* "Senator B. freely confesses that he is not *unduly* optimistic that Congress will move on electoral reform." The reader first thinks that the senator is confident, but not excessively so, that his bill will pass. But the context shows that he has no hope at all and he cites the obstacles; so that *not unduly optimistic* comes to mean *duly* (rightly) *pessimistic.*

⋇

Principle 14: Trifles matter in two ways: magnified, they lead to pedantry; overlooked, they generate nonsense.

Without yielding to pedantry, put every phrase and sentence to the test of sense, watching the small words as well as the big, and restore the intended meaning wherever possible.

1. The report is surrounded by an atmosphere of needless hysteria.
2. To everybody's amazement his apathy turned to vigor and he more than defended himself with ingenious and telling arguments.
3. There's not a scientist in the world who isn't on tenterhooks wondering when the Professor isn't going to find a hole in his favorite line of reasoning.

4. But they were nearly fatal for Charlie until Astrid rescued him from the Adriatic, and, when blackmail failed, for them both in the swirling waters of flooded Florence.

5. I thought that a disguise used once might prove to be a habit.

6. A certain brashness in common had drawn them both together.

7. The outcome of that struggle was that neither group or idea won. [Imagine a context that would make the sentence correct.]

8. [The title of a book about the storyteller Somerset Maugham is: *Somerset and All the Maughams.* Is the illogicality acceptable; and, by the way, what *is* the illogicality?]

9. . . . popping eyes, snub nose, and her mouth, if anything, on the large side. . . .

10. Uncle Ben was his last living relative, and when a vacation, annually delayed since before the war, became a reality, Peter decided to spend it with the old man.

11. An air ferry will fly your car to the British Isles and vice versa.

12. It can't be too hot or you will burn the patient's skin.

13. He kept looking at her quietly but with protruding eyes.

14. Due to a printing error as you know, New York City sales tax is 7%.

15. Granted that no list of fellowship winners will satisfy everybody, but it must not be thought that favoritism prevails.

16. He never took his eyes off Joanna, except to look at what he was eating. Sometimes not even then.

17. In the original edition the arrangement of the poems appears to have been left to chance and the result has been a total absence of method.

18. He added that any inaccuracies were more than offset by the cases we know nothing about.

19. As a novelist he has often been crowned everywhere in the world of fiction.

20 It was a trim-looking, freshly painted if capsizable skiff.

21. Gone is the light from individual lamps and its place is a warm soft diffused glow almost creating an atmosphere of its own.

22. Buy spring lamb at ———'s! It is tasty, easily digested,

and a valuable meat product. This batch of spring lamb is the cream of the crop—the ideal meat product!

23. They told him he couldn't have his cake and eat it too.

24. Statistics-hounds may note that the largest lobsters captured—tipping the scales at thirty-five pounds—are almost antiquated, probably fifty to a hundred years old.

25. [From an author's preface] Obviously, none of the people named above has the least responsibility for whatever may be found in this book. I alone am to blame.

LONGER WORDS CAN ALSO BETRAY

Anything like a list of the ordinary words that blur meaning in the work of careless writers is impossible. One can only enjoin again: "Stop and think," for you know the fundamental meanings well enough. When they are disregarded it is usually to shirk thinking and—what is not quite the same—to follow the common rut. You know, for instance, that *represent* means *stand for* a larger group of similar persons or entities. Consequently it should not be used for the whole of what is being referred to. "These books represent my library" is nonsense if you are waving at the four walls of the only room containing books. *Typify* calls for reflection too. In "Randolph Rogers (1852–1892) typified the American sculptor of his period," the implication is of a fairly standardized product of the time, the American sculptor. We know this could never be: good or bad, sculptors are not alike or numerous enough to be *typified*, as small farmers or party bosses might be. In the light of these remarks, make the effort of coming to terms with *include, compose,* and *comprise,* which are continually employed contrary to sense: *include* must refer to something larger or more numerous than what is included; *comprise* also—it surrounds, as it were, the elements of which it is *composed*. This being so, no whole is *comprised* of its parts; it is *composed* of them, and the whole *comprises* them.

*Repeat* is similarly strict: *three* blows of the whistle are *two* repetitions of the first blow. Characteristic of the thoughtless writer is the needless use of *personal* with some vague idea of emphasis: "Pick lighting suited to your *personal* needs." / "Mrs. O. was accompanied by her *personal* physician." / "Father D., whose family were *personal* friends of Cardinal Newman's . . ." / "Mr. L. displays

Walt Whitman's *personal* copy of *Leaves of Grass.*" In the last example, *own* would suffice. In the first, what can *your* needs be except personal? Even if you are buying a lamp for your mother-in-law, it is you "personally" who feel the present need. Frequently, *personal* is misused for *private,* as shown in a useful extract from an interview about an elopement: "This is personal and private. This is our personal life." The meaning was: "It is nobody's business; it concerns our *private* life"—as distinguished from public life. The notion that anybody's life could be other than personal verges on madness. Anything closely affecting the self is bound to be personal—the physician, the cardinal's friends, or the fondness expressed by A. for B.—no need to stick *personal* in front of any. But notice a somewhat different confusion arising from the same obnoxious word: "Tall, blond, energetic, yet without personally resembling his father, he . . ." One wonders first whether "he" resembled his father not personally but by proxy; then it occurs to one that the idea is: "without resembling . . . *in his person,*" i.e., in his body, physically. That last word is the one to substitute for *personally.* Perhaps the commercial use of *personalizing* to mean stamping initials on an object will in time discredit all these misplacings of the person. In a recent mail order catalogue the customer was told: "Print personalization carefully, please."

A few other hints for straight thinking may be briefly given. Remember what was said earlier about the Direction of words. *Hopefully* is an example of misdirection in logic. After widespread unthinking use, it seems now to be challenged by writers who reflect that the word can only be used to report a subjective state of mind—i.e., *full of hope.* Yet we read on an earlier page: "Sunflowers are a hopeful crop." It is he who plants them who is hopeful. The twist from the proper direction of the word takes place when the speaker attributes his hope to its object. Hence do not write: "*Hopefully* the plan will succeed"; the plan itself isn't full of hope; but "*I hope* [it is *to be hoped*] the plan . . ." Likewise, if a parent may be spoken of as *permissive,* it follows that there is no such thing as *a permissive child* in the same relation—he can only be *permissively reared.* Watch -*able* and -*ability* from the same point of view: the *thinkability* of a computer cannot mean its *ability to think,* which is nonexistent anyway. If an injured workman is logically *compensatable* under the law, what is being advertised as a *compensatable compass?*

Remember meaning—that is, shake yourself awake—when you use the following words: *lest* (= *for fear that,* not "on the lucky chance that"); *economy size* (a *large,* not a small quantity); *belabor* (= *beat with a stick,* not "make a to-do about," which is *labor* a point); *provocative* (= *intending to provoke or arouse,* not "it makes me feel provoked," which calls for *provoking*); *total* (= *the complete sum;* hence "the importance of total communications" is an idea misconceived or falsely put).

To end this topic, let us look at a few verbs. English has no future tense. It makes do with *shall* and *will,* with *am to, going to, about to,* and with the present tense: "I go to sea on Monday next." This is so instantly understood as a future that the newspaper habit, now spreading outside journalism, of "Renowned Historian Dies on Friday" and "Ex-Postmaster Dies of Heart Attack Thursday" is offensive to mind and feeling alike. Only a man condemned to execution *dies* on a stated date.

As for *shall* and *will* (*should* and *would*), the refinements they permit are so extensive and at the same time so rapidly going out of use that they fall outside our present purview. But there is a gross mishandling which is still obvious and which a little thought will prevent: "R. was reported as saying that 'if the union does call out its workers, the company *shall* maintain telephone service and it *will* be good.' " The *shall* is an order to subordinates ("Thou shalt not kill"), not a prediction. Both verbs should be *will.*

That particular confusion is generally repressed by the idiomatic sense of native speakers. A quite new confusion seems to be unchecked by it; I mean the substitution of *have to* for *must* when voicing a logical inference. The well-established, spontaneous wording is: "It must be a burglar I hear downstairs." Again and again these days, one is asked to read: "It has to be a burglar," with clear loss as a result. For if the difference disappears between a requirement (*has to be*) and a supposition (*must be*), how shall we interpret: "The lean fellow in the brown jacket had to be called first"? Was there some necessity for his being called first? Or is the writer only surmising that this is what happened—*must have been* called? I wish that conscience-stricken writers would conclude that they *must be* wrong and not tell me *they have to be* wrong, which I will not believe.

## MATCHING PARTS: ITS MANY VARIETIES

Experience shows that when one reads a sentence in which two or more elements are compared, contrasted, joined, listed, or in any way presented to the mind as parallels, comprehension is quicker and smoother if the verbal forms presenting those elements to our view are also parallel. A simple instance of the opposite proves the point: "The book cover was red, white, and torn across the corner." Here the parallel is: color and condition; two color words define the first and a phrase the second; but the construction offers all three to the mind in triple parallel, which throws us off the track. We require "red and white/*and*/torn across." In other terms, the writer gave us the parts *mismatched,* whereas the reader expects *matching parts,* i.e., the matching of parts.

Matching serves the reader's convenience by enabling him to anticipate intelligently. The self-questioning by which proper matching is ascertained is twofold: One, are the facts (ideas, agents, comments) on the same level of importance or applicability? Two, are the grammatical forms (including their length and degree of detail) a true match? Usually, it is the second question that leads to the required result: "I have been attempting to become more knowledgeable on [?] painting both by seeing and by a reading program" ("by a program of seeing and reading"; or, "by seeing and by reading").

Sometimes a seemingly perfect parallel is illusory. In "With good wishes for the season and warm thanks for all your help," the two *for*'s are not in parallel, since the season and the help each give *for* a different meaning. In what follows, the repetition of *ability* does not produce any matching whatever: "Among his other abilities he was an organizer of no mean ability." What has to jibe is *abilities* and *an organizer,* and they do not.

The most casual reading will show you—once your eye seeks out the matching—that good writing supplies paired subjects with a modifier each or omits all modification: "Almost anyone would expect a nod of recognition or a word of greeting when he meets the same neighbor on his walk every morning." Leave out the amplification after *word* and the sentence comes to grief. Or again: "She was too strong to faint, but too weak to stand up"—good and clear. Now change the ending: "but weak and could not stand up"—the thought collapses. Matching does not necessarily call for literal symmetry. Consider "but so weak she could not stand up." *Too strong, too weak* is a plain match; *too strong, so weak* is another, equally acceptable and rather more delicate.

After a negative, disharmony is frequent. One telephone company tape says: "I'm sorry; the number you have reached is not in service or temporarily disconnected." Reverse the alternatives and balance is restored, because one may negative a second idea after a positive first, but not vice versa. The reason is that the negative force carries over unless a full second subject is made to match: "or *it is* temporarily disconnected." Similar limping occurs when predicate adjectives are matched with an active verb without—again—a second subject: "He plunged into the sea. It was cool and fresh and washed away his tiredness" ("and *it* washed").

The variety of elements that can be brought into a matching relation within a sentence is of course very great. The high eighteenth-century style of Gibbon and of Dr. Johnson in some of his works consists in creating interest—indeed suspense—out of parallel subjects, modifiers, and their contrasts. Paired or tripled conceptions are set off one against the other as on a screen. With us, the matching is much more subdued; it attracts our notice when faulty rather than when properly done. Consider what is wrong with: "Dan's attitude to me was the same as his to Rose." Either *his attitude* must be repeated or *his* must be dropped, for as it stands we ask *his what?* and the true matching of parts—*same to me as to Rose*—is interfered with.

One of the easiest places to practice matching is before and after *as well as, rather than,* and the like. Innumerable writers regularly mismatch the form of the verb, starting with an indicative and closing with a participle in *-ing:* "It is not surprising that movie houses near the shopping center *attract* more customers *as well as being* cheaper than those downtown." / "He felt his work *lay at* Split Point, rather than *visiting* every other large city." / "He was the first man *brought in* from outside, *rather than being chosen* from the existing staff." Read: (*a*) *attract* . . . as well as *are;* (*b*) *lay at* . . . rather than *in visiting;* (*c*) *brought in* . . . rather than *chosen.*

With matching in mind, examine the phrase often found on the title pages of books: "Edited and With an Introduction by ————." Is the *and* logical or not? Do you prefer: "Edited [,] With an Introduction [,] by ————"? What would be the matter with: "Edited and Introduced by ————"? In the same vein of questioning, how does one interpret: "Self-indexed [?] *and* With a Pronouncing Glossary *and* Over 1100 Illustrations"?

Incoherence is the name for a complete break in construction and hence in meaning: we are led to expect continuity and possibly the correlation that matching affords, and neither is given us: "He was always kind to the child, and if the mottoes on the samplers were difficult to read or worked in Latin, he did it for her." *Did* what? And what is *it?* "He is 47, an engineer and a politician, clever in both." In both what? The effort to connect too many ideas or to start the connection with an unmatchable element will inevitably lead to incoherence: ". . . the kind of woman who, when she appeared at a party, other guests took the trouble to ask their hostess who she was." Apart from the ambiguous second *she,* the trouble here is that the first *who* finds nothing to pair with.

But beware also of the surplusage of parts: "Have you an old blanket, one that you don't care if you never see it again?" The *it* is too much and must go out, since the *that* takes care of representing *blanket* as the object of *see.* Test this pronouncement by shortening to: "a blanket that you don't care to see again," and substituting *if you never* for *to.* Of course, as in parallels, the substance of the thing said must cohere: "When you park in that public space there, you can't get in most often." The idea that matches not being able to get in is not *parking,* but *trying to park.* The *most often* I leave to you to place properly for sense.

HOWEVER YOU SAY IT, SAY IT ONLY ONCE

On the form accompanying a project submitted for a research grant, the scientist referee found a question that asked him:

"How would you rate your estimate of its originality?" The answer he put down was: "My estimate is excellent; its originality is nil." This split reply was meant to tell the form maker that *rate* and *estimate* are in fact duplicate words for one operation. This sort of duplication is the converse of incoherence, and though not destructive of meaning, it can so clutter it up as to produce a similar interruption of thought: "They were searching all last night for any survivors of a head-on crash in a tunnel between an express train and another train coming in the opposite direction." By the time one reaches the last four words one wastes time checking back to see if one only imagined the *head-on.* Here is a sentence of twenty-eight common words, of which ten merely repeat: "He got in touch and had a long conversation with his immediate superior, Supt. G——, and made certain arrangements with that official to send a substitute teacher to the school."

More often than writers notice, the repetition is on a small scale: "in ten years *from now*"; "an *unknown* stranger found on the premises"; "he had a hypersensitivity *of the senses.*" Whether you recognize it or not, *up till* (*up until*) is such a repetition, for *up to = till* and *until.* Some writers may think it is too late to stop the redundancy; but it can be confusing, as in : "He stayed up till midnight." Are we being told when he went to bed (*stayed up*) or that he remained in the house, then left (*stayed/up till*)? At times redundancy is hidden in a word of which the root idea is ignored by the writer, or unknown to him: "The words were ordinary but she sensed a mood of hostility tangible enough to be felt." *Tangible* means *touchable, feelable,* and the remark is on a par with the twice-over phrasings of melodrama: "the baffling enigma"; "the treacherous act of betrayal"; "the inscrutable countenance defying analysis." Truism, tautology, and repetition are close kin, and being on guard against any of the three will alert one to the others.

✳

Principle 15: Make fewer words do more work by proper balance, matching parts, and tight construction.

In amending the statements that follow, do not forget the demands of earlier exercises.

1. This move represented the first step in a long-matured plan.

2. A new checkless welfare system has just been proposed.

3. Hats fitted to the head exclusively.

4. Scowls Now Smiles, Hisses Now Silence [Headline]

5. The authorities ordered a count of the population broken down by age and sex.

6. The idea comes from someone who, for the sake of this discussion, wishes to remain anonymous.

7. In his singular character the dual nature alternately asserted itself.

8. All guests must have positive identification.

9. "I am very fond of him as a person," said the President.

10. With the Senate's traditional courtesy replaced by a personal clash, Senator S——, who is regarded by his colleagues as a model gentleman, proved stubborn when it came to pushing his legislation through the Senate.

11. All were costumed in a brevity usually reserved for the bath.

12. He proceeded to take a complete set of the prints of the fingers of both hands.

13. One of the buttons of his coat was mismatched with the wrong buttonhole.

14. Once on site—and there are about 600 in South Africa —the trailer can be parked while the family goes off in the car to the beach.

15. We hope as far as your summer telephone is concerned you'll suspend it for the winter months.

16. He said he knew no one kinder, more fun, with better manners or more integrity.

17. It occurred to him that the rule against cutting the deck in cribbage had to make it the easiest game in the world in which to cheat.

18. Mr. M—— fondly remembers buying sheets of poetry in Washington Square from Maxwell Bodenheim but now says the park is so unsafe he cannot walk there.

19. She seemed entirely engrossed with a train of thought that was all her own.

20. I don't advise it; the neighborhood is bad as well as being dark.

21. "I used to have a handicap"—"You may still think he does. But it's not the same. We'll send you free information about rehabilitation. Of course, your handicap may never be the same."

22. Frank has always been a favorite of mine aside from his personal life.

23. The information came from a person who fears for their life should their name be revealed. [From a Supreme Court decision.]

24. All Shakespeare's sonnets—works of passion, simplicity, and exquisitely beautiful!

25. The government was alarmed by workers' and agricultural strikes.

THE WOOLLY METAPHORICAL STYLE

A metaphor is a comparison embodied in a word or phrase without the addition of *like* or *as*. To say: "People's characters are neither all black nor all white" is to compare virtue and vice with the colors white and black without saying so. The greater part of the vocabulary in any complex language is a mass of forgotten metaphors. For language grows in response to needs, and the readiest way to name new conceptions is to adapt concrete words to abstract purposes. To do this is to speak by metaphor—as when Socrates is called the *gadfly* of Athens.

Such metaphors often generate new concrete meanings out of which new metaphors are made, and so on. These various turns can be noted in: "A man's financial position is said to be liquid when he can convert most of his assets into cash." That sentence contains six buried metaphors, those in *financial, position, liquid, convert, assets,* and *cash.* If translated backward into roots the sentence says : "A man's *finishing* [*settling*] *put-there* is said to be *like water* when he can *turn* his *enoughs* into a *box.*" By using *box* (in French, *caisse;* cf. *packing case*) to denote the contents of a money box, the idea we know as *cash* was expressed. It ought to follow that *cash box* ought to mean *box box,* but it does not, because the original image has died and been buried in the word until we no longer think of *box* on hearing *cash.*

But it is evident that *liquid* in the same sentence is on a different footing. Except in banking circles, the word is still metaphorical.

Ask a friend out of the blue: "How liquid are you today?" and the context of money will not occur to him as soon as it would if you said: "How are you fixed for cash?" The metaphor, in short, still has life *as* a metaphor. The interplay between live and dead metaphors, and live and live, and live and resuscitated, constitutes the subject of most discussions of metaphorical writing. The injunction ordinarily is: do not join two live metaphors that raise conflicting images. Anyone can see that the senator who complained of a government department as being "totally impaled in the quicksands of absolute inertia" was not visualizing properly. And the late Ian Fleming was in a still worse trance when he wrote of his hero: "Bond's knees, the Achilles' heel of all skiers, were beginning to ache."

But two things must be said about trouble of this obvious sort. One, it occurs when the speaker or writer is deliberately seeking images to express strong feelings; he is using metaphor as the poets do, as a deliberate figure of speech, and in prose this use is not the most insidious or dangerous to sense. Two, the objection felt is to the *combining* of such images, not to their mere juxtaposition. The indignant senator could have said: "The department is a quicksand; its officers are like men impaled; the whole force has been brought to absolute inertia." The successive ideas would then have been assimilable. Look up in Shakespeare's *Richard II* the sixteen metaphors by which the Duke characterizes "this England" he wishes to praise. Each would jar with the rest if they were fashioned into what might be called a "working model" of England. And this very metaphor tells us how to test any metaphoric expression—will it work? "That concept embraces many levels," says a philanthropic organization about its aims. We ask: Can a concept *embrace* anything? Yes, particulars certainly, and ideas perhaps; but not *levels,* because the concreteness of *layers* or *floors* or *measured elevations above ground* does not "work" with the abstractness of an *embracing concept*.

That same sentence also illustrates what is wrong with the modern style in which business, government, and academic life are conducted, to say nothing of so-called educated conversation: it is metaphorical without the excuse of emotion; it is unexamined, because thinking is hard work; and it is woolly, although everybody "understands" what in fact defies precise understanding. "The Governor thanked the Consul General and described the Legation as a crossroad between two great peoples." / "Our intention is to disseminate the current of creativity among all those to whom the distillation of this series of discussions would stimulate in their own sphere, and we are contemplating also the stimulation of corporate interest in support." / "Schweitzer's work is prepotent because he invariably functions symbiotically in naturalistic and religious frames of reference." No reader of the last nine lines could pass a searching quiz on their contents: they are loose translations into "Low Metaphoric" of possibly simple ideas, but those ideas were never fully conceived in a human consciousness.

For the fully conscious writer, it may be useful to distinguish among three kinds of metaphor: (*a*) the ready-made single-word expression that spreads suddenly in some professional group or other—the jargon of people who do paper work; (*b*) those produced *ad hoc* for headlines, captions, and the like, and usually not repeated elsewhere; and (c) the latent metaphors in good ordinary words, which misuse galvanizes into fresh life. To clear your mind before reading further, let me point out that names of teams, clubs, societies, etc., involve no metaphor beyond the original use in designation: there is no false imagery in "Pistons Defeat Bullets." Nor is there in the market report "Grains Uneven as Soybeans Rise." There is even charm, as sports writers know, in multiplying metaphors for technical descriptions: "Rare Treat was second to Deb Marion in a prep over the grass for that stake. She was sidelined after finishing off the boards."

All that is very well because conventionalized, but "Nervous Market on Aimless Path" and "Air of Confusion Grows in Brazil" are both reprehensible. A market on a path is not plausible, and if anything should not be called aimless, it is a path. Similarly, air does not grow, and air of confusion can only be a facial expression; it is not concrete turmoil. In short, none of these images will work. It is fortunate that they belong to class *b,* those not likely to be used twice. The danger is only to the mind of the careless creator.

Class *c,* on the contrary, begets its kind: *impervious to irregular hours; ignites a bitter contest; abrasive future ahead; volatile source of friction; something nebulously nibbling at the back of*

*her mind*—all these show the writer as not knowing or not thinking about the meaning of his fancy words. If in doubt, look up the
root ideas in *impervious, ignite, volatile, abrasive,* and *nebulous.*
For blunders of this type often come from combining a word properly used with another, also acceptable, that clashes with the root of
the first. Such is the trouble with: "Nobody fore*saw* at the time the
*repercussions* that the affair would have." / "Harvard University
has donated 18,109 pints of blood without any repercussions." If
you think of *percussion* you grasp why it or *foresight* must go and
why the Harvard blood donors are entitled to more quiet. Did the
writer of "His hand struck the table and his eyes excoriated the
face in front of him" know what *excoriate* means? Probably not;
but ignorance is no excuse, any more than plain lack of imagination: "The air was clear and cool but not cold and its freshness was
like wine in the nostrils." It's bad enough to inhale smoke!

We come now to the great blight, class *a,* which I illustrated in
the first examples on page 17, and of which we examined the
origin when discussing pseudo-technical diction: the desire to
"cover" and to sound important. On the metaphorical side, this
vocabulary has the property of raising few or no images and
thus of not at once giving away its absurdity. "Mr. D. *pinpoints*
the *fulcrum* of the whole complex *issue,* namely, control of the
currency." The words underlined are tired and we are tired,
which allows the tired writer to rearrange them with others of
their kind in endless combinations without arousing us to disbelief
—or true attention. In our daily ration of this bilge there float
bits and pieces dropped from all the specialties, together with
good words diverted from their plain sense: we find *parameter*
side by side with *gray area, focus* and *context* with *escalate* and
*infrastructure*—all denoting something other than their simple intent. Watch for *thrust, impact,* and *empathy,* and then go on to
*retooling, fulcrum, concept, angle, area, timeframes, frames of
reference, potentials, commitment, urgency, highlight, spotlight,
play by ear, major, center, viable, vital, crucial, drastic, specific*
—you will run into many more—and take note of their inability, as
used, to denote exactly the contour of any reality.

This negative power—so to speak—is what makes the metaphoric the style of evasion, deceit, and manipulation; hence the

quality of some of the answers given to a famous Senate investigating committee: "I have no ability to weigh the potentials for the sources of concern in this area," said one witness; and another, asked about the duties of a person named, replied: "He was a kind of facility attached to the office of the counsel." Utterances of this type would not have been speakable, nor would they have resembled answers, in a generation that had not been saturated with metaphors in the course of everyday affairs, public and private.

So much, everybody can see. But the perception does no good unless self-respecting writers and speakers make it a point of honor not to use any—not even *one*—of the words that make up this metaphoric pidgin. The self-forbidden words remain good in their nonmetaphoric use. If you have to report the *impact* of a meteorite in your backyard, use the word without hesitation, but forgo it in describing the effect of a new detergent on the lives of young mothers.

It remains to say a few words about certain tricks of prose that resemble metaphor, broadly speaking. One is irony, which uses ordinary words to mean the opposite of their normal meaning. It is a dangerous sort of tone unless skillfully handled: you may be taken at your word and the irony altogether missed. In any event, it is not a figurative medium that bears frequent use. A second form of the figurative is that which uses well-known references or quotations, Biblical and other, to convey a literal meaning. If you employ it, make sure you know the exact significance of the allusive word or phrase. "We scotched that" is not final, though many think so. The quotation runs: "scotched the snake, not killed it." (Note that in another Shakespeare play, a brave veteran cries: "I have yet room for six scotches more" and the true possibilities of *scotch* will linger in your memory.) Poetical tags are treacherous. Recently, someone wrote of a great new mansion which in the eyes of the wealthy owners did not prove to be "the 'fine and private place' they hoped for." The writer did not remember that by that phrase the poet Marvell refers to the grave. It would be good also to leave King Canute and the mark of Cain unused for a while. That wise king did nothing of the kind imputed to him, but told his courtiers that he could no more do what they asked than he could roll back the ocean. As for the mark, it was put on Cain by the Lord to protect him from harm, not to brand him with infamy.

An annoying transfer of ideas, quasi-metaphorical, leads to expressions such as: "On Tuesday, two flat tires and one broken axle later . . ." Time could be measured in this way only if such events occurred with regularity. Again, it would seem needless to warn against unintended puns in metaphoric expressions, if they did not crop up so often. When General Hershey headed the Selective Service, a New York headline said: "Hershey Bars Protest"; and after a long strike another announced: "Detroit Strike Paper Folds." Remember, too, that there is no synonymy in metaphor. The fact that one image will "work" is no guarantee that a closely related one will also. You may say *sunk* or *drowned* in misery but not *swamped* in it or *sodden* with it. If equivalence were possible, as someone has pointed out, one could go from *stubborn as a mule* to *pigheaded* for *stubborn,* and arrive at *pigheaded as a mule.* To close with a little puzzle, here is a curious transposition of terms. Many writers–certainly all journalists–use the phrase "I do" as signifying the marriage vow. The truth is that the words in church services and secular formulas are not "Do you take . . . ?" but "Will you [wilt thou] take . . . ?" to which the answer is of course "I will." Are we then to consider "I do" an accepted metaphor for "I will"?

♓

Principle 16: Worship no images and question the validity of all.

Take out all metaphorical language and recast in Plain, naming the fields of study or experience from which the metaphors are drawn.

1. As the architectural principle of the psychic apparatus we may conjecture a certain stratification or structure of instances deposited in strata. [Authorized translation of Sigmund Freud.]

2. Mysticism is the flame which feeds his whole life; and he is intensely and supremely happy just so far as he is steeped in it.

3. Here's the news about our colorful August White Sale.

4. Man does not live by four-door sedans alone. [Advertisement in an airport.]

5. In the Florence floods some 400,000 volumes were dismembered.

6. He called the accused a "half friend" and said he was wrapped up in motorcycles.

7. The result is that once again Winnie-the-Pooh has been the catalyst for another hilarious book.

8. The entire carpet industry is in a state of price chaos. Every one is watching the fiber front, with more bobbling considered likely.

9. Mixer had a whining note in his voice which grated with him.

10. The emphasis is toward wider indoctrination of local talent who will add considerable impact to the thrust of the regular encyclopedia salesmen, as soon as these new resource persons appreciate the soundness for them of a little moonlighting.

11. With 1300 miles of Gulf of Mexico and Atlantic Ocean coastline the slender sunny peninsula [Florida] is one huge yachting center.

12. At the fulcrum of the survey is the determination of what focal points can be relied on for gathering the data that falls within the parameters of the Commission.

13. It is only fair to add that some of his cohorts have found him abrasive in unexpected areas and also tight corners.

14. In this recession, at least so far, many of the millions of unemployed are discovering that the wolf is not at the door, that society has given them a cushion that enables them to tighten their belts a bit and live pretty much as they did when they were working.

15. Three sessions of Ecumenical Council Vatican II were required to forge the document.

16. Teeth Marks Linked to Murder Suspect

17. The fall in the stock-market is approaching window-leaping levels.

18. A key to the house was the crux of that particular angle.

19. Nudism is not my cup of tea, and I suspect it is not the cup of tea of this honorable court.

20. [Discuss the need and acceptability of such phrases as *facial tissues, no-iron sheets, human hair net, performing arts, partially sighted readers,* and search your mind for similar ones in which imagery is well or badly used, at the expense of literalism and logic.]

THE POINT OF VIEW: LEAD UP TO THE OBJECT WITHOUT A BREAK

Because the reader cannot see and interpret the actions of the person "speaking" to him, it is imperative that the writer take into account his own position, his outlook and direction, in front of the invisible person he is addressing. We were concerned with one part of this obligation when we looked at the direction of words—whether they were "standing still" or "going across" or "looking back" in their very nature and meaning. The extension of that concern makes the writer take note of what might be called the geography of the written passage: where is he in relation to the listener and to what is that person expected to cock an eye or an ear? Two examples, one concrete and one abstract, will show how easy it is to disorient the receiver of the message:

"The old bridge at Pontypridd in Wales rises steeply from each bank to the midpoint. There are a chain and a drag to be used. When a vehicle reaches the center of the bridge, the chain is hooked on behind, and the other is hooked on to the drag, on which a boy obligingly seats himself, so as to take the weight of the horse, who might otherwise go down with a run." At what moment did you lose the point of view that would have made it all clear? Next:

"I am not particularly dexterous, but by virtue of the anatomic integrity of my nervous and muscular apparatus, there are apparently no grounds in me for such awkward movements with undesirable results." Here, as I read the passage, the point of view shifts four times in as many lines. How can a reader, unwarned, be expected to jump and follow?

A practical situation of the most frequent kind will perhaps make clear how difficult it may be to choose and hold the point of view when one wants to convey an apparently simple idea. In a town of modest size, the owner of a large estate bequeathed his property for use as a public park. The council decided to pass an ordinance requiring the users of the park not to let dogs run loose. The debate was as follows:

*Chairman.* The motion reads: "Resolved, That no dogs shall be brought to Wildwood Park except on a leash."

*Councilman A.* That wouldn't keep a dog owner from letting the dog go once he was in the park.

*Chairman.* How would you re-phrase the resolution?

*Councilman A.* Dogs are not admitted to this park without a leash.

*Councilman F.* Mr. Chairman, I think the notice should be addressed to the public, not to the dogs.

*Councilman S.* There's not much of a difference that I can see, but what about saying: Dog owners not allowed in this park unless they have them on a leash.

*Councilman F.* That sounds to me as if a dog owner could not come to the park unless he brought his dog.

*Chairman.* Would Mr. A., who made the first objection, try his hand again?

*Councilman A.* Perhaps this will do. *(Reading)* Nobody without his dog on a leash will be allowed in this park.

*Councilman S.* I don't own a dog. Must I get one before I am allowed in the park?

*Councilman F. (impatiently)* Keep it simple: No dogs in this park without a leash.

*Councilman A.* It implies, but doesn't say, they must be *kept* on the leash.

*Councilman F.* Very well: All dogs must be kept on a leash in this park—and don't anybody tell me that means all the dogs on one leash, because it doesn't!

*Chairman.* One last small improvement: All dogs in this park must be kept on a leash. (Unanimously carried.)

In novel writing toward the end of the nineteenth century, "the point of view"—that is, its strict observance—became for some authors an inescapable rule of art. Nothing in the story could be told that the narrator might not have seen or heard for himself, his place and his opportunities being clearly defined. In ordinary prose these limitations do not apply. It is enough if the expositor sticks to a line of thought or description and refrains from jumping to and from the position of his reader or of a third party. *Continuity, linking, coherence,* is the desideratum. In description the advice is easy to follow: look at the scene from a convenient point and describe it from left to right or top to bottom or here to there or in any other consecutive way without skipping. You can always add or retract, or contribute miraculously acquired information later on. Take care also of ordinary truths about physical realities. When one reads: "His next concern was the back staircase which led upwards out of the kitchen," one detects a writer either careless or self-centered. Stairs do not lead upwards more than downwards and they generally lead out of some room. The reader can easily imagine the back stairs or kitchen stairs if you tell him just that; he will not think of the cellar stairs. Do not clutter up his practical view of the simple facts.

Just as the direction of words must be respected in syntax, so the normal direction of ideas must be in composition. In a paragraph that speaks of some persons' longing for relief from loneliness comes the sentence: "It was at once to satisfy their ego and exchange excitement for boredom." *Exchange* in the abstract is neutral and works both ways, but here the point of view requires "exchange boredom for excitement." You can exchange only what you possess.

Certain verbs such as *rent, lease, dust,* etc., also look both ways and need something more to show a direction. "We rented the back cottage" may mean that you moved in or that you moved out. Often the failure to attribute an act or attitude to a person prevents our knowing what happened, which is a pity. Look at: "Mr. O.'s decision cast a glow of goodwill on the stockholders, who left the meeting exchanging smiles." No one can say whether Mr. O.'s decision embodied goodwill, which he thereby cast at the stockholders, or whether a quite neutral decision brought forth goodwill from them. It would be nice to know.

Frequently, single words will cut across the line stretching from the point of view. This interference always occurs when something that can only be known after an event is mentioned as preceding it: "I should hate everything I've ever done to be proclaimed to a shocked world." The world would not be shocked until after the proclamation, which therefore would not be made *to a shocked world.* Such anticipation is frequent in poetry, but in prose all modifiers must be scanned in the light of rational sequence, especially absolute or superlative terms. You cannot ask for "an excellent cup of coffee"; you ask for a good one and then you find it excellent.

The same consideration dictates that increase or decrease of magnitude be orderly, not haphazard; the reader wants to be led by jumps or degrees always upward or always downward. "He is a crook and not as honest as he might be" reverses the expected gradation of censure. We hear a positive accusation followed by a mere suspicion. Remember that the word *climax* means *a ladder*. Whoever uses it must make his way rung by rung, not skip about as if it were the keyboard of a piano: "He called the government morally bankrupt, subject to investigation, and criminally liable." The first epithet is the strongest, the next weakest, and the third middling. Put them in order of increasing strength and not only does assent follow more readily, but the wording is seen to need amendment for parallelism (matching parts).

*Emphasis,* to which what we have been discussing is related, will occupy us in the following section. All that needs to be said about it here is that if the point of view is not held to, misdirections are given about what is important. Take as an example the malpractice of using dates or other indications of time as modifiers ahead of the subject. "His 1954 bankruptcy was held against him when he was nominated for office." To a good reader this clearly says that he had a 1954 bankruptcy and other ones on other dates. This indication is given by the invariable rule of the preposited adjective of time: "his June payment was overdue" implies other monthly payments not overdue; "your September 10 editorial" recognizes that an editorial appears every day. To perceive this relation of the unsaid to what is said, the writer must keep his eye on his bearings and never forget the position occupied by his object, by his readers and—through "triangulation"—by himself.

⚶

Principle 17: In each portion of the work, begin from a point clear to you and the reader and move forward without wobble or meander.

The three paragraphs under number 7 below are to be recast into proper shape. The other items speak for themselves.

1. Police have as yet made no progress in solving the case of Jane S—— and her lunchtime murder on P—— Street.

2. A private plane with four aboard including the pilot crashed near here, killing all occupants. No further details were immediately available.

3. The work was discovered by a curious and delighted 20th century.

4. 1913–45 Roosevelt Romance Reported.

5. For the billing [and cooing?] month of June the charge will be 7.2% higher.

6. The big house was so beautifully balanced that its size went almost unnoticed. . . . She was a big woman, five feet ten inches or so, but, like her great mansion, so precisely built that her size was unnoticed.

7. As I wrote, my memory awoke and presented in the order of time, clear recollections of event with which I was connected in the earliest years of the improved service and they were chronicled so that those who joined the devoted corps later might become familiar with the details of its inception, inauguration and development; the hardships and disadvantages under which the work was performed; the desperate struggle preceding its firm establishment, and the gradual breaking of the clouds between the rifts of which could be seen the coming of the magnificent service of today.

As the story progressed, the educational methods employed to strengthen the minds and memories of the clerks, to increase the efficiency of their work while its scope was enlarging, and its character becoming more complexed, the system of discipline instituted to insure obedience of orders, instructions, regulations and laws, and thus gain the confidence and support of the public, were introduced and discussed.

The strength and favorable consideration thus obtained, fostered and advanced the work the service was created to perform; improved facilities for distribution, storage, and dispatch of the mails were furnished more readily by the railway companies, and the frequency of train service and consequently of dispatch of mail was increased.

8. Classify the following compounds into kinds and discuss each group of similars as to clarity of meaning, point of view, and propriety of form: *self-service, self-image, self-indexing, self-starter, self-will, self-colored, self-control, self-addressed, self-identity, self-adhesive, self-regard, self-mailer, self-conceit, self-centered, selfsame, self-despair, self-opinionated, self-unconscious, self-important, selfishness.*

## TIME OUT FOR GOOD READING IV

Certain authors of unassuming books, or of unsigned notices, instructions, and captions, are notable for the ability to make plain in words what most of us would need gestures and diagrams to convey in full. Such persons are in fact distinguished writers, though their names are unknown or unremembered. Here is a passage from Alfred P. Morgan's *Tools and How to Use Them* (1948), which illustrates what has just been said.

### Hints for Sawing

Human beings are blessed with ten strong, amazingly dextrous fingers and a world filled with raw materials from which can be fashioned almost anything that may be desired. But fingers alone cannot cut wood and metal and stone. Not much progress can be made in driving a nail with the fist. It is obvious that hands, even though they are guided by an ingenious brain, must have tools to accomplish much.

Anyone possessed of ordinary coordination can easily learn to handle tools efficiently. It is not difficult to use, or to learn how to use, most of the ordinary tools with skill. Do not be dismayed by the dexterity of a skilled workman. Proper instruction and practice will make you skillful also.

First, you must understand the tools you propose to use, their purposes and limitations; then, the proper way to hold them and apply them to the work.

To get the most out of a tool, we do not, for example, pick up a hammer and merely whack at a nail with it or push a saw back and forth to cut wood. We learn the *technique* of using each tool. Starting right is half the secret. If we start right, we soon acquire skill by practicing. If we start wrong, practice will not bring skill.

Striking a blow is not all there is to using a hammer. There can be artistry in its use or in the use of a saw, a wrench, a screw driver, a plane, or in fact of any other tool. The skilled mechanic is skilled in the use of his tools because he knows more about his tools than the novice and has learned the technique of using them. His tools have become extensions of his hands and brain. . . .

The piece to be sawed must be held firmly in a vise, or on a work-bench, a box or a pair of horses. Small work often can be held firmly on a bench or table by the pressure of the left hand. A bench hook for this purpose (see sketch) is a great convenience. Pieces of considerable length are best supported on a pair of saw horses, or on two boxes or two chairs, and held firmly by the pressure of one knee.

As a saw progresses across the grain of a board, the weight of the board tends to close the cut and bind the saw so that you can no longer push the blade back and forth. If the waste end is a short, light piece you can hold it up with your left hand while sawing and prevent the slot from closing on the blade. You will need an assistant to hold a long or heavy piece. Moreover, if you do not support the waste end properly, it will break off just as you are finishing the cut and take a large splinter from the corner of the other piece with it. The splinter can be glued back in place but it is preferable to avoid this.

The proper position for sawing permits long easy strokes using nearly the full length of the blade. Take your time, and be careful not to jerk the saw back and forth. It is difficult to keep the kerf beside the marked line where it belongs if much of the cutting is done with only a few inches of the blade.

Watch your grip on the handle closely when you are learning to saw. It should be firm but not tight. The saw should run freely. A tight grip prevents the free running of the saw and tends to swerve the blade away from the line. The thumb should be against the left side of the handle. Keep the index finger extended along the right side of the handle to help guide the blade. If the blade starts to cut into the marked line or to move too far away from it, twist the handle slightly in order to draw it back to the correct position.

To keep the saw at right angles to the surface of the work is the most difficult thing to learn in sawing. The beginner should make an occasional test with a try square, as shown in one of the illustrations, to keep the saw in a perfectly vertical position and to help develop the knack of sawing square. Check the position of the blade with the try square from time to time until the tests show that you can get along without it. That stage in your skill will not be reached the first few times that you use a saw. It will come only with careful practice. Accurate sawing is done with long, easy, relaxed strokes, guided by the hand and eye, and is mastered only with practice.

All the cutting action of the teeth on a hand saw takes place on the forward or pushing stroke of the saw blade. Do not try to make the teeth cut on the backward or pulling stroke. Exert a little downward pressure of the wrist on the forward stroke and do not apply any pressure on the return stroke. Do not try to guide the blade on the return stroke. Relax and lift it more than pull it. If the tip of the blade vibrates when the blade is brought back on the return stroke, you are not allowing the saw to run freely but are bending or twisting it slightly.

Look carefully for nails in the path of the saw when second-hand lumber is used or repair work is done. A hand saw will not cut nails. If it is drawn or pushed over a nail, the sharp points and edges will be knocked off the teeth.

❖

Except for a few special words easy to look up or guess at (*kerf, waste end, horses*), the only object referred to that needs illustration is *bench hook,* and even that becomes clear when one is reminded that it is not really a hook but a contrivance made of wood, against the raised end of which a board may be pushed for sawing.

Observe the natural skill with which the writer keeps his sentences short without letting the prose become choppy. The avoidance of descriptive clauses by a neat use of modifiers (*all the cutting action of the teeth; the blade on the return stroke; lift it more than pull it*) is sheer art. In order to find any fault in this section it would be necessary to suggest that the last two paragraphs would be better placed somewhere earlier—but where?—so as to end with "Accurate sawing . . . is mastered only with practice," a maxim that goes for accurate writing too.

# Composition
## or How Does It Hang Together?

# V

From the beginning of this book you have been asked to scan words, expressions, and their combining forms in the light of resulting meanings. You have thereby acquired a sharper sense of what goes on when words are set down "side by each." Now, judging from the title of this penultimate section, it would seem as if you were at last reaching the art of writing itself. Composition, in any of the fine arts, is generally said to be the test of the master, the rest being detail and less important.

These are reasonable thoughts to have at this point. But I would ask you to put them aside and not lose your grip on the central purpose of this book, which is to develop in yourself the highest possible consciousness of words-as-meanings. You have not been badgered about "details," nor are you finally coming to "art." In short, the discussion of how to compose will use the same test as before—Is it clear? Does it suit?—but will apply it over a wider range of matter. The matter itself is no different from what it was earlier: sentences with faults. Only, we shall now consider their external faults as well as their internal ones, and their interaction as wholes in the building up of still larger wholes.

I shall shortly specify the tests that correspond to these demands, but first it is best to dispose of some ideas commonly associated with composition. In the old rhetorics it was usual to divide prose writing into descriptive, narrative, expository, and persuasive (hortatory). These genres still exist but they are no longer set apart by differences of style, or regarded as constituting distinct pieces of work. Even the novel cannot be all narration: it includes description and it often expounds a thesis and argues for it—all four genres between two covers. In modern prose tone may vary, but the language that suits storytelling or argument as such is one and the same.

### WHERE IS A SENTENCE? WHEN FOUND, OF WHAT KIND IS IT?

Nobody has been able to define *sentence* satisfactorily—which shows how important the subject is. As in poetry, love, thought, and faith, the reality is familiar but it eludes definition. None the less, as a writer you cannot escape the duty of knowing when you have written a genuine sentence. A rough test is to see whether there is too much or too little between the first capital letter and the final period to give voice to a self-supporting idea. "Go!" is a sentence. "Which, by the way, that was a good piece of work" is not a sentence. Cut out *Which* and you have one. Take note here of the difference between a bad sentence—our Exercises are full of examples—and a non-sentence. The one just repeated from page 111 is, I believe, the only non-sentence in all I have quoted, headlines and captions excepted.

The reason for using sentences and no substitutes is twofold. The form enables you to verify the coherence and continuity of your thought. In the false form above, *Which* necessarily relates —to what? The gap in thought is disclosed by the expression. Again, the form assures the reader that he is receiving the full message at no cost of stumbling or backtracking. The redundant *which* in our example makes him expect one kind of construction and he stumbles when it is not there. He probably returns to the previous sentence to see if he has missed anything: he has been treated with discourtesy fore and aft.

Sentences come in three forms, which it is a great convenience to recognize; for as in all technical definitions, the knowledge permits the workman to spot and repair trouble quickly and efficiently. The simple sentence has the general form $A \rightarrow B$: some agent acts on some object or person or is acted on by it. A is subject, B is predicate. The compound sentence consists of two simples paired or contrasted: $A \rightarrow B$ *and* (or *but*) $X \rightarrow Y$. The complex sentence is made up of two parts, of which the main one is a simple or a compound, and the other is a group of words that could not stand alone yet contributes to the total meaning. This second part is called a subordinate clause: *"Although the boat was without sail or rudder,* it managed to keep its head athwart the breakers." The first eight words by themselves leave us hanging; the last nine would keep us happy and informed regardless of the first clause. That clause modified the otherwise self-supporting idea to come. How should this form be represented? Perhaps Z] A → B. Suppose the boat to have reached the shore safely, and we are free to add an X → Y at the end. Another subordinate clause [Z, also could come at the end, or indeed at any point where it did not drag down the rhythm or confuse the thought.

Now consider this sentence: "The traffic light shone into the glass-sided phone booth where the man dialed and turned green." We spot this at once as a case of bad linking, but we are now concerned to make it right without changing the form of the sentence—i.e., without making it two sentences, a compound. Take it from me that a comma after *dialed* will not make it right; we must recast: "The traffic light shone into the glass-sided phone booth and turned green where the man dialed." Absurd— a mere shifting of a bad link. "The traffic light shone and turned green in(to) the . . . booth where the man dialed." Just as bad and contrary to fact: the light is not in the booth. "The traffic light shone into the booth and turned green as (or when) the man dialed." A good enough sentence, but inaccurate: the original suggests a different timing of the green light and the dialing. One more effort: "Into the booth where the man dialed, the traffic light shone, then turned green." This is it. The meaning agrees with the data, the links are rightly placed and thus no longer ludicrous, and best of all, the sentence is *balanced* and *in movement*—in dynamic equilibrium, if you like a bit of jargon.

EMPHASIS AND MOVEMENT OUT OF PATTERN AND PERIOD

To keep using that sentence of ours, we find motion given by suspending the meaning in the first clause: "Into the booth . . ." What then? "Where the man dialed . . ." We still don't know what is to happen. We learn it when the green light shines and completes a vivid night scene.

Observe that in ending with *green* we have preserved the main emphasis of the original bad sentence. For the emphatic places in a sentence are beginning and end, the end being the more so. By our rearrangement we have kept this primary stress and we have improved the secondary, since *shining into the booth* is a more important visual fact than the traffic light itself, which we are not even looking at.

Is the meaning of emphasis clear from this casual example? Because the word *emphatic* suggests a loud voice or someone banging the table, one can easily forget that emphasis in speaking and writing is nothing else than pointing to the object you want your audience to attend to. Remember the three divergent emphases in the spoken words discussed on page 2. All three interpretations were equally possible because no clue was in the words or could be inferred from their placing. They did not form a sentence. We now know the emphatic places; but placing may be insufficient: the words in themselves must have a certain "weight," a result of length or sound. We do not say: "I'm not as lucky as you're," because the ear and the mind demand a stress on *"you* are," a stress that the contraction prevents, since contractions are for sliding over the unimportant.

Similarly, a short, weak word will usually not support the load of preceding ideas. It will lack all emphasis, even though it comes last: "It was of no use to pretend that under such conditions of general and mutual suspicion, though not indeed of their own making, the friendly relations so happily sprung up between them could prosper, and would not rather dwindle and leave his spirit—certainly the more eager of the two—wan." Several things could be changed to advantage in this spaghettilike sentence, but the one that cries out for attention is the last word. Even a two-syllable adjective such as *bereft* would work better than the wispy *wan,* which makes such a silly effect after *two.* In truth, only a phrase of at least two strong *sounds* would balance the long preparation.

Looking back at the less pretentious elements composing the sentence about the green light, we may say that in it all the virtues of a right sentence are comprised: (1) it *is* a sentence; (2) its meaning is the one intended, in accord with the facts; (3) it is in balance and in motion as well; (4) the emphases direct the reader to the correct view of relative importance. The effort of turning the words this way and that may seem disproportionate to the result, which is but a vignette in color. But composition is nothing else than this putting of the elements in the best pattern. Fortunately, skill in framing sentences comes with practice; and when the habit of composition has been acquired, it so shapes one's thoughts as they arise that no tinkering is required except in circumstances of special complexity.

This fusion of thinking and writing as one act of composing enables a writer to elaborate, refine, interweave, and imply ideas with a great economy of words and effort. It is the form of the complex sentence that permits this work to be done, for a series of simples and compounds will produce the effect of addition rather than organization. Scan and parse the following construction several times until you appreciate how cunningly it tells its tale:

> Stranger still, though Jaques-Dalcroze, like all these great teachers, is the completest of tyrants, knowing what is right and that he must and will have the lesson just so or else break his heart (not somebody else's, observe), yet his school is so fascinating that every woman who sees it exclaims: "Oh why was I not taught like this!" and elderly gentlemen excitedly enroll themselves as students and distract classes of infants by their desperate endeavors to beat two in a bar with one hand and three with the other, and start off on earnest walks round the room, taking two steps backward whenever M. Dalcroze calls out "Hop!"

I am not recommending that you write sentences like this—until you can do it; and even then, so long a pull at the complex form must be justified by a scene or mood to be conveyed, as it was in Shaw's sentence about Dalcroze. Its clear complexity illustrates a number of new points about structure. By the placing of its details as much as by their contents, it creates a storylike effect that cannot be obtained from the purely declarative style:

"John hit the ball. The ball hit the window. The noise brought the owner to the door. The owner scolded John." The complex form gives and withholds information, subordinates some ideas to others more important, co-ordinates those of equal weight, and ties into a neat package as many suggestions, modifiers, and asides as the mind can attend to at one stretch.

A second point to note in Shaw's 110-word sentence is that it presents no barriers to consecutive thought. It may indeed require you to store up impressions before their full bearing can be seen, but it gives no false leads, it never compels you to return and reread. You will remember the likeness to a skeleton, which I suggested was truer of sentence structure than the analogy with a house of bricks. We feel in our long sentence the force of the better image: the sentence runs, it virtually flies, because it is not rigid but has joints; it is always on its feet and never thrown off balance by the continual insertion of fresh ideas.

Let us now ask, as we did about the smaller-scale effort of the green light and the booth, what gives the necessary push to this remarkable composition of Shaw's: The first two words, "Stranger still," arouse curiosity and the assertion "J.-D. . . . is the completest of tyrants" makes us want to know in what ways this "great teacher" imposes his will. But it is not only fact or substance that impels us forward; it is the third word in the sentence, "though." The *periodic style,* in short, is always good for creating suspense. That is why it should be reserved for matter interesting in itself and not wasted on trivial details or "bridge passages" between important subjects.

Come now to the place where the sentence, after offering six distinct ideas, takes a turn and (so to speak) lets out its suspended breath over the remainder of its course. That turning point is YET; and we might suppose the momentum was spent, but no: by including the word *so* in the predicate—"a school so fascinating that"—we are pushed forward again and willingly pass in review the picturesque features of the school.

The last lesson to be drawn from the example is the most valuable: what makes for smooth reading is the continuous presence and *activity* of the original subject—one only—until the comments to be made about it are exhausted. Violating this simple law produces the catchall, nonstop sentence, invertebrate and mindless: "Soon the ruins came in sight and the porters threw down their packs, when Dr. Benvoglio said: 'This is a great moment;' some of us started looking for tent sites and others went searching for water, wells being said to be not far off, and even the map indicated a number, though drought of course might have dried them up." There is no reason for that sentence to cease and desist; it pursues one like a stream of lava down a hillside.

Be warned, then: follow through! Grasp the subject and do not let go. You may, incidentally, look upon this principle as another application of right linking, and one that shows how the same uses of the mind recur in the several duties of the writer.

But you will not be able to maintain your hold unless what you begin with is the true subject of your thought, the subject that organizes everything in sight around its central importance. In our instance, that subject is "Dalcroze," equated with "great teacher." All other ideas are *predicated of it,* are its predicates —that he is a tyrant / knowing what is right / having the lesson just so / breaking his heart (not somebody else's)—YET (the turn by which we temporarily leave Mr. D. behind and attend to the closely related subject no. 2) "his school" / so fascinating that / "every woman" (first subordinate subject) exclaims about it / and gentlemen enroll in it who . . . ; "gentlemen" (a subordinate subject, like "every woman") explains the sort of school in question, until it adroitly and logically carries us back to Mr. D. shouting "Hop!" At every point the cluster of fresh facts is attached to the subject continuously in our grasp.

This faithfulness to one subject till justice has been done to it is the rule of clear thought. It governs not only the good sentence of whatever type, but also (as we shall see) the good paragraph. What is more, it dictates its grammatical counterpart: adherence to the same voice of the verb, active or passive. Except for special reasons, then, connect the verbs by the one subject. Instead of: "Bonaparte hastened across the Adige, but no reinforcements had come up," keep the principal actor as subject: "B. hastened . . . but found that no . . ." Similarly in the passive voice: "The documents were photographed and enlarged, but the experts declared they were genuine" (". . . *and* [not *but*] were declared genuine by . . .").

After our study of the dinosaur skeleton dug out of Shaw's prose, the composing and perfecting of ordinary sentences ought to be easy. The chief mistakes to which they are liable are wrong coordination and wrong subordination. Decide which of two ideas is the one uppermost in your mind, the other being a modifier, afterthought, or curious detail. It may even turn out that the two ideas are only chance associations of your memory and *cannot* be related, at least in one sentence. Thus: "Cicero was a Roman statesman and philosopher and he lost a daughter he was very fond of." No coordination or subordination is possible: just try to fit in a *but* or an *although,* a *who was* or *who lost,* and you will see that the nonsense persists. You would need two or three additional ideas about Cicero to connect the pair of facts rationally.

With a legitimate *although, when, in spite of,* etc., the subordination is often forced upon the wrong clause: "He had run six blocks when he found himself at his own door." / "The candidate was certain he had applied in time, although the foundation refused him the grant." / "Many great men have suffered from severe physical handicaps in spite of their successful careers." It takes little thought to discover that the logic of cause and effect requires *when he had run, although the candidate was certain,* and *in spite of physical handicaps.* Again, the connection of ideas between a description and a clause in apposition must be perceptible or the joining is fallacious; this error is frequent in biographical notes: "Born in Australia in 1939, he has published two novels and a long travel diary." The fact that the opening clause is not a completed statement does not make it any less resistant to union with the main clause: even if you made two full sentences out of the facts, you would not dare to put an *and* between them, because birthplace and literary output are entirely independent.

These diverse features of the three sentence forms permit an agreeable variation of pattern from sentence to sentence, all the while following, not dictating, the thought. Nobody wants variety at the cost of sincerity and truth. But every reader is entitled to a succession of *un*like formulations, which refresh the interest and renew the forward push. If you allow your thoughts to pursue different motives and attitudes—now concessive, now additive, now in opposition, now in amplification—you do not need to think mechanically of ever-fresh openings for your string of sentences. You will vary spontaneously: *There is . . . ; Having looked . . . ; Tall and handsome, Mr. X. . . . ; It is indeed . . . ; Usually . . . ; In the summer . . . ; Although she said . . . ; Because no one remembered . . . ; The sun was rising and . . . ; To divide by nine . . . ; That he remembered . . . ; What everybody knows . . . ; Then came a message . . . ; If only . . . ; Nobody imagines that . . . ; All that matters is . . . ; What I suppose . . . ; For the reason is . . . ; Whether or not . . .*

I have no idea what subject could give rise to the series of beginnings I have set down at random, but I am confident that such a sequence is possible, and it is manifestly more enticing than a brain-hammering alternation of: *There is, It is, The day, The man, There is, The job, It is, The next day, This is, There is.*

If, in the miscellaneous list of good openings for sentences, *And* and *But* have been omitted, it is because they deserve special comment. Both have suffered from ignorant prohibition, though it is plain from American and English literature that the most exacting writers use them without hesitation as normal openers. Reason says further that if *For* is allowable, so must *And* and *But* be. The only question about any of these three is whether in a given instance it is better to write a comma or semicolon followed by *but* (*and*) (*for*), making a compound sentence, or stop with a period and start a new one. The use of *and* will probably be more frequent for compounding than for starting fresh, but in that second role *And* is useful as a way of adding the new thought to a general idea developed in several previous sentences, rather than to the one stated immediately before the *and.*

Each of the preferable starts so far mentioned is in positive form. Further variation can be had by asking a question: *Is it not also true that . . . ? What is the actual difficulty . . . ? Who would suppose . . . ?* This rhetorical trick must not be overdone, but it is useful when it springs up spontaneously after a longish course of argument or assertion. It then suggests conversation, in which you pound away at a contrary opinion and, suddenly aware of your friendly listener, stop and ask him: "Don't you think so? Isn't that right?" The question in prose is said to be *rhetorical* because the writer who asks expects and gets no answer; but the reader gives a silent one nevertheless and he is grateful for the opportunity to give it to himself.

It hardly needs to be said that varying the length of sentences is a source of pleasure essential to the reader's satisfaction. In the rat-tat-tat style that we sampled earlier, the comic effect (tedious if protracted) was due to the chopping up of discourse in equal lengths. Mingling short, long, and medium statements provides change of pace. Listen to Henry James talking to himself in his notebooks about the plan of one of his novels, *The Portrait of a Lady:* "The obvious criticism of course will be that it is not finished—that I have not seen the heroine to the end of her situation—that I have left her *en l'air.* This is both true and false. The *whole* of anything is never told."

I chose a diary to make the point, because it is likely to be less worked over than other prose. Notice in the extract how like spontaneous thought the length and sequence of the remarks are. The writer first gets down on paper what bothers him—a longish sentence, with two matching pieces that repeat. Then comes the verdict on the complaint and it is brisk. Last comes the quiet reason why he will not change his mind. Not only has James copied (as it were) his self-questioning, but the push and pull of long and short has transferred the mental struggle accurately into your mind.

The framing of good sentences cannot be divorced from the raw material supplied by the thinking mind. One's first notion may be imperfect and need refining, but its rightness at the end depends in part on its potential goodness at the start; for the affinity between form and contents is by definition reciprocal. Take a rather subtle case. The logic books use the sentence "Man is mortal" to illustrate a universal affirmative proposition. It is about all mankind. Shakespeare states another universal on a different subject in the form: "Men were deceivers ever." Query: Why is it best to have the first generality in the singular and the second in the plural? the first in the present tense, the second in the past? the first stark and three words long, the second adding *ever?* When you can explain to yourself the point of each of these differences you will know what you must contribute of your own before any rules of writing can help you. You will also have taken a step toward making the composition of paragraphs and essays easier and less mechanical.

✶

Principle 18: The writing of a sentence is finished only when the order of the words cannot be changed without damage to the thought or its visibility.

Study the passages below and the questions about each, and spend a few minutes pondering before you write a diagnosis of their ills and a prescription in general terms for their remedy. Then alter in the text what must be altered.

1. [In the following paragraph, what attitude in the writer causes the inadequacies you are about to enumerate?]

Harriman met the threat to his empire with gusto, organizing a couple of trick paper-railroads to conflict with the Hill locations all the way. Much of this portion of the war was fought in the courts, although the opposing crews in the field made it something of a personal matter by carrying on fist fights, night raids on one another, and several attempts at dynamiting equipment. It was during this battle that Harriman was stricken with appendicitis and had to go to the hospital for an operation. Just as soon as he could sit upright in bed and hold a telephone in his hand, he called Jim Hill long distance to say that he, Harriman, was feeling as fit as a fiddle and would soon be back at the front. Aye, they had warriors in those days. . . .

2. [Can you find any reason why the rule about complete sentences should be purposely breached at the end of the following passage? What have you to say about elegance and speed? And if the sentence ought to be left as it is, does anything else require change?]

I am wondering if, after all, I have made clear the picture that is before my eyes: the languid cruise, the slight relaxation of discipline, due to the leisure of a pleasure voyage, the *Ella* again rolling gently, with hardly a dash of spray to show that she was moving, the sun beating down on her white decks and white canvas, on the three women in summer attire, on unending bridge, with its accompaniment of tall glasses filled with ice, on Turner's morose face and Vail's watchful one. In the forecastle, much gossip and not a little fear, and in the forward house, where Captain Richardson and Singleton had their quarters, veiled hostility and sullen silence.

3. [Make a list of possible improvements before carrying them out in this short series of faulty sentences.]

Ben Jonson supplied the idea, and book of the words; and, alas! quarrelled with Inigo Jones, alleging that he obtained more than his fair share of credit. Jonson was a man of many parts. He started life as a bricklayer, served in the army and became an actor and playwright. Then he quarrelled with another actor and, fighting a duel, killed his man.

4. [Here are two standard formulas used by accountants in their reports to the public and the firms they audit. Express and explain your preference.]

a. We have examined the books and vouchers of the Funds and Trusts and certify the above accounts to be in accordance therewith.

b. We have examined the balance sheet, including the summary of investments of the charitable and educational trusts and funds as of June 30, 1972 and the related statements of current funds and transfers in fund balances for the year then ended. Our examination was made in accordance with generally accepted auditing standards and accordingly included such tests of the accounting records and such other auditing procedures as we considered necessary in the circumstances.

THE PARAGRAPH: ANOTHER PIECE OF KNITTING

The oldest writings, on stone or vellum or parchment, run on from the first word without a break, even between words. The reader's convenience, someone discovered, would be served by some spacing here and there. From this stroke of genius has come the space between words, paragraphs, chapters, and other familiar divisions. If you put yourself in the place of the inventor of this device, you will see at once that the paragraph must contain some reason, not immediately clear, for beginning and ending when it does. It is a slice, but of what thickness? That cannot be left altogether to chance; even a slice of bread varies only between certain limits.

The traditional answer to the question is that a paragraph corresponds to the development of a complete thought, with all its qualifiers and connectives set forth in full. But books only one hundred years old show us that paragraphs then were two or three times as long as ours. Taste has changed, and yet "complete thoughts" must remain the same. In this predicament all that can be said is that "a paragraph" now varies in length between ten and twenty lines, though not arbitrarily. For one thing, the length ought to be adapted to the width of the page or column. In a weekly magazine in three columns, paragraphs are best made shorter than in a full-page quarterly or a standard book: the reader's convenience is paramount. For the same reason it is desirable to break up any page of print at some point with a new paragraph.

The change of paragraph should of course go with some turn in the thought. The "full development" test will not really help you, because it is hard to say what a complete thought is. It may need 600 pages if you take a broad definition of *an* idea; or an idea may fit in a sentence if you concentrate on a thoughtlet, part of the big thought. But if you ask yourself after writing for some 10, 12, 15, 18, 20 lines: "Have I settled some point and am I now ready to take up the next?" you will have a rough guide to paragraphing. Do not be afraid to make, from time to time, one paragraph six lines long and the next twenty-two. The aim is not packaging in uniform containers; it is reproducing in visual form the weight and contours of each portion of *your* thought. A perceptible difference of length will at the same time contribute to variety of effect, so useful in sustaining attention.

What matters more than length is, as in the sentence, good internal form. A paragraph is ideally one piece. If anything is a brick in composition—and there is some doubt about that—the paragraph is it. To ensure internal strength while also marking the turns in thought described above, the practice has grown of using a *topic sentence* at or near the beginning of each paragraph. That sentence tells what the paragraph is to be about and indicates the turn that the journey has taken. An example from page 163 will suffice. When I had finished the previous paragraph and begun this one, the last sentence now in the first was not there. It was an afterthought, but one that clearly belonged somewhere in this neighborhood. To decide exactly where proved easy: it had to do with *length;* the previous paragraph was discussing implications of *length*. Clearly, one more implication of *length* belonged in that paragraph and at the end. It would have been absurd to insert the sentence at the head of the next paragraph, where I had already written: "What matters *more* than length," which is to dismiss length, to say to the reader: "We have done with it, at least for the present and as it affects paragraphing." Poised with a new sentence in hand, I saw the idea-link above and the new topic sentence below, both dictating where the afterthought should come.

That would be the whole philosophy of paragraphing, if certain writers did not habitually prefer to announce the new topic at the end of the preceding paragraph. They probably think that they secure greater continuity. If the paragraph is a well-knit construction, why not knit the ends together, top and bottom? There is merit in the idea, but it has (as I see it) two drawbacks. One is that it eliminates breathing space, and indeed requires filling the space with adroit phrasing, to prevent the new paragraph from sounding as if the indention were a mistake. Two, this filled-up space deprives author and reader of the opportunity to make a jump in thought. In a well-conducted essay or story not everything need be said. Yet excellent narrators and expositors will end one paragraph with: "The marshals came, took away the furniture, sealed up the door. He was finished. After such a resounding failure, there was only one thing to do—to go west." And the next paragraph will begin: "But to go west was not to be done or even thought of with any ease of mind." Preferable, to my mind, is the practice that would end the earlier paragraph at *finished*. The next would then start with "There was only one thing to do," omitting the surplusage about the failure, which is there in order to atone for splitting the two remarks about going west. It knits all right, but the drama obtainable by presenting new hope after "He was finished" has been thrown away.

## BRIDGING VERSUS JUMPING ACROSS

Whichever of the two techniques you adopt, discussing them has brought out the issues raised by the act of cutting up prose into short, manageable lengths. The last of those issues contains the beginnings of another—the so-called problem of Transition: how to go from one thought to the next, between sentences as well as between paragraphs. For simple needs there exist a number of transitional words and phrases, of which the commonest are *and, but,* and *for.* Yet it often happens that to move across the "idea space" separating two sentences requires more complex means: we feel that it is not possible to pass immediately from one statement to the next, yet we cannot think of any additional remark that would pave the way.

It is at this point that the set phrases for transition—*In addition, None the less, Be that as it may, etc.*—are resorted to. A great American stylist, John Jay Chapman, refers in one place to a book he was reading, "complete with however's and moreover's." He was indicating a certain contempt for the style that relies excessively on these joints, and he was right. Ideally, the perfect composition would consist of sentences so formed that the transition to the next would occur, without a word, in the reader's mind. You instinctively feel what an amateur the writer is when you come across: *Thus we see, In addition, In conclusion,* alternating with *Nevertheless*'s and *However*'s in endless series. How do we reduce our need of them to a minimum, and what should that minimum be?

As before, as always, the best answer is not a mechanical formula, but a conscious thought about what we are doing. The transitional words and phrases are the guiding touch to the elbow of someone you are piloting through new sights: look at this and now at that. Or if you prefer, transitional words are signposts, which the reader relies on to stay on the road. When so conceived, they can be reduced in number by making the sentence itself do the work: "In such an atmosphere there could be only one sequel to the Madrid explosion. All Europe burned to emulate it. Vengeance! More blood!" By means of the phrase "only one sequel" we are made alert to hearing that sequel described in what comes next. Transition has taken place in our minds. We do not need any towropes in the form of set transitional phrases.

Suppose the wording had been: "In such an atmosphere the Madrid explosion provoked widespread concern. *The result was* [or *In consequence*] . . ." There, in this dull transitional matter, is the price you would pay for not having laid the ground of mental transition plumb in the middle of the earlier sentence. The lesson then is: think ahead; try to couch your thought in such terms as will prepare the reader for your next. He sees it coming because you foreshadowed it adroitly. Think of your sentences—or some of them—as leaning forward against the next, making that next necessary before it comes. These images I am using refer, of course, to the ideas in the sentences. But, you will say, one cannot have an endless lean-to; something has to stand upright and be the backstop. Quite right, and it is there, after the stopping place, that you do need transitional terms. You can use them without hesitation; they will be fewer (and stronger for being fewer) than if you had not taken pains to interlink your previous sentences in the manner described.

Remembering now that guiding the reader by bridgelike words should be minimal, we go on to choose those suitable to our subject and our temperament. For my part, *however* is a forbidden word, the sign of a weakness in thought. I use it once in a great while, when I cannot get rid of neighboring *but*'s and do not want to add one more. (I do not refer to the adverbial *however,* as in *"However much* you take, this drug will not hurt you.") *Moreover,* if slipped in after the beginning of the sentence, is useful in showing that the previous subject or reason is still with us. The concessives *of course, naturally, true* (or *it is true*), similarly inserted in the body of the sentence, give little nudges for the reader's benefit. *None the less* can be kept for places where its meaning will be literal: not less by any amount. *In addition* is a grim presence at the head of a paragraph. Much better is something like: *"Besides* [this disadvantage]," which

insinuates the idea: "the foregoing items make up a disadvantage
—and there is more to come."

You will of course adapt these suggestions to your needs. Their
upshot is: amalgamate the transitional idea with the sentence by
(*a*) keeping it away from the beginning and (*b*) making it serve
as a comment upon what has been or is being said. Transition in
these explicit forms is best when it seems like the writer's giving
quiet hints and directions in his own voice. Notice, though, the
qualification *quiet*. The intrusion of the writer is not a happy one
when it takes the form: "I propose in this paper to show . . . I
have now demonstrated . . . Next, my object will be . . ." Excellent in scientific reports and didactic works (such as a handbook
of rhetoric), such phrases elsewhere chill the marrow of well-
intentioned readers by making them feel lectured at. In argument
or demonstration, where a tight grip on the reader's attention
can hardly help being explicit, confine yourself to the gentler
modes of shoving people about: *Now it appears to me . . . ; What
I contend for is . . . ; Consider a little . . . ; If I insist on . . . , it is
because. . . ; So obvious does this conclusion seem . . . ; Before
quitting the subject, I . . . ; I fully admit . . .* and others you can
summon up for yourself.

HOW TO START AND STOP

If you think back on your experience, you will surely remember
that your decision whether or not to read a particular book, story,
or essay was much influenced by the look and contents of the
opening paragraph. Readers are shy birds that have to be coaxed
to come nearer. Nothing, then, is more desirable than a good
opening if you want to lure rather than rebuff your potential
reader. Your first paragraph should not exceed medium length
and may fittingly fall below it. Likewise the opening sentence,
which ought to be capable of being absorbed in one breath. For
this purpose it should be fairly simple in structure, though not
necessarily a simple sentence in the technical sense. And by the
same reasoning, its contents should catch the eye, hold attention,
evoke interest. A rhetorical question is often used, but the device runs the risk of sounding artificial. "What is TNT?" may leave

the browser cold—he already knows or is quite willing not to know. If instead of using the common name you write "trinitrotoluene" and it turns out to be TNT, then the browser feels that he's been had by a mere ploy.

I use a made-up example so as to be brief. If it shows the sort of attitude *not* to adopt for an opening, the alternative is to reflect soberly on your theme and choose an aspect of it that will put the reader in the place, mood, time span, or other relevant state from which he can best see your subject and comfortably begin to learn your views about it. Here is how an introducer of Henry James's short stories "takes you in": "The list of things Henry James will not do for you, his reader, is rather forbidding." Immediately you want to know what is on that list, and the trick is done: you're caught, and in a legitimate way that creates no resentment. For your opening, then, frame a declarative sentence that goes straight at the heart of things, awakens a serious curiosity, and in its quiet, assured finality establishes the competence of the demonstrator.

For closing, finality is of course still more in order. Nobody wants merely to stop, but rather to end. And since the ending of any good experience leaves regret, the feeling of loss must be compensated for by a feeling of gain: what do I, the reader, possess in exchange for my willing attention to this past discourse? Sometimes a summary answers that question most aptly. At other times a conclusion arrived at, a new idea, the net result of the investigation, is the proper close. In an introduction to another writer's work, the end should not be ultimate, but rather like a bow and a lifting of the curtain to reveal the guest of the evening. It may be something of the same kind in an introduction to one's own book, the guest being Chapter I overleaf. In a self-contained essay, the close may recall the beginning—we have come full circle after a variegated journey. When this device is adroitly used it gives the reader a pleasant sense of retrospect, as if he now had a complete view of the ground covered and could call the land his own. In short, like an opening, a close has work to do. Neither is a detachable frill. So inescapable is this function that a writer often finds his true beginning ten or twenty lines below his first sentence and his true closing ten or twenty lines before he stopped writing. Watch for those happy indications of your unconscious judgment.

Without losing sight of *meaning* as our criterion for *wording*, we have in this Section V turned our minds more and more to spontaneous thinking as the prime ingredient of writing. Almost everybody thinks not in single words, nor yet in complete sentences, but in blobs of ideas and words between the two—say, a subject with two or three notions clinging to it that one wants to bring out. That first portion once put in shape pulls along another and another, and by then one probably has a sentence, compound or complex. It is very difficult to think more extensively in one stroke, though it often happens that the fragments come so fast, the next pushing the one in front out of sight, that the blur interferes with the task of formulation.

To spare oneself confusion of this or any other sort, it is useful to contrive aids to memory (for the ideas) and aids to order (for the form). These props are the familiar ones—notes and an outline. About both, the first piece of advice is that you should make them congenial to your temperament and, once chosen, habitual. You may prefer notebooks to cards for note taking—very well: use what you like, but invariably; it will save you time and annoyance. If you use cards, use small ones (3" × 5") so that you use a separate card for each fact, title, or memorandum to yourself. The cards are then easily shuffled for grouping. If you use a notebook, leave a margin for the key word, letter, or number which you will insert later as an index to the contents. Suppose a fact or quotation on topic X, the proper word or symbol in the margin will enable you to spot it easily as you leaf through your notes. It is of course possible to put two or more symbols opposite one item if it relates to more than one subject.

You will have guessed that in such a scheme the notes and the outline are connected, though as with the hen and the egg it is hard to say which comes first: your notes as you survey them give you some vague idea of what the scope and the parts of your composition will be; you can begin to list topics. Yet until you have made a first tentative outline of the finished essay you cannot tell exactly where any of the notes is to find its proper place. In other words, the notes and the outline must be played with in combination, each by its nature presenting you with choices to follow or reject until the whole is set. Notice that the interplay and the choices are matters of thought. You are thinking deeply about your subject when you shuttle between your notes and your plan, and this activity, far from being wasted effort, is of great help in the subsequent writing.

I shall return to the outline shortly, after suggesting here a trick or two about note taking. The first is: always take notes in your own words—I mean, of course, facts and ideas garnered from elsewhere, not statements to be quoted verbatim. The title of a book, an important phrase or remark, you will copy as they stand. But everything else you reword, for two reasons: in that effort the fact or idea passes through your mind, instead of going from the page to your eye and thence to your note while you remain in a trance. Again, by rewording you mix something of your thought with the acquired datum, and the admixture is the beginning of your own thought-and-writing about the whole topic. Naturally you take care not to distort. But you will find that notes taken under this safeguard are much closer to you than mere transcripts from other books; they are warm and speak to you like old friends, because by your act of thought they have become pieces of your mind.

The old cookbook said: "Take enough butter." I say: "Do not take too many notes." Both recommendations are hard to interpret except by trial and error. If you take too many notes, they will swamp you. You will shuffle and review them over and over and be left bewildered. It will be almost as bad as having all the relevant books and encyclopedias piled on your desk. So take notes only upon what you judge to be: the main *new* points, the complex events or ideas, the striking statements (for quoting), and also your own thoughts as they pop into your mind while reading in preparation. Do not omit these last—they will not come back at will, even when you return to the item that gave them birth, and it is galling to have to say, "Now, what was that bright idea I had about *this?*"

Let me illustrate the taking of a "thoughtful" note. Here is the original: "The circus became popular during the second half of the 18th century. We are told that in the early days of George III's reign 'a man excited the curiosity and called forth the wonder of the metropolis, by riding a single horse, on full gallop, while standing upright in the saddle.' " The note upon this might be: "Circus a pop. institution by 2nd ½ 18C. In 1760s (London) new notable attraction was the [now familiar] stunt of riding gallop horse while standing on saddle." You observe the abbreviations: invent your own, taking care that they do not overlap and lead to misunderstandings when you transcribe the note (mark off your own thoughts by square brackets). For the same reason, do not be too telegraphic in style. It is both better for writing practice and safer for transcription if the note is so framed that it could be understood by a stranger. With such a technique you are also equipped to do *précis writing,* that is, make a condensed but usable version of a longer document.

Now we can go back to the outline which is to grow out of your notes. What I said about choosing a kind congenial to your ways of thought relates to the degree of fullness. Some writers are unhappy unless they have in front of them, before writing, a complete "map" of the forthcoming piece, chapter, report, or book. The main heads have subheads and these sub-subheads, and so on, not ad infinitum but halfway there. There is something admirable as well as comforting about so much foresight. It gives the writer who can draw up such an outline the feeling that he can simply throw a few verbs, pronouns, and articles around each indicated point, in the exact order of the outline, and have the finished work as it were fall ripe into his lap.

I have sometimes wished that I could write so predictably, and in my early days I prepared a good many of these full outlines, only to find that my thoughts while writing would not follow the track I had laid down. Connections that seemed self-evident when envisaged abstractly turned out to be weak or artificial when it came to the task of setting down one sentence after another. Accordingly, I gave up the master plan and devised a substitute that I find more serviceable and no less orderly.

It consists of the appropriate number of main heads—from three or four to twenty or thirty (in a work of book length). The great thing is that they should really be *main* heads—all equal in weight and therefore, when written out, in length. The only exceptions to this even division of the whole (approximate, of course) are the Introduction and Conclusion, if appropriate. The same relations obtain on a smaller scale for an essay. The role of equal measurement is to ensure Proportion. As Sherlock Holmes says to Watson on a famous occasion: "If page 534 finds us only in Chapter Two, the length of the first one must have been really intolerable." Proportion facilitates the understanding of a subject by automatically impressing on the mind the correct view of relative importance. Being based on the notes, the outline will also tell the writer whether he has neglected to study adequately this or that part of his subject; for he has seen the equal importance of topic 5 (let us say) and he sees also that his stack of notes on that topic is slim in comparison with the rest.

Under the main topics come, at first in guesswork order, the subtopics. These are not likely to be of equal weight and they may not even remain under the heading originally assigned, let alone in the ranking first guessed at. The course of writing may disclose new connections and thus the greater utility of a reassignment on both counts. Here is the working outline of the present section of this book:

V. Composition
   General considerations (four genres, Meaning)
   The sentence (kinds, structure, Variety)
   Emphasis & Transition (Thinking and Meaning)
   The Paragraph (& other divisions)
   Outline (2 kinds, Proportion, Opening)
   What makes for interest (Thesis, Objections, Pace)
   Writing to read aloud

I should add that this brief and none-too-explicit memorandum was only produced after I had covered two or three sheets of legal-size paper with lists of topics, grouped by what I thought were kinds, with no main topic to label them by. Many of these single-word subjects were crossed out because they showed themselves on reflection to be mere facets of the real topics buried in the miscellany. Gradually, the main heads emerged, commanded their battalions of twenty to thirty subtopics, and finally boiled down to what you see above.

If you analyze the section itself you will notice how and where I have deviated in the heat of writing. I call it heat not because one does or should write in a fever, but because the deliberate choice of words and links and transitions is easiest and best when it is made from a throng of ideas bubbling under the surface of consciousness. On this account, I strongly recommend writing ahead full tilt, not stopping to correct. Cross out no more than the few words that will permit you to go on when you foresee a blind alley. Leave some words in blank, some sentences not complete: Keep going!

You may at times, when going, find yourself going—in circles; that is, dealing with a topic a second time soon after others have been taken up. If so, the remedy is to make a quick "shorthand" outline of what has actually been set down, using a single key word for each item in the passage. By looking at the list of these key words in order, you will soon discover where your mind took the wrong track and how you may recompose the material more consecutively.

You have, of course, another guide to the right sequence: the notes in front of you; but let them spur, not drag you onward. In short, *write from memory*—as far as possible—with only occasional prompting from the notes, and make everything correct and shipshape later. Once you have "something down," as professional writers say, the job of verifying, improving, cutting, and polishing is pure pleasure. Unlike the sculptor, the writer can start carving and enjoying himself only after he has dug the marble out of his own head—pity the poor writer!

You may ask what will set the caldron of ideas bubbling. *Wanting to tell* is the answer. The desire presupposes an audience—a group at large or a particular person, who may be the writer himself, as is true of the diarist. There must also be something to be told, of which you have the secret. I mean by this that your own view, experience, or information constitutes something apart that nobody knows until you disclose it. If you are too modest about yourself or plain indifferent about the possible reader and yet are required to write, then you have to pretend. Make believe that you want to bring somebody around to your opinion; in other words, adopt a thesis and start expounding it. Or else, imagine the need to instruct someone in a piece of learning you possess. Or describe to the Geographic Society on the other side of the moon what earth valleys and mountains are like. In a thesis or argument, think of the objections you must forestall, framing and answering them. In a didactic piece, think of the confusions and errors you must remove to make the teaching clear. In a description, think of the unknowns that must be depicted before the whole can be rightly imagined. With a slight effort of the kind at the start—a challenge to utterance—you will find your pretense disappearing and a real concern creeping in. The subject will have taken hold of you as it does in the work of all habitual writers. They do not continually think of some editor, much less of a book club subscriber: they think of the subject—and the words.

WRITING FOR THE LISTENING EAR

Yet there is one type of composition in which a clear conception of the audience must be formed and their needs consulted in a special way, without letup from beginning to end. That is the paper or lecture which will be read aloud. What has to be said about this situation might more logically have followed our discussion of the periodic style, but pedagogically it might have created confusion about the way to write interesting complex sentences. Hence the postponement. We have been, throughout, reaching the mind through the eye. The very first notion I put before you in this book was that of the difference between the spoken word, made clear by the voice, and the written, made clear by many complicated stratagems. Now we close the circle, returning to the spoken word, to which the voice gives much assistance. But in a formal lecture, the word is spoken only after being written, and that double treatment calls for what is virtually the opposite of the periodic style. The reason is evident: that style invites you to pile up modifiers, conditions, and comments before the reader knows what they apply to, and it produces (as Shaw proved to us) marvels 110 words long. But no listener, however sharp or intent, can perform the feat of following by ear and retaining by memory the turns and twists and factual contents of a long complex sentence.

The paper that is to be read must therefore be written mostly in simple and compound sentences and—to prevent monotony —in complex sentences of the shortest kind. The *If, Although, Whereas*, etc., clauses must be no more than a few words long and their cargo of ideas as light as possible. The heavy work of exposition must be done by the main clause. In general, short and long, simple and short-complex must be mixed, not only for variety but for additional emphasis, a short simple sentence serving to clinch a point or, again, to introduce a new topic.

In a speech, too, there is more occasion than in writing to indicate changes of subject in so many words: "Now I want to turn to . . ." (or "take up," or "remind you"). Everything that helps the audience know where they are or what they should be thinking of will be gratefully received. You must therefore observe still more than you usually do the principle of matching parts, the exact tethering of pronouns and danglers, and the close linking of modifiers.

Group receptivity to spoken ideas is heightened also by a judicious use of the I-you attitude. It need not be explicit in every paragraph. Let it appear from time to time: "If I were to say to you . . ."; "Some of you must be thinking that . . ." and the like. Elsewhere, simply avoid the impersonal ("One supposes . . ."; "It will appear to some," etc.) and choose instead words that establish the mood of conversation. You are not lecturing *at* them but only *before* them. Beware above all of talking down. The lecturer's proper tone is one of respect, which elicits the same feeling in return.

Other modifications of your written style will occur to you if you pursue the line of thought I have sketched: if your subject allows, use as few technical terms as possible, not because they may not be understood but because they may not be heard aright;

they are not common words and many are alike in sound. More than ever, watch the sound of your prose. You will have to *speak* those sentences, so you must assemble words that your tongue can wrap itself around. Avoid the noun plague in your compound sentences, or you will be giving out *-tion, -tions, -sion, -sions* like a steam engine; and remember that *s, ce, sh* coming in a row are disagreeable as well as a possible danger to your delivery ("She sells seashells by the seashore"). If you can, change the pace in keeping with the divisions of the subject, and give the last section a spirited rhythm. The feeling conveyed that even this good talk is coming to an end cheers the patient sitters and will augment the pleasure of the whole as they look back upon it.

One conclusion follows from the opposition between the canons of good writing and those of good written speeches: unless you are threatened with jail and a heavy fine, do not allow a written lecture to be published without extensive rewriting on your part. I say this, fully aware that there may be special circumstances that justify publication direct. But if you have learned to write *prose,* and you reread your speech in print, you will be displeased at the form of those very passages that made the lecture good.

✸

Principle 19: In whatever paragraphs or essays you write, verify the sequence of ideas and take out or transpose everything that interrupts the march of thought and feeling.

Criticize and correct all the faults as usual, but bear in mind the great importance of the principle just stated.

1. [This first passage is fundamentally good prose, far better than much written today by men who call themselves educated. The writer, Fred Dodge, was born to white parents on an Indian reservation in California in 1854. He had very little schooling. In his late twenties he worked with the Earp brothers to clean up Tombstone, Arizona, and other wild towns of the Southwest. Later he kept a journal, from which this paragraph is taken. As you think of small improvements you might make, consider whether the author's use of capitals serves a partly conscious and useful purpose.]

My position in the Court room, by reason of being Guard for the Person of the Court, was sitting up beside him near one End of the Court's Desk—which is higher than the floor of the Main Courtroom. His Desk was Slightly on the order of a Crescent, and directly in front and below the Court's Desk was the Table for the Attys. Shaped like the Desk of the Court. Where I sat, I could keep a good lookout over the Prisoner, the Attys., the Jury and the whole Courtroom. I had my Short Double Barrelled Shot Gun sitting right by me but out of Sight of all but the Judge. We had listened to all the Speeches made by the Attorneys for the Defence and Mark Smith, the Dist. Atty., was making his Closing Argument. Mark was a Personal and close friend of mine and I thought a lot of him. He did not fear anything or anybody and he had flayed the Witnesses for the Defence and had come to where he had taken up Barney Riggs himself. (I seemed to have a hunch that some trouble was coming.) Mark Smith was in his Argument up to the actual Killing, and he was picturing Barney Sneaking up to that Pen like an Apache Indian— "And," (Dramatically) "He did then and there Murder Hudson." Barney was sitting behind Mark Smith and there was a large and heavy Inkstand on the Attys'. table, and Barney jumped to his feet and grabbed that Ink Stand and Shouted, "Yes, You Son of a Bitch and I will murder you." All in a few seconds, I left my chair and jumped. I just touched on the Table and then onto Barney Riggs' Shoulders, crushing him to the floor and taking and throwing aside the Ink Stand, jerking Barney up and throwing him into his Chair. Mark Smith was the quietest man there—he stood still and when I had Barney in his chair, Mark turned to me and said, "Thank you, Fred," and went right on with his Argument. I stayed pretty close to Barney until Mark finished the Argument and the Case was at an End. How I ever made that jump, I cannot tell, even to this day. It was a long jump and was Commented on by many— But I must have helped myself when I touched on the Table and from there on to Barney.

2. So at ten o'clock that Thursday morning, Mr. A. was ready. The near side-door of the car could not be opened from the outside, and scarcely from the inside. He waited patiently while T. fumbled with the catch. The car was not vintage; it was merely old, and in the condition described by honest dealers as *rough*. The front seat could hardly have accommodated a more robustly built man than Mr. A., since T.'s bulk occupied three-

fourths of it; and the shock absorber on his side had collapsed. But, as he pointed out, it was a serviceable vehicle and would probably outlast him.

3. [The following was spoken, not written, but it contains phrases obviously derived from writing habits. Can you spot them and show how they spoil both speech and prose?]

I would feel that most of the conversations that took place in those areas of the White House that did have the recording system would, in almost their entirety, be in existence, but the special prosecutor, the court, and, I think, the American people are sufficiently familiar with the recording system to know where the recording devices existed and to know the situation in terms of the recording process, but I feel, although the process has not been undertaken yet in preparation of the material to abide by the court decision, really, what the answer to that question is.

4. Whether the poem is quite complete I do not feel sure; it seems to end very abruptly. It is true that, as Mr. Sisam says, "it is the only example before 1400 of the swift and dramatic movement, the sudden transitions, and the restrained expression of the ballad style." Nevertheless I do not think that it can properly be regarded as a ballad, certainly not as a "popular" ballad. It is one of a group of religious poems, of which another on Twelfth Day has been claimed, although not by Child, as a popular ballad, or possibly only a "literary imitation" of one. Both poems are in the same hand, but of that on Twelfth Day the manuscript also contains a rough draft in red chalk, partly overwritten, which at least suggests that the scribe was also the author of both. I feel sure that they are of purely ecclesiastical origin.

5. The newsboy was commonly a worldly character, once he had made a run or two on the cars. In the early period he was anywhere from twelve to eighteen years of age. He worked either pretty much on his own, that is, his job was a concession, and all he made from it was his own, or he worked on commission for some individual capitalist such as the aforementioned Skelly of the Erie. Working on commission has a tendency to make a lad hustle, as the phrase has it, and no young Americans of the latter part of the last century were better known for their hustling qualities than the train newsboys. The most successful of them were good showmen as well as alert for every chance to turn an honest or even a partly honest dollar, or perhaps dime.

## TIME OUT FOR GOOD READING V

Robert H. Jackson (1892–1954) was an Associate Justice of the Supreme Court when the case of *Terminiello* v. *Chicago* came before the court for review. The petitioner had been found guilty of disorderly conduct by a Chicago jury on the evidence that his speech to the Christian Veterans of America had caused several disturbances among some two thousand persons inside and outside the meeting hall. Claiming the right of free speech and challenging the Chicago ordinance, the petitioner appealed and obtained a reversal of his conviction. Mr. Justice Jackson wrote a dissenting opinion from which the following paragraphs were taken. Though the words "I begin" are the first given here, they are preceded by twelve pages reviewing the case and quoting from the trial some of the inflammatory remarks.

### The Law as Guarantee of Free Speech

I begin with the oft-forgotten principle which this case demonstrates, that freedom of speech exists only under law and not independently of it. What would Terminiello's theoretical freedom of speech have amounted to had he not been given active aid by the officers of the law? He could reach the hall only with their help, could talk only because they restrained the mob, and could make his getaway only under their protection. We would do well to recall the words of Chief Justice Hughes in Cox v. New Hampshire, "Civil liberties, as guaranteed by the Constitution, imply the existence of an organized society maintaining public order without which liberty itself would be lost in the excesses of unrestrained abuses . . ."

This case demonstrates also that this Court's service to free speech is essentially negative and can consist only of reviewing actions by local magistrates. But if free speech is to be a practical reality, affirmative and immediate protection is required; and it can come only from nonjudicial sources. It depends on local police, maintained by law-abiding taxpayers, and who, regardless of their own feelings, risk themselves to maintain supremacy of law. Terminiello's theoretical right to speak free from interference would have no reality if Chicago should withdraw its officers to some other section of the city, or if the men assigned to the task should look the other way when the crowd threatens Terminiello. Can society be expected to keep these men at Terminiello's service if it has nothing to say of his behavior which may force them into dangerous action?

No one will disagree that the fundamental, permanent and overriding policy of police and courts should be to permit and encourage utmost freedom of utterance. It is the legal right of any American citizen to advocate peaceful adoption of fascism or communism, socialism, or capitalism. He may go far in expressing sentiments whether pro-Semitic or anti-Semitic, pro-Negro or anti-Negro, pro-Catholic or anti-Catholic. He is legally free to argue for some anti-American system of government to supersede by constitutional methods the one we have. It is our philosophy that the course of government should be controlled by a consensus of the governed. This process of reaching intelligent popular decisions requires free discussion. Hence we should tolerate no law or custom of censorship or suppression.

But we must bear in mind also that no serious outbreak of mob violence, race rioting, lynching or public disorder is likely to get going without help of some speech-making to some mass of people. A street may be filled with men and women and the crowd still not be a mob. Unity of purpose, passion and hatred, which merges the many minds of a crowd into the mindlessness of a mob, almost invariably is supplied by speeches. It is naïve, or worse, to teach that oratory with this object or effect is a service to liberty. No mob has ever protected any liberty, even its own, but if not put down it always winds up in an orgy of lawlessness which respects no liberties.

In considering abuse of freedom by provocative utterances it is necessary to observe that the law is more tolerant of discussion than are most individuals or communities. Law is so indifferent to subjects of talk that I think of none that it should close to discussion. Religious, social and political topics that in other times or countries have not been open to lawful debate may be freely discussed here.

Because a subject is legally arguable, however, does not mean that public sentiment will be patient of its advocacy at all times and in all manners. So it happens that, while peaceful advocacy of communism or fascism is tolerated by the law, both of these doctrines arouse passionate reactions. A great number of people do not agree that introduction to America of communism or fascism is even debatable. Hence many speeches, such as that of Terminiello, may be legally permissible but may nevertheless in some surroundings, be a menace to peace and order. When conditions show the speaker that this is the case, as it did here, there certainly comes a point beyond which he cannot indulge in provocations to violence without being answerable to society.

Determination of such an issue involves a heavy responsibility. Courts must beware lest they become mere organs of popular intolerance. Not every show of opposition can justify treating a speech as a breach of peace. Neither speakers nor courts are obliged always and in all circumstances to yield to prevailing opinion and feeling. As a people grow in capacity for civilization and liberty their tolerance will grow, and they will endure, if not welcome, discussion even on topics as to which they are committed. They regard convictions as tentative and know that time and events will make their own terms with theories, by whomever and by whatever majorities they are held, and many will be proved wrong. But on our way to this idealistic state of tolerance the police have to deal with men as they are. The crowd mind is never tolerant of any idea which does not conform to its herd opinion. It does not want a tolerant effort at meeting of minds. It does not know the futility of trying to mob an idea. Released from the sense of personal responsibility that would restrain even the worst individuals in it if alone, and brave with the courage of numbers, both radical and reactionary mobs endanger liberty as well as order. The authorities must control them and they are entitled to place some checks upon those whose behavior or speech calls such mobs into being. When the right of society to freedom from probable violence should prevail over the right of an individual to defy opposing opinion, presents a problem that always tests wisdom and often calls for immediate and vigorous action to preserve public order and safety.

I do not think that the Constitution of the United States denies to the states and the municipalities power to solve that problem in the light of local conditions, at least so long as danger to public order is not invoked in bad faith, as a cover for censorship or suppression. The preamble declares domestic tranquillity as well as liberty to be an object in founding a Federal Government and I do not think the Forefathers were naïve in believing both can be fostered by the law.

❖

Judicial opinions resemble legal arguments in that they seek to establish a position on the issue at hand, but they differ in being obliged to weigh the merits of all contrary positions. The judicial tone is therefore less assertive and strident than counsel's in court, and as a further result it is difficult for opinions to sound free, conversational, lively. Ask yourself whether Justice Jackson succeeds in being at once judicial and easy in manner. How does he handle constitutional and, more generally, legal questions? Has he any peculiarities of style that you deplore?—admire? Whether his propositions satisfy you or not, what about his prepositions? Has he a proper regard for the definite article? Is he anywhere writing for effect—or for posterity? Or rather does he show himself in earnest for present purposes? Can you point to the verbal evidence for your view?

# Revision
## or What Have I Actually Said?

# VI

A good judge of the facts has declared: "All writing is rewriting." He meant good writing, for easy reading. The path to rewriting is obvious: when rereading after a shorter or longer lapse of time what one has written, one feels dissatisfaction with this or that word, sentence, paragraph—or possibly with the whole effort, the essay or chapter. If, as I shall assume, things are not totally bad, the rewriting affects only bits here and there. The criterion is as it has been throughout: Meaning. If words you have set down puzzle you once you have forgotten how they came to your mind, they will puzzle the stranger and you must do something about them—rediscover your meaning and express *it,* not some other or none at all.

The truths behind these reflections *guarantee* that the piece written at midnight on the eve of the deadline date will be bad. It is scarcely looked over in that desperate hour of fatigue and self-reproach; it is no piece of prose, but the possible embryo of one. Without time to reread and some calm thought to effect repairs, you defeat your purpose: the hastily cobbled thing you produce cannot succeed, whether its aim is to persuade, prove, enthrall, or merely show such powers of writing as you possess. Any of these ends can be achieved only after a series of revisions. Recall your experience as a student and imagine being allowed to go over your written final examination on three consecutive days, though without looking at your books or notes in between: the final final would surely be fuller, better organized, more intelligent than the

## REVISING UP TO THE VERY END

A proof from *Eugénie Grandet*, corrected by Balzac

first. You would have thought and remembered, filled gaps and corrected first impulses to a point well above your normal achievement when limited to a single try. Your article or report must be treated the same way. It must be gone over and patiently rewritten if it is to represent what you intend and what you can do.

Rewriting is called revision in the literary and publishing trade because it springs from *re-viewing,* that is to say, looking at your copy again—and again and again. When you have learned to look at your own words with critical detachment, you will find that rereading a piece five or six times in a row will each time bring to light fresh spots of trouble. The trouble is sometimes elementary: you wonder how you can have written *it* as a pronoun referring to a plural subject. The slip is easily corrected. At other times you have written yourself into a corner, the exit from which is not at once apparent. Your words down there seem to preclude the necessary repairs up here—because of repetition, syntax, logic, or some other obstacle. Nothing comes to mind as reconciling sense with sound and with clarity in both places. In such a fix you may have to start farther back and pursue a different line altogether. The sharper your judgment, the more trouble you will find. That is why exacting writers are known to have rewritten a famous paragraph or chapter six or seven times. It then looked right to them, because every demand of their art had been met, every flaw removed, down to the slightest.

You and I are far from that stage of mastery, but we are none the less obliged to do some rewriting beyond the intensive correction of bad spots. For in the act of revising on the small scale one comes upon gaps in thought and—what is as bad—real or apparent repetitions or intrusions, sometimes called *backstitching.* Both are occasions for surgery. In the first case you must write a new fragment and insert it so that its beginning and end fit what precedes and follows. In the second case you must lift the intruding passage and transfer or eliminate it. Simple arithmetic shows you that there are then three and not two sutures to be made before the page shows a smooth surface. If you have never performed this sort of work in writing, you must take it from me that it affords pleasure and satisfaction, both.

At the end of this section I shall set down a list of ten questions that should reawaken the chief ideas we have discussed and guide your eye and mind in reviewing, revising, and rewriting the substance of your papers. Here I want to take up equally important matters of form. In actual revision, of course, you do not separate the two. You attend on the spot to everything you see. And your reader will not separate form and matter either; he takes in your page as a meaning communicated, not as an exercise in writing. So the division that I am making for convenience is artificial and must be forgotten as soon as its purpose has been served.

### THE LOOK OF THE TYPED PAGE: CLARITY ONCE MORE

I begin with what you may think trivial: the aspect of the copy. It is not trivial, any more than a *but* for an *and* or *flaunting* for *flouting*. In the finished product everything matters that belongs there, just as the smallest cotter pin matters to the working of a machine. Don't be misled by anecdotes about "the operative word"; all words are or should be operative. By the copy, which concerns us here, I mean the black marks presented to the reader's eye. They include: the words as typed, their spelling, syllabication, and punctuation, and the corrections, typed and longhand, added afterward. With the use of photocopying and word processing, more and more persons are likely to receive the copy in its original form. Its appearance matters more and more. For convenience again, I shall give Punctuation a separate treatment, after I have dealt with the rest.

What the effect of the copy is on the reader—editor, publisher, colleague, teacher, supervisor—your own experience will tell you. Everybody wants a block of print or typescript to be inviting, so as to overcome the usual reluctance to reading. It is the reverse of inviting to see on the page a group of uneven lines, spattered with dark blots produced by erasures, overtypings, and handwritten words and signs. If on such a pockmarked surface the blemishes are hard to interpret, the reader's reluctance and irritability increase. Lines, loops, and arrows showing transposed sentences are then the last insult; no one whom you address has signed a contract or taken a vow to read your stuff at all. By neatness and ease of physical reading you are merely giving yourself an added chance.

Do not underestimate the effect of the smallest flaws on the alert sensorium. For example, *butterfly* raises an agreeable image of fields and colored wings; *butter fly* gives a quite different picture. So the first task of the reviser is to see to it that all the words have their letters and spaces duly distributed. A series of *hte* for *the* diverts attention from what you are saying and begins to make one wonder, childishly, whether the next one will be right. On your part it is rudeness to let them appear, either because you have not even seen them or because you think the profundity of your message makes all else unimportant. Under the same stricture, all capitals and periods must be there; inadvertent duplicates *(the the)* must be reduced to one; wrong spacing repaired by ⌒ ; and similar faults taken care of in the traditional way of editors and printers. Go to your dictionary for the conventional signs of correction.

Omitted words or additions of new phrases must be written above the typed line, straddling the point of insertion (marked by a caret: ∧ ), and closer to the line affected than to the line above. This tells you by inference that typed, as well as manuscript, copy must be double spaced, precisely for these corrections to be made in legible form. Learn to shape letters like typing, of the right size, and neither too lightly penciled nor too dark, so that they may be read without drawing attention to themselves. If the number of corrections and additions is too great for the original copy to survive as the main body of print, retype the whole page. But you need not do this to alter paragraphing. The eye will easily take in ¶ and *no* ¶.

Spelling is of course part of the general grooming, the neglect of which is harm done to your meaning, let alone your standing. Many good writers, it is true, and some great ones, have been poor spellers. When this is acknowledged, it usually means that they habitually misspelled certain words, or were never quite sure which of two spellings was right. This failing is forgivable in anyone. Quite other is the handiwork of the encyclopedic bad speller, the one who never misses a chance to misspell—not even following his own precedents—and who offers to the view a broad pattern of wrong syllables. He shows that he has never paid complete attention to what he was doing, in either reading or writing. Granted that some people are lacking in visual memory, it is possible by concentrating on a few "catchfool" words to master their confusing or unexpected spellings. Go after rec*ei*ve and bel*ie*ve if they still defeat you. Learn through the etymology that super*sede* is not one of the inter*cede* group, idiosyn*crasy* not one of the demo*cracy* group, and aut*arky* not one of the an*archy* group. In looking up a word there is often something useful beyond the spelling. If this effort still leaves you uncertain about many words, then you owe it to yourself to go through a course of phonics or to consult an oculist or both.

In any event, do *not* spend time or thought in worry about alternative spellings: *traveller* and *traveler, theater* and *theatre, brusk* and *brusque,* are equally acceptable, though consistency is to be desired. But don't assume that *indict* and *indite, lineage* and *linage, relics* and *relicts,* are alternatives: anything unfamiliar or that looks fishy to your intent gaze, look up—and you will find the reason why. You can work out for yourself the cause of the *k* in *picnicked,* the *k* which should also appear in other verbs formed from words ending in *c* (*arc, tarmac*), just as the *u* should reappear in *catalog*[*ue*] when *-ed, -er,* or *-ing* comes at the end. The reader's convenience, always!

THE POINT OF POINTING: TWO SYSTEMS

To punctuate means to point, in both senses: putting in little black points and pointing as with a finger. Since space is lacking to give here a complete manual of punctuation, you will be best served if I first sketch the theory of modern punctuation by contrasting it with the old. Ours has been in use for about eighty years, and anyone who reads books written before the First World War will come across classics of our century punctuated in the earlier way. You can keep your own practice clear by understanding the principle of each mode. The old was "oratorical," that is, based on the needs of a speaker reading the text aloud. It indicated pauses in the sentence more than it did the relation of its parts; it was therefore abundant. Ours is spare; it is—or tries to be—logical, cares nothing about speech pauses, and forever strives to avoid punctuating at all. I have lately seen in books reputably published attempts to get rid of the serial comma: "Their new flag is red green and black." Compare a passage from Scott: "But, hist! here comes the landlord, with tidings, I suppose, that the chaise is ready? It was no such thing: the tidings bore, that no chaise could be had that evening, for Sir Peter Plyem had carried forward my Landlord's two pairs of horses, that morning, to the ancient royal borough of Bubbleburgh, to look after his interest there."

Note first the comma after *bore,* which separates subject and verb from the direct object clause that completes their meaning. A pause there suits the voice and contributes emphasis. That comma is forbidden—no hope of reprieve if caught—by the modern system, which says: no single comma between subject and verb, none between verb and object, logic must prevail. A *double* comma does not interfere with logic, because the pair sets off what they enclose and declares it removable; hence subject and verb are still felt to be in direct line without obstruction. Thus: "The master, having called all hands on deck, ordered a reef taken and all hatches battened down."

Other places where Scott's use of commas differs from ours are: after *But, landlord, tidings, horses, morning,* and *Bubbleburgh.* These six would be canceled by a modern copy editor, leaving only three out of his nine. Ours is an economical system, but it has some disadvantages, as we shall see. Meanwhile, observe that the exclamation point, question mark, and colon served then as they do now, and that the three commas retained do the work of setting off *I suppose* and of separating the two halves of a compound sentence: *that evening, for Sir Peter . . .*

In revision, your punctuation must be closely scanned for adherence to the fundamentals: (1) No "obstacle comma" of the sort just described. (2) All "set-off commas" in pairs, not one of the two missing. (3) All long compound sentences to have a comma (or semicolon) at the point of division. (4) No commas to set off short adverbial modifiers that can be taken in stride (*that morning,* in Scott above). (5) All declarative sentences to end with a period. (6) All exclamations and questions to have their proper marks (Compare *Stop!,* a sign in front of a hole in the road, with *Stop* to mark a bus stop. Distinguish also what is said in exclamation, though in question form, from a true question: "How could I ever have done this!" / "How could he extract the insulin from the pancreas?" And remember that *Will you please . . . ? Would you kindly . . . ?* are real questions).

It would be pleasant to be able to leave the rest to common sense and the good habits acquired by reading. But reading itself —reading good books—shows so much heedless punctuating and failure to punctuate, so many dropped hyphens and wild dashes, that a few more hints and warnings are indispensable to the careful reviser.

Until further notice, the serial comma continues in force; and except in text set in narrow columns where space is scarce, it is best to use one before the terminal *and:* "red, brown, black, and white dogs" eliminates any thought of a black-and-white dog. No less needed is the comma to signalize a modifying clause or phrase at the beginning of a sentence, particularly when the meanings of the separated parts would merge and mislead: "On the whole, avoidance of such issues was an integral part of the stated conditions." (Not: "On the whole avoidance . . .")

With or without a risk of "merging," a long opening modifier takes a comma, by a hangover from the oratorical mode of punctuation. Modifiers in apposition at the end require separation for both kinds of reasons. "Government Aide Quits Criticizing Administration" needs a comma, one would guess, after *Quits.* Instances occur where guessing is less easy: "However, the technical questions may be resolved, the dispute will never make a great difference to the public . . ." Is this: "However the questions may be resolved, the dispute . . ." or, "However, the questions may be resolved, [and] the dispute will never make . . ."?

The logic system demands a comma before the relative pronoun (*who, which,* etc.) of every non-defining clause. This injunction implies that you must know a defining clause when you see one. We encountered its role before, but I describe it here again: a defining clause is one that gives a diagnostic clue to the subject being discussed, selecting it from others of its kind. In "The man who is wanted is bald, stout, and about thirty-five," *who is wanted* sets that man apart from men who are not wanted. This essential information is referred to as *defining* the man, hence the "defining clause." Now look at: "The expedition returned with more knowledge and more specimens than had been counted on, and also with several cases of jungle fever, which is another story." The last four words are a free gift of information, not necessary at all; they define nothing—certainly not *fever*—and being non-defining, their separation from the essential thought must be marked by a comma.

If you follow the practice of making *that* the usual (not invariable) word for introducing defining clauses, your revising to make sure of this particular comma will perhaps take less effort. In "The notebooks that Coleridge left behind are of various sizes and shapes," there is no temptation to put a comma after *notebooks*. It is when *which* replaces *that* and when *who*(*m*) comes into play that you must quiz yourself about the presence or absence of "definition." And every writer will admit that it is sometimes hard to say whether a *which* (*who*) clause unmistakably defines or merely comments. In such a doubt, use a comma: "After the great earthquake[,] which Voltaire made the subject of a poem, the ideas of providence and divine justice were less easy to defend." Note, finally, that the *which* and *who*[*m*] may be preceded by *in, of, to,* etc., with the same comma needed or not needed.

The comma sometimes replaces the colon before short phrases quoted with or without quotation marks: "Excuse me: he did not say, What of it? He said, So what?" Again, the comma is often felt to be inadequate before *and, but,* or *for* in long compound sentences, the reason being that each part of such a compound already contains commas and there is danger of creating false pairs or other confusions by introducing one more. It is then that the semicolon comes into its own, marking separation at a level one step higher.

Some writers make little or no use of the semicolon, usually because they deal in narrative composed of short sentences. But the semicolon's power to hold apart equal portions of thought more sharply than the comma and not so sharply as the period is very useful, especially when the writing does not retell events but expounds ideas. In really well wrought prose of that kind the order and phrasing of the sentences can be so managed that most *and*'s, *but*'s, and *for*'s are eliminated; the semicolon, in the very act of separating, also does the work of organizing ideas that would otherwise be too tightly joined by those overfrequent connectives. After two or three statements thus associated by semicolons comes the period, which shows that a wider break in thought has taken place. Notice for example the relations established in the two previous sentences by this mode of punctuating. Or again: "Demonstration was to Lincoln the one proper goal of argument; he never seems to have considered it within his power to convince by disturbing the judgment through the emotions." To understand the double role of the semicolon, take a conscious look at its makeup: clearly it separates, because its two elements—dot over comma—take up more vertical space than a comma and thus keep apart the words before it and after. Equally clearly it unites, because no capital letter and extra white space follow it as they follow the period. In its form you can read its function.

The colon, needless to say, introduces quotations long or short and serves also to establish a kindred sort of confrontation. Both uses rest on the same principle: the colon is a sort of equal-sign (as this very sentence shows). In "She said: Go away!" the two parts look at each other over the fence and with mutual effect. She said what?—"Go away!" What's "Go away!"?—It's what she said. Likewise in pairs of sentences that present complementary ideas. "Optimism on this point is only willful blindness: we all have the hard fact of failure before us." B explains A and in a sense repeats its point—"Optimism is blind: [I say so because] failure is in front of our eyes." There is no warrant whatever for using the colon to add afterthoughts, especially subordinate clauses and non-matching ideas. One English novelist permits himself just such inconsequence: "For him there was no truth except in tangible things: though he was not ambitious." A comma is all that group of words requires. If you lack any feel for the colon, leave it alone—except for quoting in the usual way.

A surprising result of the modern "logical" mode of punctuation is that many good sentences that would be clear in speech can no longer be written, because they cannot be punctuated. No room for a comma or anything else can be found in: "What will happen if they do not need not now be considered." In the old mode, commas around *if they do not* would have made all clear. In revising, this very natural form of utterance must be watched for and recast. It is only fair to add that the modern style permits distinctions not otherwise available. One may write: "Criticism as I understand it is the effort to . . ." and also: "Criticism, as I understand it, is the effort to . . ." The difference in tone is that between assertiveness and diffidence. Or again, in a dedication: "To Arthur for believing" offers a work for him to believe, whereas "To Arthur, for believing," offers gratitude for his past belief in the author. It is of course possible that these subtleties of the new system are too "logical" to be noticed. On some occasions a comma that is not needed for logic is employed in the old way, oratorically, for a slight pause and its emphasis: "He had replied with a long explanation, not altogether courteous." Since much punctuation in printed matter today comes from the copy editor rather than the author, these shades of thought should perhaps be classed as "aleatory art."

But some things remain clear. Delinquency about hyphens is peculiarly irritating to readers of typescript. In the first place, the hyphen is not a lesser dash, and if used in typing instead of a dash it connects in painful intimacy words that on the contrary the writer wanted to keep well apart. Imagine this sample recurring frequently: ". . . relating various urban problems-such as drug abuse, housing, and welfare-to community law." The dash is indicated in typing by the use of *two* hyphens together, preferably close to the preceding word and spaced away from what follows, thus: *problems-- such*. In the second place, the hyphen does not mean *to*. "From 1890-1914" is illiterate; write out the *to* or reword: "the period 1890-1914," which if read aloud has nothing sounded between the dates.

Hyphens are needed to join words that would be read separately and inaptly unless united by the little sign. (Compare *once-born* with *once revered*.) All *two-word adjectives* before nouns must be hyphened. In revising, do not miss a single one of the places where you have written: "in the *eighteenth*[-]*century* manner"; "She was his *long*[-]*lost* sister"; "Then came the news of the *hoped*[-]*for* victory"; "It was a *head*[-]*on* collision." Look out for the ungainly but sometimes unavoidable postponement of the second word, as in "both hand- and machine-made goods." That first suspended hyphen must be there, and not glued to the *and.* In longer combinations all the spaces must be filled: "a never-to-be-forgotten experience." By logical extension this gives us: "a set of Robin-Hood-and-Knighthood-in-Flower characters." And the same hyphening must be done with genuine proper names: "a Mary-Pickford-Douglas-Fairbanks silent film." If, as is usual, the series looks a trifle silly, find another wording: designations do not all have to become quasi adjectives.

Many two-word terms are hyphened to show that they signify one thing permanently, not just for the nonce: a *walk-up* (apartment), a *set-to, bric-a-brac, hangers-on,* etc. Others have become fused: *a setback, a giveaway, a floorwalker.* Still others are allowed to stay apart without losing their oneness: *a picture gallery, an office machine, a vacuum cleaner.* There is no rule and no consistency among writers, editors, printers, and theorists. All that need be said is: suit yourself, but do not go in for innovative fusion, especially when the visual elements will mislead: "We built the first *homeoffice* typewriter" is condemned by the fact that *homeo-* words are numerous and a few quite common, such as *homeopathy* and *homeostasis.* I would also disallow *nonobjective,* which everybody first reads *nono,* and similar compounds with *non-* and *co-.* But there is a fury at work in the people to make war on hyphens, and the number of unreadable hashes of words grows daily.

Readability should none the less continue to govern the splitting of words at the end of the line, where most hyphens live. You will find several codes of *syllabication* (as the practice is called) proposed or enforced by editors and others. The doctrines seem to me more interesting than important. What is important, I repeat, is to read without stumbling. Therefore: do not break a word in such a way that the first fragment makes a false meaning (*ear-liest, pea-sant*); do not break before or after a natural division in a compound (*outw/eigh*); do not break in a manner to suggest false pronunciation in either half (*intrig/uing*); do not break before or after double consonants (*fatt/ening*); do not break monosyllables (*thro/ugh*). In short, use your head, your eyes, and your sense of humor. A great many words, you will find, resolve themselves into their elements, being compounds of English, French, and Latin roots and movable particles: *anti/dis/estab/ lish/ment/arian/ism*—not that you will use this artificial word; but its parts may well be strewn over your page in smaller combinations.

The difference between dash and hyphen has been explained earlier. Now the use of the dash deserves a word. It is the separating mark par excellence, but its playground is inside the sentence, not outside. Only Sterne in *Tristram Shandy* and Keats in his letters are free to play fast and loose with the dash and substitute it at will for the period. Within the sentence a pair of dashes sets off a shorter or longer interruption of the main thought by an aside. The matter thus jammed into the stream of words can be a sentence by itself, though its effect on the reader's memory of what precedes must be nicely calculated. The paired dashes act like parentheses, but with this difference that the dashes within one sentence must not exceed one pair. Otherwise, it is not possible to tell which dash goes with which. The rounded shape of the parentheses takes care of that difficulty, which is why a sentence requiring two interpolations will use either one pair of dashes and one of parentheses or two pairs of parentheses. Count your dashes in revising.

A second use of the dash is to separate the final portion of the sentence from the earlier, often with a jump in thought suggestive of impatience, afterthought, or summary. It is very important in revising for punctuation to eliminate accidental triplets: two dashes acting like parentheses, followed later in the sentence by a disjoining dash. This state of affairs confronts us in: "Respectful of his last work as the critics were—critics in that age did not turn and rend established authors—they could not admire its subject, treatment, or style—everything in the book offended them." Replacing the third dash by a colon will restore parenthetical power to the first two.

This quick run-through of punctuation leaves but one mark that revision must make certain of: the apostrophe. Compel your brain to grasp the difference between *it's* (= *it is*) and *its* (neuter possessive). After all, no genius is needed to test which is called for: expand to *it is* and you will know. A comparable effort and no more will tell you whether it is horse*'s* hoofs or horse*s':* count your horses. As to the question, Is it Dicken*s'* Works or Dicken*s's* Works? I am utterly indifferent. Write it one way and your editor will insist on the other as she or he propounds rules about monosyllables and disyllables that carry (to me) no conviction. I consult my ear and would consequently repel "Artaxerx*es's* army." Finally, remember that joint possession takes but one apostrophe and *s* at the end: "Wordsworth and Coleridge's *Lyrical Ballads,*" not Wordsworth*'s*.

THERE ARE ALWAYS TOO MANY WORDS AT FIRST

One great aim of revision is to cut out. In the exuberance of composition it is natural to throw in—as one does in speaking—a number of small words that add nothing to meaning but keep up the flow and rhythm of thought. In writing, not only does this surplusage not add to meaning, it subtracts from it. Communication is most complete when it proceeds from the smallest number of words—and indeed of syllables. The reason is that in absorbing ideas through words a kind of friction is set up by the stream of syllables employed. Compare "He was delighted with the gift" and "He was very much pleased with the presentation." The first slips in and is registered before the other is half through; and the second, with its repeated *pl-pr, ch-tion* makes a lot of mental noise, reducing its movement and leaving a sense of wasted effort.

You will be surprised to see the number and kind of words that can be got rid of to advantage. They include: *all, own, of, and, whole, one,* and often the possessives. Find them in these sentences: "They were seen talking outside of the house." / "This idea is an interesting one." / "All of them had decided to go abroad." / "She went on knitting and not one of them minded." / "For his own part, he was ready to give up the whole claim." / "In the preface to his *Secret Agent,* Conrad tells us . . ." With care, the reviser will come upon dozens of these pointless noises, and not solely the ones I listed. Longer words such as *however, almost, respective(ly), successive, entire, thorough, always, perhaps,* and many others can be classed among the idle by the vigilant reviser. It is not of course the words themselves that are useless, but the words in this or that place: remember the adverbial dressing gowns (page 100). Revision is the time when survivors of earlier purges are to be eliminated. With them must go any word or words that may unaccountably recur in your paper. For at times a verb or noun or modifier will obsess the mind and be served up in every possible context, not as a conscious choice but as an unnoticed automatism. Revision should dispose of it.

Other inadvertencies of eye and ear may be found as well: if not *lay* for *lie* or similar catchfoolery, then wrong terminations— *phenomena, criteria,* for *phenomenon, criterion;* odd unconscious echoes that betrayed your pen (*massive men* for *mass of men*); the various jingles—*way* and *say* already mentioned, to which must be added *day* and *today;* the strings of *-ate, -ation, -otion, -ance, -ence, -ity, -bility,* and the like; the heedless use of *etc.,* a neuter implying *things,* tacked on to names of persons, which require *et al.;* the carry-over of oral usage in *myself,* when *me* is actually more modest; the unfortunate tautology *the reason is because* in place of *the reason is that.*

The list could be stretched without harm—except to the space at our disposal. In these concluding pages I want rather to link up with your work of revision a few of the warnings given earlier and most often needed. The reminder will jog your memory about the faults that *every* writer is subject to in the rush of getting words down. Only in revising does he catch and correct them; here they are:

1. Ambiguities: "As Mayor of this city I write to you to report a serious violation of the zoning law." Who is mayor—you or the recipient?

2. Misconceptions and malaprops: "The proposal to move the observation of all national holidays to a Monday would make us forget important dates in our history" ("observance").

3. Metaphorical mush: ". . . profound impact still exercised for this pervasive belief on the imponderables of the public mind" (*for?*).

4. False leads: ". . . contract will be given to G. Co. instead of to L.S., whose design officers of both services favored."

5. Incomplete and run-on sentences: "Her eyes were dark and angry, her face white, except around the eyes, and angry."

To these bugbears may be added a fresh one, most easily tackled in revision:

6. Gibberish of any sort, notably in matter translated from a foreign language. In that language the statement is doubtless clear and sounds normal. It must not be strange and muddled in your version, as, for example, the key phrase in a news story about the opening in Berlin of a musical based on Kafka's book *Amerika:* " 'This is murder of Kafka,' shouted a wildly booing and jeering section of the audience." Nobody ever shouted any such thing in any language. Search for the true equivalent and allow nothing in this vein to subsist in your work. And while we are on the subject of foreign languages, let it be said that foreign phrases must be spelled correctly, with the right accents in French, umlauts in German, and so on. It is *bête noire* with an *e* and *crime passionnel* with two *n*'s and nothing tacked on the end, no matter what you see in magazine articles and stories.

PARTS AND PROPORTIONS AGAIN

When in successive rereadings you have scrubbed the face of your text free of the many blots, specks, and warts that are bound to be there, you will have gained in addition a sense of how the march of your ideas affects a close reader. The paragraphing may here and there seem abrupt or contrary to the actual relation of the topics. You then study the contents of those paragraphs and divide one or both at some other point. The change may entail some rewriting of sentence openings or closings or wholes. It is surprising how even one adjustment of this kind can strengthen an essay. Indeed, it often happens in writing that the need for some seemingly mechanical correction brings about an improvement in substance by indicating a more exact relation between ideas.

There is, in truth, little that is purely mechanical in composition. Since the workings of the reader's mind depend altogether on what is physically presented to his eye, it follows that arrangement is the basis of effect. This is why a last consideration before you let go your copy is the marking of its large divisions: after the paragraph, the part. Rarely is it advisable to serve up a stretch of eighteen or twenty pages without a break. If you have done a proper job of thinking and composing, it is virtually certain that in your essay or chapter you have embedded an introduction, an exposition, a development, and a conclusion. These deserve to be marked in some fashion—by the figures 1, 2, 3 . . . (or I, II, III . . .) or by asterisks or simply by a white space—any of these preceding the block of print that forms a unit. In a narrative, which has perhaps no development, there are still episodes, after the exposition of who is who and where. In short, every organized sequence has parts, and the span of attention required to comprehend each should be divided visually into corresponding sections. As I said before, equal parts measure equal importance, but that is a flexible rule. It does not mean that in every twenty pages there shall be four sections of five pages each. What serves as introduction may either merge with exposition or be set off from it. The conclusion may be two sentences at the end of the third and final part. Contents dictate form.

THE REVISER'S GUIDE

Here is, as promised, the set of questions that must be answered favorably to your copy before you can call your revision finished.

I. What is the tone of my piece? Have I indulged myself in language that is toplofty, patronizing, technical for mere showing off—or have I been simple & direct throughout, never falsely modest, but always sincere and respectful of the reader?

II. Is the movement of my prose satisfactory to the mind and the ear? Are my sentences on their feet, varied in rhythm and length, and carrying each its full weight of meaning and implication—or are many of them rendered obscure by my inattention to matching parts or thrown off balance by the weight of modifiers and afterthoughts?

III. Have I tested and retested the meaning of each statement of mine to preclude ambiguities? Have I made fast every pronoun to its proper mooring—the slightest error is fatal—or have I allowed my private comprehension of the sense to blind me to one confusion after another?

IV. On the same subject of ambiguity, have I linked modifiers, clauses, and compound sentences in the clearest manner possible —or have I produced a number of danglers, manifest absurdities, and other false leads that will require the reader to start the sentence again and do the work I have left undone?

V. Can I say, looking at single words, that every one of them means and connotes what I think it does? Or has my diction been spoiled by threadbare clichés, pseudo-technical jargon, unthinking metaphors, and that excess of abstract words known as the noun plague?

VI. Still on the subject of words, have I been strict as well as clear—or have I committed any illiteracies, malapropisms, ludicrous confusions by echo, or heedless jingles by alliteration and rhyming syllables?

VII. I turn now to my theme and ask myself whether the ideas of which it consists have been set down fully and in consecutive order—or have I again relied on *my* understanding of the subject to bridge over gaps in thought and to disentangle snarls in description?

VIII. In the layout of my paper have I devoted space and furnished detail in proportion to the importance of each topic—or have I concentrated on what interested me and skimped the rest, whether owing to a poor outline or the neglect of a good one?

IX. Since readers have in common the desire to be enticed and to experience afterward a sense of acquisition, have I contrived the most engaging opening for my subject and the ending best fitted to leave an impress on the mind? Or do I fumble my way at first and leave matters in the air at the last? To which query I would add: do the divisions of the paper provide breathing spells at once significant and agreeable?

X. Have I reread my copy and made it both correct and sightly? Or have I been inattentive, ignorant, lazy, and rude about typing, spelling, syllabication, punctuation, inserts for correction, and other marks for the reader's convenience?

The answers to all those questions should be Yes and No as the sense of each contrast dictates. "But," you may say, "will you look at all those demands! Just to think about them is exhausting." Very true, and no one expects that you or any other writer will fulfill them all every time you set pen to paper. They are nevertheless your proper goal. To strive toward it may indeed be exhausting; that is the price of *exhaustive* literary expression, by which I mean *ex-pressing*—squeezing out every last drop of meaning from your mind and putting it in words *right*. No conscientious writer should complain of the trouble. Writing is a social act; whoever claims his neighbor's attention by writing is duty-bound to take trouble—and in any case, what is life for, unless to do at least some things right?

⌘

Principle 20: Read and revise, reread and revise, keep reading and revising until your text seems adequate to your thought.

The requirements in this final exercise hark back to any of the applicable guidelines and not just to those in Section VI.

1. Captain Porteous was wrought, by this appearance of insurrection against his authority, into a rage so headlong as to make him forget that, the sentence having been fully executed, it was his duty not to engage in hostilities with the misguided multitude, but to draw off his men as fast as possible.

2. For three consecutive centuries the idea of church reform possessed the mind of Europe and repeatedly brought it again and again to civil war.

3. My situation was now an exceedingly awkward one.

4. The lamps arced and spluttered and the scene was as a Kaleidoscope.

5. His tenure of office ran roughly from March 1960-October 1965.

6. As he read dissatisfaction spread from his eye to all his face.

7. He turned abruptly away and picked up his own papers.

8. With everything shut, it was swelteringly hot, just under the roof.

9. Money was limited, enthusiasm was wanting in the faculties, and public opinion.

10. She was the second wife of the late silent screen star Rudolph Valentino.

11. The girl was arrested for being concerned with two unknown men in robbing seven thousand from a department store.

12. In "seeding" Hurricane Ginger when the plane first

penetrated the storm, it was enveloped in white clouds and rain began to sweep the windows.

13. All Language Schools offers itself as world's language authority.

14. Her fiance had been killed in 1918 just six months before the Armistice when she was a young girl of fifteen.

15. This cartridge is equipped with a diamond and sapphire styli.

16. The great nineteenth century poets tended to die young but the greatest perhaps were the longest lived, as Wordsworth, Goethe and Victor Hugo.

17. It was also laid down that in future examinations would be one of the entering obligations, for Graduates and Associate Members.

18. Unles one is allert to recieve impresisons he cannot expect to be much of a success with the Signal Core.

19. The gold set stones pendant from her earlobes were carnelian.

20. He would not be a free man until he had done his small share in the fight against the terror that had killed his father, and had fulfilled his promise to Philip.

21. Improving quality of life by limiting it's quantity is Population Center goal.

22. I can pass with some brevity over the events of the next day.

23. It was as far as he could judge a frank story.

24. His lips were dry and brownly incrusted. . . . The size of his head was exaggerated until it seemed a deformity by long thick fluffy waved hair.

25. The Association was instrumental in distributing 74,975 free tuberculin tests to 2,232 physicians in all five boroughs who requested them.

26. Snoopy, a more-or-less Beagle seems bewildered by the tiny creature held in the hands of their mutual master, 13-year old Mike L. of Oklahoma City.

27. The restaurant was closed on evidence of active rodent signs.

28. When you take off this straight jacket, you introduce a lot of wild cards into the game on which we will have to ride herd.

29. You may say I have been reticent to a tactical fault, but you won't mind me going ahead now that I can be beneficient to others.

30. The offer was made to coopt the director of the rival firm along with original founder but he proved entirely unwilling to listen and so in the end the whole scheme proved ultimately nonoperative.

31. They looked again at the dead man: it was a face of a wicked Roman-Emperor.

32. There had been moves made to harass him, to expropriate his property, or deface it—it rancored him—then one day the olive branch dawned.

33. Six bathrooms were simply wicked: though no one would argue it is not an important consumer good.

34. The control group were not on the whole milk diet, as the text says.

35. To hear him cry out "How are the mighty fallen?"—No: he was too far distressed for worlds.

36. She gave us a foundation to move in any direction we liked.

37. This has a great deal of empathy to me.

38. "Because of the difficulty of providing negatives," the commission wrote in its report, "the possibility of others being involved cannot be established categorically."

39. The boy wearing kilts was given a place of honor near the altar.

40. The architect responded that the design was sympathetic and would complete the corner in an interesting and eventful way.

41. No sales representative will be seen without prior appointment.

42. It is unrealistic to assume that a person trained for a specific level of library employment has a fighting chance of surviving metamorphosis to emerge as a higher form of life on the library's evolutionary scale.

43. The idea is a floating palace so fabulous that it becomes a shot in the arm for river travel.

44. Bobby was more likely to pick up something useful about the man than would be an officer.

45. *The Communiqué:* Europe—Sides agree that European

conference on security and cooperation should be convened "without due delay" [sic] but set no time. [The phrase marked *sic* above was repeated in the news story next to the front-page communiqué.]

46. November 30, 1973. Name of Texas Gulf, Inc. changed to Texasgulf Inc.

47. Hamlet spoke of a single skull. McMahon was referring to a single scull (see 23 July, p. 350, table 1).

48. You could never forget him for his vultural features.

49. Keep tag on her, she's dynamite . . . lives in a shack without a stitch of furniture . . . we'll wait and let them strangle in a few at a time.

50. Mona, as Anna Karenina, directing her romantic feelings towards Karenin as a lover rather than Vronsky as a husband—that was it.

## TIME OUT FOR GOOD READING VI

"Perfect" prose is rare, if indeed it is not a mere ideal limit toward which we strive. What is most regrettable is not that the ideal is seldom reached, but that so much potentially good prose collapses repeatedly into gross error. Here are a couple of excellent paragraphs written by a lawyer in a small town who, if asked, would not say he had had a superior education or prided himself on "a prose style."

### Two Gifted Amateurs

In the event of a partition suit, of course, all previous agreements made by us would have no force and effect, as we would be willing to take our chances with a division of the entire property pursuant to the best judgment of the receiver and surveyor appointed by the court.

It appears as though this matter can still be satisfactorily resolved by a little cooperation on the part of you and your client, and we still would like to have an agreed partition in order to prevent a lot of unnecessary expense and in order to prevent much wasted time.

❖

Yet this same user of simple-&-direct, in another letter, writes "between he and his brother." It seems a shame that grammar-school teaching did not rid him of the solecism. In the seventh grade of a respectable public school, one boy who was running for office wrote an election speech of which this is part:

❖

Some friends of mine have joked about "When Matt talks, people listen." But what I want you to know is that when you talk, I will listen. I believe that the president and I can do a good job of putting your ideas into action. I am pleased that we are going to have a student council and I hope to represent you on it.

One of the changes I would like to see is fewer detentions. As you know, the present system allows only two days for us to bring in our absent notes. I would like to extend this to four days because when you return to school you are thinking ahead and not focusing on the fact that you have been sick. It is also hard to get mothers (some of them) to write these notes. (They aren't unwilling, just unavailable.) One teacher told me that it is necessary to give detentions for late library books, report card slips, and absent notes because that is the only way we will bring them in. I do not agree. I suggest that staying until 2:45 P.M. is sufficient punishment for what I view as relatively minor crimes.

❖

Again, this engaging vote getter goes on to say: "I may even be able to use my power to *bring about soft-drink machines.*" The speech, it is clear, was carefully worked out and revised more than once. But apparently the way to analyze relations between verbs and their object had not been imparted to this talented child.

Both our gifted amateurs, it is clear, could profit, the one from closer attention to the structures of speech, the other to the structures of thought.

# To Use or Not to Use

## VII

For fifty years, more or less, educated users of the English language have treated it as one of the free natural resources—do with it what you like, the rich lode is self-renewing. When someone ventured caution or reproof, he or she was denounced as a spoilsport. "Language has eternal life and is not subject to loss or disease."

But recently the tune has changed. The mood of conservation and environmentalism has reached language. Though demagogues here and there still encourage the free-for-all, the public at large takes a strong stand on the opposite side. An editorial in *The New York Times* asserts: "The Decline in Literacy Is No Illusion." Columnists all over the country, seconded by public officials, business executives, and editors and publishers, cry out that much of what they hear and read is verbiage unworthy of homo sapiens—incoherent, ambiguous, pedantic, and ugly. Newspapers and magazines publish lists of linguistic offenses, and even reviewers of books now dare to mention bad prose and are no longer thought bad mannered for doing it.

Schools and colleges have long tried to stem this peculiar brand of civilized illiteracy. Their efforts are frantic now, and often fruitless, because they have caught the corruption they mean to arrest. Even so, "deans of writing" are busy and "remedial programs" cost millions, purely for repair work. Most lately in New York City, a "high school of writing" has been created on the pattern of the high school of science, and there is a Homework Hotline through which parents and pupil can get help about grammar, hard words, and improper fractions. But in the schools themselves, as a survey of teachers in

Chicago showed, the best grades still go to pupils who use the prevailing academic jargon, not those who write simple-&-direct. The upshot is that language skills, as jargon itself puts it, are now in demand, advertised and paid for like rare accomplishments.

Recovering literacy is difficult in proportion as the surroundings are polluted with its opposite. Not just ill-taught schoolteachers but even those who genuinely lament the state of affairs help to perpetuate it. The bureaucrat, the advertiser, the scholar, the doctor, the lawyer, the technologist, all complain of impediments to their work from some aspect of poor writing in learned journals or the public press, but few see the general causes or notice and correct their own misdoings. Yet anyone who really suffers and wants to join the crusade must become aware both of causes and of types of error. There is no other way to be vigilant instead of self-indulgent.

Two of the causes in the decline of *all* modern European languages have been: the doctrines of linguistic science and the example of "experimental" art. They come together on the principle that "anything goes"—not in so many words, but in unmistakable effect. Modern grammarians have thundered against "rules" and fought the idea of correctness. Everybody, they said, has a "right" to his or her "native speechways"—i.e., uncorrected—hence it is snobbish and humiliating to correct them. Language lives by change; what is right now was wrong two hundred years ago, so let each of us be as "wrong" as we like now; it will all come out in the wash of Time.

From the opposite quarter, the "right" to manhandle the language is justified under the Freedom to Experiment that artists invoke against critics and philistines. The outcome has been poetry and prose, good and bad, that inspired imitation both conscious and unconscious. Advertisers and novelists popularized every species of poetic distortion. Playing with language became everybody's sport, encouraged also by the urge to rename things more "scientifically." Word play in casual conversation should perish with the occasion; and for public or permanent purposes, fiddling with words is tantamount to tampering with the currency or defacing common property.

A third cause, unrelated to the first two, has been the sort of appeal made by those who have tried to promote clear writing. Their slogan has been "effective communication," but they have gone after the obstacles piecemeal and without showing the bad emotions behind the bad habits. It is of course true that communication is a main purpose of language, but the person who fails to communicate thinks he is succeeding. Otherwise he would pause and ponder. If he thinks at all about the receiver's mind, he is unable to imagine its workings; and he has no detailed insight into his own. To him, the puzzles or absurdities he has created with words remain a closed book.

Therefore a better motive and better means must be found to extract fair writing from people who are adult, serious, schooled, and entrusted with the world's work. The motive, first conscious, then habitual, should be the search for *exacting expression.* It is the parallel to making a pencil sketch that resembles the jug or the face in front of you. Concentrate on the idea (event, information, experience, feeling, memory), and after turning it over and over to see all parts, find words that match it as closely as possible. That will happen only after turning *them* over and over in the mind.

This restatement of the goal of writing has the advantage that it calls for comparing two phases of your own mind, instead of your mind with that of a stranger. To put it another way, the writer must think like an artist of the representational school and follow his model with a trained and practiced hand. For language is not an algebra or a code, whose elements can be put together mechanically and where mistakes show up virtually by themselves.

To "copy" one's own idea in words presupposes a working knowledge of those words, which means learning their worth and avoiding confusions among them. That is the positive side of diction. But because of long habit and the continual influence of bad examples from without, the clear writer must also fend off a host of verbal suggestions from within, must by conscious negation reject jargon, pretentiousness, the wish to be coy, arch, jocular, folksy, learned, mysterious, elegant, and inventive: these and a dozen other feelings underlie the phrasings that come first to mind when one begins to write. Those feelings are not fully conscious, or the words would probably be dismissed at once; rather, they are whispered temptations and they must be *made* conscious if one is to be master of one's vocabulary instead of mastered by it.

The language we have now has suffered damage wholesale, the

faults encountered come not as single spies but in battalions and thus cannot be guarded against by simply memorizing a few enormities. They must be classified by origin and tendency so that the alert may spot them as they occur in ever-fresh forms: words misunderstood or misapplied, idioms distorted, prepositions used at random, jargon and imagery blanketing thought, neologisms proliferating without need, grammar and syntax defied to no purpose. These types of disorder and their subtypes do not yet warrant the term "degeneracy" which has recently been applied to the state of our ailing speech, but they show that the sense and instinct for language, the so-called *sprachgefühl,* is at low ebb. George Orwell pointed out years ago that bad writing was often a sign of political deceit. Today it is clearly a sign of unlovely moral traits as well—vanity, pretentiousness, pedantry, complacency about one's ignorance, disrespect toward the listener, and a curious mixture of slavish imitation and desire to appear original.

This chapter and the next offer such a classification of words and phrases to guard against, both because they blur meaning and because they imply attitudes no one would consciously espouse. The inventory is necessarily incomplete, but—it is hoped—suggestive enough to start the reader on a fuller one of his own, a private dictionary of misusage and verbal seducers. The list will grow, for no attentive writer can fail to spot in what he reads a dozen fresh solecisms a month (a week!); and the cumulative familiarity with these old offenders will shorten the time it takes to wipe the mental slate clean as one sets out to write.

It goes without saying that painstaking writers differ in taste and sensibility and do not all agree on the innumerable choices that writing entails. What matters is that choices should be made, and made for a reason that can be talked about. What will persuade one writer to use or avoid a turn of phrase will leave another unmoved; but at least the argument will have been heard. So it is in the sections that follow. No one is bound to reach the conclusions arrived at, but the type of reasoning toward them is of the kind that all writers do use in choosing their words. It can therefore also help those less accustomed to doubting their own expressions, less practiced in the art of choosing words.

INNOVATIONS: HOW TO SIFT

Novelty in language takes two forms: newly made-up words (neologisms) and new meanings thrust on old, usually specialized, words. The conscious writer comes across both kinds continually and must make up his mind which, if any, he needs. There is nothing wrong with the new as such. The question is, does this particular novelty fill a need, add a nuance? And: will it last, or turn yellow and be swept away like last summer's leaves? Lastly, is it fit by its shape and sound to join permanently the great company of English words?

These tests rule out at once such compounds as *radiothon, sportagon, cargomation,* and all other pseudo-technical combinations with *-thon, -tron, -atic* at the rear or *auto-, hydro(a)-, perma-* at the front. Those scraps from Greek and Latin only show ignorance of several languages at once, notably the *-thon,* from Marathon, which is meaningless in itself and which falsifies history, since the famous run from Marathon to Athens, if it ever took place, was not particularly long or taxing. There are other, better ways to indicate endurance.

The claim often made (as it was for *cargomation*) that "the idea is so new it created a new word" is null and void; these "creations" only serve to make the "innovative" person or group believe that something grander is afoot than a mere *machine handling* of cargo or a protracted *radio campaign.* As for the "new idea," it usually consists in a combination or application of means or devices all quite familiar and deserving no more than a parallel combination or application of familiar terms. We should have done better than the now indispensable *condominium,* which spawns the rootless *condo* and leads to *condo-park complex* for nothing more unusual than a big house on a big lawn.

A good new word for a truly new thing should sound as if it had been born, not cobbled together out of shavings and leftovers. For example, *clone* is good, because, though derived from the Greek for *twig,* it is short, does not show off a learned ancestry, and its meaning, once grasped, is unmistakable. And of course it was needed as soon as genetically duplicate creatures could be produced.

Restlessness, as well as vanity, causes people to coin or combine words for which there is no need. Out of the nursing profession has

•

come *wellness* to replace *health,* perhaps because *health* is modifiable: poor health, failing health—neither likely with *wellness.* Words in *-ness* are a last resort; they are clumsy in form and show the loss or lack of a noun to match a quality. When *sloth* was commonplace there was no need of *laziness; health* deserves its monopoly.

New words in *-ize* belong to the same unfortunate class. If we moderns had a proper sense of the language, we could have avoided *containerize,* for we had *box.* "Let us box your shipment; our ships *box* the whole cargo." But it wouldn't have sounded like the heroic, scientific conquest of mind over matter. Its evil tendency is to break up all of life into distinct, registered, impersonal processes *(finalize, folderize),* of which there is no end: a fresh example, *laymanize,* only means "make more readable."

Nor is *-ize* the only way to make "process verbs." The National Institute of Mental Health (not yet Wellness) promotes the Search for Alternative Pursuits. First we are told that "alternative is not just a synonym for substitute, since it implies being more satisfactory and not merely a replacement." The distinction is imaginary—why not say Preferable Pursuits and cut the explanation? We are further told: "Exercise your capacity for *alternativing.*" Query: Is it pronounced *-tivving* or *-tyving?* It should be pronounced detestable, and a prayer uttered against the temptation to manufacture verbs out of the objects or actions of everyday life.

Verbs of this kind often generate further nouns: The Postal Service announces a program of *route demotorization,* which a thoughtful critic insists should be *repedestrianization.* Even when new words such as these do not offend by length and multiple accents, the chances are that the root meaning will be unfairly dispossessed. A writer to the press who learned that a new drug would be "tableted and distributed" expressed the hope that the phrase would come to the attention of those engaged in putting the Old Testament into modern English, as it "described so neatly and accurately what Moses did with the Ten Commandments."

ILL-ADVISED TRANSFERS

The second type of novel words comes under cover of an existing usage, which is invoked if the interloper is challenged. That is how *gift* as a verb has been argued for. Since we say "a gifted musician," why can't we say, "Look to us for your Christmas gifting"? The obvious reply is: No need; we are used to Christmas *giving.* To which it may be objected, "Oh, but that means charity; we mean *gifts.* " Exactly; why not say so: "Look to us for your Christmas gifts." "But won't that sound as if the shop were impersonating Santa Claus?" Really! Adults reading Christmas publicity know very well it is not offering goods free.

A question persists: why the *gifted* musician? To fill a visible, recurrent need. The talented person is said to have *gifts;* the adjective to describe him or her could not be *given*—hence *gifted.* And that very usage makes it necessary to exclude the new verb; otherwise *gifted children* will mean alike those endowed with talents and those well supplied with presents.

This last example illustrates an important generality. In weighing the merits of a new word or phrase, or the new extension of an old one, it is imperative to think ahead. The experienced writer knows that the use or abuse of words entails consequences not immediately apparent. If he chooses a certain locution now, it may cause difficulty later on. The sequel may lead to a form, a sense, or a combination that is ambiguous, puzzling, ludicrous, or simply in disharmony with the spirit of the language.

A good occasion for thinking ahead was certainly missed when someone launched the new and popular *acerbic.* English has long had the Latinate adjective *acerb,* meaning sharp; but according to the apologists of the bastard form, "it didn't sound like an adjective, so *-ic* was tacked on." Of course, *superb* is an adjective and recognized as such by most people. Are we going to be faced with *superbic?* Thinking ahead, one sees what will happen when *acerbic* calls for its noun: it will have to be *acerbicity,* on the model of *public, publicity; specific, specificity; catholic, catholicity;* and so on. But we already have a noun correctly formed from the true adjective—*acerbity.* So by using *acerbic* we open the way to a silly long word, by-pass a compact old one, and expose ourselves to having copy editors "correct" *acerbity* for lacking a syllable. Looking still farther ahead, one can foresee *exacerbicate.* Already *acerbic* has given *acidic* a foothold *(acidic rain)* and the acidic test awaits us. But this is an even worse offense, for *acidic* has a genuine technical use, to mean not *acid* but *acid forming.* Hence acid rain and acid remarks are not *acidic.* (Here an aside suggests itself. There was no need to bring into common use the rather literary *acerb* unless one knew the foregoing to begin with. No need to go foraging for the new in unfamiliar regions: we had *sharp, cutting, sarcastic* ready for ordinary use.)

HIDING THE FACTS

Yet another source of unwanted "creations" is circumlocution—roundabout phrasing—chosen either to veil a plain fact on purpose (euphemism) or by inadvertence, or again as a way of dignifying the commonplace by a hint of public importance. Thus a mere *patient* can be found anywhere, but a *dental consumer* is a grand addition to the national statistics. It was apparently not wonderful enough for the astronauts to *walk in space:* they *engaged in extra-vehicular activity* (EVA). Aircraft tested and found faulty were declared "not operationally suitable"—soothing words after the crash. When criminal charges against juveniles are dismissed, they are termed "adjusted at intake," the opposite being "felony augmentation." Museums do not sell a painting from their collection; they *deaccession* it. When broadcasters in England have finished making a film, it goes to Continuity Acceptance for—well, censorship. And from our State Department we learn of "premature unauthorized partial disclosure"—a leak, finally explained in full.

Anyone can see how serious is the disease. But are there not also some simple-&-direct neologisms that came just in time to nail an idea down—*meld, computer, disinformation?* To be sure, *meld* is simple and English-sounding, but it is in fact a word of German origin used hitherto only in the game of pinochle. It means *announce (melden)* and its entry into the vernacular to mean *combine* is a mistake and a needless addition. Its appeal probably lies in its vague echoing of *merge* and *weld.* But we have *mix, blend,* the aforesaid *merge,* and the intense *fuse,* to say nothing of *weld* itself—all applicable to ideas, plans, projects, bureaus, and works of art that *unite* (another one!) several purposes or their means.

*Computer* certainly belongs to the good kind—no fancy tricks with Greek, short enough , and plain. Only a slight fault can be found with it: it sounds like a synonym for *calculator,* and the thing itself is not a mathematical machine but a logical one. The result is that many people who think they have "no head for math" keep away from "computer science" because of its name. Some have found by accident that they had good "logical heads" and have become able programmers. The French for *computer* is *ordinateur,* which gives a truer idea of what happens inside.

As for *disinformation,* the art of spreading lies in a foreign country, it is the prefix *dis-* that is regrettable; for it suggests *undoing* what is present or was done *(disable, dispel, dismantle)* rather than *doing badly on purpose,* which is the meaning wanted. If *misinform* does not sound vicious enough, we could have had *malinform,* on the pattern of *malpractice, malversation, malocclusion,* and other kinds of *malefaction.* And come to think of it, why not *malarkey?*

But compared to the rest, *disinformation* and *computer* almost deserve a prize. Their qualities far outweigh the one flaw that might have been avoided in each if the specifications here cited were more generally understood by the baptizers of the new. One more feature must be added to the list: a new word should be sayable. Among recent innovations, two at least flout this requirement. How does one utter *parenting?* The accent has to fall on the first syllable, but that muffles the proper sound of the second, and the result is a nasal rendition of *parroting.* Even worse is the verb *mentoring,* which has arisen out of the belief among business women that they need a mentor within the firm in order to succeed ("upward, downward, and outward mentoring"). Now, *mentor* is a spondee (equal stress on each syllable); does it become men*tor*ing and lose audible connection with its origin? Or does it lose it the other way by rhyming with *entering?*

There is, in fact, no need and no excuse for either verb. *Being* a parent (or mentor), *serving, acting, failing as* (or *in the role of*), amply suffice. Verbs that reduce human life in this manner to a series of processes and methods spring from a childish aping of "science," but all they achieve is to diminish the users' sense of wholeness and selfhood. (See NOTE on page 215.)

THE FAKE TECHNICAL EVERYWHERE

The reference to science a moment ago could equally well have been to technology, the two being no longer seen as separate by the public

NOTE ALSO page 100 and: The investigation should be *fruit-worthy* (by the mayor of a large city)/ *verificability* (from the White House)/ *truismatic* (from the Supreme Court)/ It will be forced to *deconglomeratize* itself/ For the all-upholstered look in your living room you will want to-the-floor-draped stools/ Take the *phonetastic* journey with New York Telephone/ Chekhov's story is *intertextually* related to Tolstoy's *Anna Karenina* (= what follows shows the two have some points in common)/ Between certain altitudes, planes above the control tower are *transiting* in all directions/ I see us as a multiform dynamic university with a vital outreach into the world/ We furnish a nurturing potential as a panacea for the stresses of life/ This is not a partnership but a *duopoly*/ 2-Mamina is the name that has been given to radish sprouts/ There will be an *audioanimatronic* figure of Mickey Mouse/ nostalgia for the hysterics of being an official problem inventor/ Rather than using (= use) the phrase "fraud, abuse, and waste," she would prefer "program misuse and management inefficiency."

mind, thanks to the jargon that looks the same for both. Continuous with it is the pseudo-technical vocabulary produced by manufacturers and advertisers. The thought at work in such creations has recently been disclosed in a business report about a company that makes gloves (excellent ones) and calls them *Isotoner.* That trade name, we are told, was designed "to indicate that the gloves apply a measure of pressure to the wearer's hands. 'The term has no medical or therapeutic meaning,' Mr. Fischer says. 'It may have come from the word "isometric," which is defined as having an equality of measure.' " In short, the word is a foundling ("it may have come") as well as meaningless; it has no technical force; its parts form no legitimate whole; and it is intended to suggest something remarkable which turns out commonplace, since all gloves exert some pressure when put on.

It may be urged as an excuse that this work of art was fashioned for trade, not general, use. But nowadays much talk and writing is carried on in trade names, and the christening of new products is bound to affect our sense of language. We get accustomed to the vaguely portentous which is at the same time jerry-built. Our minds are filled with vocables that are quite different from *stone* or *wheel, fear* or *cod liver oil,* in the relation they bear to experience. The new words pretend to be indicative but remain arbitrary and abstract. We do not know how water (or a monster?) works in *hydramatic* transmission or what notion of strength (or is it farewell?) goes into *valium;* the simple days of *frigidaire* are long past.

The intention of the pseudo-technical is to impress with modernity and seriousness; and so they multiply, having by this spurious look become indispensable to business success. In one city, and perhaps in others, one finds a *Cardio-Fitness Center.* "Heart fitness" would be too humble and less reassuring. Nearby, a beauty specialist promises: "I'll *oxygenate* your skin with a spray of steam" and "your skin will never forget it"—which would be true if he actually used steam.

This means of being important and up-to-date occasionally brings in words truly technical but in false or vague applications. In business and casual talk one has had a surfeit of *parameters.* The chic word now is *paradigm,* borrowed by science writers from grammar and identical in sense with *model, pattern,* as *parameter* was with *limits* — when it was not mistaken for *perimeter.* The overuse of *metaphor* has long been a disgrace to otherwise responsible people in science and the arts, and one is not surprised to learn that an attempt was made some time since to popularize *synecdoche.* The story is instructive and, for once, has a happy ending.

The pedantry originated in a report of the Senate Select Committee on Intelligence, which stated that certain assassination plots by government agencies had been "concealed by synecdoche." The term comes from rhetoric and means mentioning a part as a sign of the whole: thirty sails = thirty ships. Fortunately, an article in a local paper rid Washington of this new menace to sense. For the pedant who unearthed the Greek word was unable to see that if by synecdoche the part is made to *represent* the whole, the device is not for concealment but for its opposite; it could not mean "suppressing part of the truth."

Fake technicalities are fake precisely because the bright-eyed innovator lacks the bright mind to make sure he understands what he is about. Current writing, for example, is full of *quantum jumps (leaps, steps)* variously intended to mean big, sudden changes, or scientifically contrived improvements—e.g., "the quantum jump in interest rates"; "With this new product Rococotex takes a quantum leap into the 21st century." This jumping in and out of centuries is silly to begin with, and the quantum jump of physics is neither large nor sudden nor applicable to anything in common life. It is simply discontinuous: the electron that jumps does not pass through the space between its orbit and the one it occupies next; it disappears from the one and reappears in the other, emitting a photon (light) as it does so. So a quantum jump means the absence of physical existence between point A and point B. Only a vaudeville magician is really entitled to use the image— unless one wants to say it in anger: "Go take a quantum jump!"

LEAVE THE GENUINE WHERE IT BELONGS

By a twist that could be expected, the habit of "being technical" with special words makes writers careless at other places where they should be technical with familiar ones. Thus, in reporting in two successive articles a train wreck with casualties, the writer used *rail* and *track* interchangeably, together with the verb *split apart.* It was impossible to know whether a rail—a single piece of metal—had split; or whether the track—two rails held together by ties, plates, etc.—had *spread* apart. Again, it rightly annoys specialists when newspapers refer to submarines "cruising under the thick North Pole *icecap,* " when they mean the polar *ice pack,* which is possibly twenty-five feet deep, whereas the icecap that covers Greenland is more than a mile thick.

The test of a good technical word is fixity and, if possible, simplicity. In chemistry and biology, the long, unpronounceable terms are at least made up of simpler parts that are fixed: "The Maleonitriledithiolate and Toluene-3, 4-Dithidate Square Planar Matrix Systems" raises in the chemist perfectly definite images. In workaday life, a good many technical words turn up that could serve more often—for example, the roadside *berm,* that is, the *prepared* shoulder of the road; underclothing that has "warmth and *wicking* ability," meaning that it transmits perspiration evenly away from the body; the useless condition of a fitting made of rubber that has *perished.*

The reaching out for singularities and neglecting their technical sense accounts also for the intrusion into common prose of Latin terms borrowed from the professions. The architects have lately revived *atrium* for what is actually a deep well within a skyscraper and certainly not open to the upper air. They had *court* at their disposal, but it did not sound new and special. Novelty hunting, again, is what prompts the fancy variation *academe,* in the belief it means the academic community, when in fact it is another form of the hero's name Academus, whose grove was the Academy.

Apropos of these foolish flourishes, the most paradoxical tendency of the day is the combination of this reckless annexing of Latin words and making of Greek compounds with the mouthing of hostile clichés about the ancient languages: they are "dead" and "useless." Yet law, logic, and theology are drawn on for Latinisms that are equally out of place: "This is a *mea culpa society"* (= guilt-ridden). "You have reported a *de minimis of a de minimis"* (strictly meaningless, but perhaps = a fraction of the small amount?). A writer to the press complains of the government's *"ad feminam* attack" on a certain person, believing that he is adapting *ad hominem* and that the phrase betokens hostility. On the contrary, it is an *appeal to; ad* does not mean *against,* nor *hominem male.* Classical tags, too, snatched from heaven knows where, are used with no awareness that they are only part of a full sentence. Thus a newspaper and a gourmet shop both use *De Gustibus* as if it meant "Fine-Tasting Things." Under any other name they would taste as well. (See NOTE on page 219.)

VOGUE DEGRADES AND DESTROYS

Mankind is subject to infatuations of all kinds, one of them being the craze for some word in good use, which suddenly is found everywhere in talk and print, applied correctly enough, but without cease. It seems to sound a special note that enchants the ear and to glow with a fire to light up every situation. By that time, good writers avoid it, because in their eye the fire is dead and the central meaning of the term is but a memory in the minds of the well-read.

Such a word is *compassionate.* Like other vogue words, it has attained popularity without bringing with it its distinctive connotation *(suffering with)* and it has displaced the clear common word *kindly.* We have *compassionate reviewers* (who never say a mean thing) and *compassionate citizens* (who favor progressive taxation).

NOTE ALSO pages 22, 90ff., and: The recommended procedure would be operant conditioning/ The son talked of paradigms, the paradigm of the government's case, the paradigms of the critics' case, but the truth is that I never really heard the question/ this five-function electronic executive time-minder/ Their effect is de minimus [*sic*]/ He was not the author of the whole but he catalyzed the important second clause/ She'll say *ipso facto*—closed case/ paperworkitis bureaucraticus/ It's at once intimique and feminique/ Every so often I get into a syndrome about it/ The objection to Dick Cavett's humorous coinage *légumophobia* misses the point/ You mean the opposite of what you say—in short, an oxymoron./ "Elders are no longer elders in the Presbyterian Church in the U.S.A.—they are 'Presbyters.' Interestingly enough, the Greek word for elder is 'presbuteros.' "/ "My effort will be in terms of . . . addressing the key management decisions."/ Rimbaud's work engaged the general turbulence of modern culture/ Foul play was suspected and a suspect was developed/

---

*Sensitive* has likewise lost its force from being used to characterize issues and documents, instead of persons and plants as it was designed to do. Strange pairings of ideas often result: "The motion picture is a great artistic achievement, but its subject matter is extremely sensitive and contains scenes of extreme violence." A sensitive person may now be one involved in secret operations or about whom controversy is rife. And the negative has become a term of abuse. The mayor is called insensitive if he does not agree with the demands of some group, the contract for garbage disposal being the most sensitive of current issues. To be sure, in the past it might have been called "ticklish business," which implies a form of sensitivity, but the usage caused no ambiguity and left a good word in its proper place.

In their vogue currency, the words just impugned are at least used with some glimmer of sense. Others have achieved pointlessness—for example, *gap*. It emerged in connection with *credibility* (see page 13) and has moved on to linkage with *gender, publication, influential, literacy,* and other dubious allies. "A proposed study will explore the creative gap in the school system." Can anyone say what the opposite edges of the chasm are? *Gap* has fallen into its own void. It deserves oblivion except with a capital letter, as in Delaware Water Gap and *Ruggles of Red Gap;* though it would be a pity to lose the wise critic's dictum: "This book fills a much-needed gap."

*Credibility* itself has suffered from the battering of the gap phrase and caused an unfortunate flight to *credence* as if it were a synonym. Indeed, the whole *cred-* family has degenerated and one finds (in a university alumni journal): "It's incredulous that these quiche eaters could perform so impressively upon their female cohorts [*sic*]." Or again: "They evidently suspect his credence." Only a total retreat to *belief, trust, faith,* and their adjectives, verbs, and negatives, will restore order.

In the mysterious *creative gap* above, and nearly everywhere else, *creative* is also a vogue word of no meaning: "A creative closet for not much money." The word has been nullified by the assumption that every person is a potential creator and that workaday jobs in which a little gumption is called for give scope to "creativity" or "creativeness." From another quarter, *creative writing* has contributed to the downfall, through being used to distinguish fiction from other prose. The word was better understood in more rural days, when "to create" was to carry on and have a tantrum for no reason—making something out of nothing is the true sense of *creation.*

It would be a long assignment to list even the main verbal vogues to be avoided. But here are a few more: *Profile:* "reduced food profile" in a government cafeteria = shorter menu. For the next fifty years, *profile* should be kept to describe the human face exclusively. *Surface* as a verb implies something deep in water (or earth) and that rises by itself. A paper lost in a filing system doesn't surface; besides which, the very frequency of the word is annoying. Recently, an ambiguous adverb has been overfancied by political writers: they use *arguably* as if to offer a concession to opponents whose argument they anticipate: "I have given my reasons, arguably idiosyncratic." But when one compares a number of examples, the tone and context are found to vary, so that the word may mean either: "you could argue . . . but it isn't so"; or, "you could argue . . . and there is a fair chance that it is so." The same trouble beset *no doubt* and *doubtless* in the past, but these have been so weakened by that very fact that they now suggest a mild *of course.* The negative of *arguably* is not ambiguous but superfluous: "Inarguably, many European countries were overrun by German troops during the two world wars."

CENTRAL MEANINGS ONLY

The best way to offset the harm of vogues is to stick resolutely, in speech and writing, to each vogue word's central meaning. *Address* an audience or a postcard, but not a problem or a question. Call a substance or a temperament *volatile,* but not an issue or a situation. Express sympathy far and wide, but keep *empathy* for aesthetics or psychiatry. Remember *Tiny* Tim and avoid naming things *minuscule* or *minimal* ("I tried to create a warm environment by using objects that are crisp and minimal"). The critic's verb *distance (d)(ing)* is hollow too. One finds it usurping the place of *detached, impersonal, judicious,* and even *apart*—enough to condemn it in the eyes of critics who really want to show powers of discrimination in their studies of literature. And speaking of studies, forgo adding *in depth,* except for those of Jacques Cousteau and other oceanographers.

By resisting vogues and respecting central meanings, the writer not only reaffirms the original reason for which the particular word was designed; he also sustains the life of the several other words that the voguish one suppresses. The dull substitute may continue popular for a while, but it will pass, and the vote cast against the unthinking use may shorten the time. The writer has moreover kept his self-respect by keeping the words that are in everybody's mouth out of his own. (See NOTE on page 222.)

MALAPROPS: IGNORANT AND PRETENTIOUS

Mistaking a word's meaning or confusing that of a pair that sound alike makes up the common variety of malaprop: *flout* and *flaunt, appraise* and *apprise, infer* and *imply.* When words such as these are misused by people who have been poorly educated (or not at all), the fault is excusable. But in the ordinary language of today, many words are made into malaprops because of someone's pretentious reaching after something rich and rare, for which he or she has not paid the price of exact understanding. A sports broadcaster declares that foot-

---

NOTE ALSO: *ambivalent, drastic, phenomenal, abrasive, priority, prioritize, approach* (noun), *communicate, supportive, concept, (re-)position* (verb), *ironic, interact, interpersonal, interface, (major) thrust, protagonist, macro-, micro-, escalate, replicate, share (= tell, impart), option, values, upcoming, ongoing, problem, affinity for, identify, identify with, ethnic* (with objects or *= foreign*), *historic (= old), conventional (= standard, traditional), establishment (= institutions, officialdom, leading figures), gentrification (= cleaning up), undocumented (= illegal), methodology (= method), technology (= machine* or *technique).*

---

ball is a *microplasm* of civilization. He could have said "the image," or "it is like . . . on a small scale"; but no, he had to go stumbling after *microcosm.* Again, in announcing someone's appointment to head a subsidiary, the president of the corporation said: "We exercise no editorial autonomy over the publishing division." "The editors remain independent" was too simple. *Authority, hegemony, autonomy,* rattling in the speaker's head, produced the opposite of what was meant.

A new case of galloping malaprop—that is, one taken up at once and spreading like measles in school—is that of *testament:* "Great literature is a testament to the society that produced it" (letter column) "The new national holiday is a testament to the man who led the civil rights movement" (editorial) "A wonderful testament to her beauty and talent" (movie critic). Apart from the Old and New Testaments, the word has hitherto been restricted to the phrase *last will and testament,* plus a figurative extension *political* or *artistic testament,* which denotes a person's last thoughts bequeathed to posterity. This central idea is being lost. The OED quotes only one use (dated 1533) in the new sense of *testimony* and calls it "erroneous."

It is entirely superfluous, for we have not only *testimony* (which gives the noun and adjective *testimonial*), but also the simple word *witness,* which fits easily into the three examples above and any others. It provides in addition an idiomatic construction: "a great society

. . . *witness* the literature it produced"; and just as readily available is its associated verb: the film *testifies to.* If this variety of means is buried under *testament,* we shall be reading about *testamentary dinners* given to the living, juries listening to *testaments* in court, and candidates for positions producing their *testaments.* Perhaps, too, the recent attempts at another malaprop, *fundament* for *foundation,* will prosper in echo fashion: "That event was the fundament of Polish nationalism." The innocent who look up the accepted meaning of this impostor will be shocked to the bottom of their souls.

These malaprops are clear-cut; but there is another sort, which come into being through the user's ignorance not of central meaning but of implications. When that ignorance is general, we have a vogue malaprop such as *mundane:* "A mundane sex life can be compared to a TV dinner, but it's not a gourmet banquet." The remark is nearly meaningless. *Mundane* means worldly, the opposite of spiritual, lofty, *disinterested.* An apt use of the word (and its opposite) was made in the report that in the kissing of the bishop's ring, "the more mundane of the faithful try to bite out the stone when it is large and when they imagine the bishop is thinking of heavenly things." Sex life, of whatever kind, is inescapably mundane, and so is a gourmet banquet. The attempted comparison suggests that the writer meant *ordinary, commonplace, humdrum*—elements of the mundane, no doubt, but not the whole of it.

Another example illustrates the opposite error—enlarging a word's scope: "an *avid* supporter of the Liberal party"/; "an *avid* runner"/; "President Eisenhower was an *avid* golf-player." *Avid* means hungry, greedy, moved by physical appetite. One can indeed devour a book with *avidity,* because the metaphorical *devour* (now almost a cliché about books) prepares the way. Other figurative uses of *avid* need the same mediation: *avid* for revenge, because one can hunger for it; *avid* for power, because one is greedy for it. But not *avid* for running or supporting the Liberals. It may be a curious side effect of the frequent *avid* that it is affecting *fervent:* "The mayor has been *fervent* in calling on Washington for" something or other. Fervor connotes love and devotion, not vehemence as such. For both the words in course of spoiling, the vocabulary offers *eager, pressing, demanding, passionate, fierce,* and *vehement,* depending on the context.

A third kind of corruption is due to ignoring or not knowing the way in which two meanings have come to be associated in a single word. Of late, *legend* and *legendary* have been turned into advertising superlatives with ludicrous effect: "This silk lingerie is fast becoming a legend"/ "Announcing the return of a legend whose time has come again"/ "W.S. Offers a Legend" (nothing more than an expensive cognac). Now, *legend* primarily means a tale unsupported by facts, a myth, a "good story." It is Lady Godiva's negligee that is legendary, not the silk undies you can buy down the street. Moreover, a legend comes to us from the past; that "its time has come again" kills it as a legend, for then we'll find out if any of it is true.

What has led to these absurdities is that legends grow about famous men and women even during their lifetime. Anecdotes, witticisms, scandals, mostly invented, cluster about their heads and they come to be called *legendary figures*. In this way *fame* and *legend* overlap. (Compare *fable, fabulous.*) But this fleeting association of ideas is no warrant for giving up *legend* to the lingerie counter and the distillers. It would be as galling a loss as that of *disinterested.* Consider: "The acrimony between tenants and landlords is legendary." It is *traditional* and true, not legendary and false in the way Washington and the cherry tree is legendary. Worse still, the wretched word is acquiring the sense of *well known to all:* "The teams' notoriety in jumping cities for a better return on the dollar is fast becoming a legend." (Note in passing that *notoriety* in this sentence and *acrimony* above verge on malaprops.)

In this last category examples abound. *Restrictions* are called *strictures,* which means reproofs, criticisms; Greek and Latin are termed *derelict* languages; people who leave a large estate for a park are said to be *disbursing* it; others promise to *reconnoiter* the topic for discussion; doctors have named types of infection *opportunistic* from being the result of casual copulation, and social workers use the same word for unpremeditated rapes; "In a very few years all the young writers had *coalesced* around him." And as a critic has said, thanks to *cohort,* reduced from a troop of several hundred soldiers or followers to a single sidekick, we can now interpret Byron's lines intelligently:

> The Assyrian came down like the wolf on the fold
> And his cohorts were gleaming in purple and gold.

Those "co-horts" were the grand vizier on his right and the chief eunuch on his left. As for the Assyrian who was the "hort," his name was Sennacherib.

It must be admitted that if they neglect a certain old-fashioned form of exercise, speakers and writers have a hard time ascertaining the precise use of all the common-uncommon words they use. That exercise is reading, reading, reading. One of the largest banks in the country has made an interesting discovery and, because of it, rewritten its bank-card agreement "in the belief that you will be able to use your account more effectively if you have a better understanding of how it works." That belief applies to words. There is no other recipe for using them more effectively than understanding how they work, and this in turn can only be found by reading good writers.

How does one know which are good? The signs are unmistakable: They are clear, they do not use jargon or vogue words, and they keep you reading by something in the march of the thoughts they have set down. Two sorts of reading are recommended: books on subjects about which you already know a good deal and others about which you know little or nothing. The first enable you to observe how skillfully the language fits the facts; the second show how unfamiliar matter is made intelligible and attractive. In the course of reading, the *limits* of words are acquired automatically. There is then no temptation to say: "I have *sojourned* from a liberal position to a more conservative one"/ "The buildings of that decade are already *debilitated*"/ "They are finally *asserverating* [*sic*] their potential role." (See NOTE on page 226.)

IDIOMS AND THE SMALL WORDS

In learning a foreign language, it is the smallest words that give the most trouble. What they *do,* for those foreigners, differs from what they *mean* on the surface. Besides, foreign verbs and adjectives take prepositions different from ours; and still worse, those small words combine with nouns and verbs to form *idioms*—phrasings that say something (often absurd) and mean something else quite useful. It is these arbitrary combinations and habits of thought that give a language its distinctive character.

Respect for such phrasings and for the right attachment of small words make one sample of prose "idiomatic" and another "foreign

NOTE ALSO: with amazing affrontery/ This idea undergirdles the whole scheme/ a smoldering volume on a shelf/ They put her in charge because she is so deciduous/ Intelligent TV is in trouble/ Loitering shall mean spending time idly, to linger, to be dilatory/ These commitments are appropriate yet do not interface in any way with important principles/ a massive change and the decimation of the lives of many workers/ Let him go his torturous way/ The number of serious injury accidents will deteriorate/ The bomb was reported diffused/ This artist goes in for enormities/ takes the reader with him to inspect every faucet of life/ There was still a heartbeat, but he was very critical/ She was at the edge of her tether/ When I think of this college I am deeply accelerated (an alumnus and trustee)/ Their friendship precluded open altercations/ The Secretary of State will revisit his previous article/ The place was so sordid it was Dickensian/ It was an atmosphere of seizing hostility/ Mr. and Mrs. C. are at home receiving the kind felicitations of their friends (after the suicide of their son).

sounding." In a conversation manual of the 1880s, compiled by a Portuguese who knew no English and used a dictionary to guess his way, we find page after page of such locutions as: "Bring us some thing for to breakfast."/ "Have you pain to the heart?"/ "There is the postman, I go to put it him."/ "Apply you at the study during that you are young." These sprightly remarks are readily understood—they are "effective communication"—but they are not in English. Let those who say there is no right or wrong in language ponder these specimens.

At the present time, English is being subjected to a loosening of the bonds that hold idioms together and prepositions with their customary verbs and adjectives. It is true that over the centuries these linkings have varied, and one can find usages in Shakespeare or Swift that parallel modern vagaries. But going back to those authors also shows that they stuck to their choices—as we should stick to ours. It is understood that in England today they say *chat to* and *cater for;* over here, *chat with* and *cater to*. They also have the idiom *chatting up*, in the sense of exchanging small talk, often with an ulterior motive. Disregard of such set ways only makes work for reader and writer. Uncertainty wastes time, whereas uniformity has the great merit of not distracting the mind from the meaning to the words.

A frequent cause of faulty connection is to assume that a preposition seen with a verb will serve with the corresponding noun. Thus we come across "a writer with distinction" for "of distinction," because to *write with* distinction is correct. Confusion is likewise overtaking *compliance:* is it *in, to,* or *with?* Here verb and noun go in parallel—it is *compliance with,* as we are reminded by the frequency of *comply with* in laws, instructions, application forms, and the like. What probably derails the thought when the noun comes up is the accepted *acquiescence in,* an act that somewhat resembles *compliance.* Beware of echoes of sense or sound; they are false guides where idiom rules.

The only way to be sure about idiom—as with connotation—is by reading. It will not only teach the cast-iron phrases, it will also teach the variations in meaning made possible by using different prepositions with the same word. See agree *to, with, on* above (pages 33, 61–63) and note the recent special meaning of *agreed* without any preposition: "rely on agreed principles." It might seem needless to add that varying the preposition for mere elegance is at once foolish and fatal, yet it happens quite often. In a recent article about useful relations within a business firm, the writer began by describing "a one-on-one mentor relationship." The sense is surely *one-to-one,* since no hostile surveillance is implied. That same writer would evidently have concurred, since later in the same piece she reverts to common usage and writes *one-to-one.* If doubtful at first, she had a ready test: it is impossible to say: "they met face on face"; "they see eye on eye." Factuality settles it, just as *one-on-one* has correct applications in the textile and ceramic industries, as well as in basketball.

An important pair of idioms has already succumbed to this kind of error, which begins in thoughtlessness or doubt: "The first railroad *dates to* the 1830s." The norm for historians, museum curators, journalists, and the plain man has been to say: This *dates from* . . . or this *dates back to* . . . The *to* belongs to *back,* not to *dates.* As a result of the muddle, we now have a brand-new construction never needed before: "He dates the document to 1855." It is particularly silly when one considers what assigning or writing a date means; does anyone say: "Please date your letter *to* January 5"? Simplest is best—and right: "They date the painting 1583."

Apart from idiom, abide by the general rule: the fewer words the better. Try your phrase without the preposition and you may find the colloquial additions to be disposable. Say "they visited their grandmother" as you would say "visited the Taj Mahal," not *visited with* in either case. The same goes for *consult,* meaning ask for answers or instructions. If extended give-and-take is involved, then one *confers with.* With *expound,* no preposition—the word is the same as *expose.* One expounds a theory. The urge to say *expound on* may come from *expatiate on,* which originally means *digress* and has thereby acquired the connotation of *going on and on* about a subject.

For both brevity and best usage, cut as many as possible of the barnacles that have grown on expressive verbs: *miss out on, check up on, rest up, pay off, stop off, face up to, start up.* Omit *as to* in front of *whether:* "the question *whether to go or stay.*" And if one starts out with "all the more," what comes after the intervening words is *that,* not *in that* or any other combination. "He was all the more tired that he had eaten nothing since breakfast." If the construction sounds incomplete because of its frequent perversion, drop it altogether. (See page 122.)

WHY TAMPER WITH THE EXPECTED?

A different kind of decision is called for when a familiar idiom is twisted or curtailed. Take *hard put to it,* now often replaced by *hard put* alone. The attentive writer asks first: is it as clear? Then: is it more elegant thanks to its omission of *to it,* which demands another *to: hard put to it to . . . ?* Lastly, what about parallels?: *feel out of it, put one's foot in it, get away with it, see someone through it*—all expressive turns, in which *it* has no discoverable reference. No one could write *I feel out, he put his foot,* and so on. And going back to the questioned idiom, if *hard put to it to . . .* seems overlong, why not use *hard pressed,* which is shorter, or the even more direct "I found it hard to [run the last lap]"?

One type of *it* that certainly cannot be got rid of is the anticipatory *it,* as in *suffice it to say.* Removing *it* is ill*it*erate, because grammar (not idiom) is at stake. Even though sentences that ignore the call for *it* may seem complete, they limp: "This is a rule that in spite of all the objections raised is vital should be observed" (*it* is vital)/ "What was expected might result did result" (*it* was expected)/ "The time has already elapsed which was originally thought would see the work finished" (*it* was . . . thought). The last sentence will serve to make the point of this digression clear: a subject is needed for "was originally thought." It cannot be *time,* because "time has elapsed . . . which would see" is a whole sentence by itself. To insert "was originally thought" needs *it* for the thinking to be done by some agency, live or indefinite.

Grammar, as in this case, can be worked out by analysis, but idiom either does or does not give up its secret when one looks into its origin. People who say "go by the boards" (plural) do not know that the board (singular) is the rail of the deck—recall *man overboard.* Accordingly, trash—or jewelry—goes "by the board" when thrown or dropped into the sea. Once explained, the image readily keeps the writer from using the plural. But the person who says: "I have no bones and no contentions that we are perfect" has no recourse but to learn by rote the meaning of *make no bones* (have no hesitation) and the proper use of *contention.* He then concludes that here they contradict each other.

Some verbs occur in two related forms, one of which seems to possess—or to suggest—a preposition: *tend, attend; minister, administer.* What they suggest cannot be relied on, nor does *at-* or *ad-* save the trouble of using a preposition; there is no shortcut to idiomatic rightness. It is: *tend* the sick; *attend to* one's needs; *minister to* the world's woes; and *administer* a soothing potion. The most frequent misusage is *administer to.* Of course, the unrelated sense of *tend* (tendency) uses *to: people tend to forget,* where the preposition belongs to the infinitive *to forget.*

An unfortunate slippage which is retrievable by taking thought is very likely due to the otherwise benign influence of interior decorators. They are always "doing a room *in* pale yellow" and mistakenly go on to cover its sofas *in* ribbed velvet. The advertiser offers "A lucky elephant covered in rhinestones." By imitation, the novelist writes: "It was an old farmhouse built in pale-gray stone, its low-pitched roof covered in pinkish tiles." Really and truly, things are built, made, carved *of* some material and covered, roofed, lined *with* some other. Regain the idiomatic sense by stepping out of the house and seeing that the roadway isn't covered *in* mud and remembering that watches are made in Switzerland but not *in* platinum. The very idea of making or building is *partitive,* for which English uses *of;* it is not *static:* "They made a shelter *of* pine boughs, rather than take refuge *in* the cave."

DELICATE ARTICLES

Choosing among *a, the,* and their omission demands another act of thought, for it determines different nuances of sense and can sabotage idiom. What Gertrude Stein wrote is: "Rose [the name of a particular girl] is a rose is a rose." The repeated predicate is an emphatic assertion of the girl's loveliness. The public has changed it to: "A rose . . ." and then made the misquotation into a catchphrase by varying the noun. The result is not emphasis but a sort of mulish tautology, excusable only if one were irritated at somebody else's obtuseness. Another nonsensical *a* (see pages 54–55) negates the difference between a common noun and a proper name. "It was a happy child who met the returning pair"—yes; but "it was a happy Jane who . . ."—no. There is only one Jane, *the* Jane who welcomes her returning parents. The misusage continues its mindless course in the newspapers: "An ailing Yuri Andropov did not appear." So there is more than one? What about the Andropov who ruled the Soviet Union, *the* Mr. Andropov? The Scots have lately reminded us of what *the* means: "Only one Scotch in all the world has the right to call itself *The* Glenlivet." One thinks at once of the practice of calling the head of the clan *The* McQuern, *The* McDonald. But, back to Russia, imagine the case where additional modifiers had to be used: would anyone write, "*a* poor old ailing Mr. Andropov could not get out of bed and attend the meeting"?

With words denoting classes of persons, not individuals, *a* not only may but must be used. "Claude Monet's father was merchant at Le Havre" is illiterate unless it is an unconscious gallicism. As for *the* in front of terms stating a generality or an abstraction, it is so frequently omitted unidiomatically that the error can only be explained by the growing influence of foreign tongues on English. "Loss of the *Jane Vosper* cost the insurers plenty" should be *the loss,* for it happened only once. "Loss of ships cost the insurers . . ." can omit *the,* because it forms a kind of fused noun, a single general subject. But it does not authorize: "Passage of the bill was a mistake"; "Education of children in this city is a disgrace," any more than it would permit: "Game of baseball is joy of my life." (See pages 52ff.)

One idiom made up of short words—not prepositions—which has usurped the place and meaning of a common verb deserves notice here, because instances are now found that defy interpretation. The idiom and the verb are *has to be* and *must* (see page 130). The standard usage to indicate supposition after a knock at the door is: "It must be John." But *must* also serves for compulsion: "You must take it or leave it"; so when ambiguity is feared, *must* is replaced by some form of *have to.* "There *must* be lemon in that dish" could be read two ways; hence "There *has to be* lemon . . ." (or it won't taste right). Until recently, *have to be* always marked emphatic compulsion.

Now the terms have been switched: "You have to be joking!" Since I know I don't *have to* at all, and since "You must be joking" is still written, with the old meaning, we have eliminated instant comprehension and recreated ambiguity with no device to fall back on. One example among many shows the depressing fact. A report from the Department of Defense, not yet made public, was commented on by an expert who had not seen it; he said: "It will have to be critical." What, if anything, does the remark mean? Of the two possibilities: "I bet it's going to be critical"/ "It ought to be critical," the first used to be made clear by *must* and the second by *has to.* And supposing an authoritarian chairman, the *has to* would also serve for "I demand that it be critical."

WHICH WAY DOES THE WORD POINT?

Knowing the "direction" of a word is closely allied to the sense of idiom (and connotation) and to the use of prepositions. It goes with the awareness of how far two ideas that one wants to join are related and how far they are not.

For example, *public education* means the schools paid for by taxes. When a reform group uses the same phrase to mean that it "conducts a continuing program to inform the general public," it creates an annoying confusion; *public education* is not the same thing as *educating the public.* Likewise, if one turns a noun into a passive verb heedlessly, false or silly meanings will follow. From *paint* one makes the verb *to paint* and one can say: "This door is painted." But from *alarm* (against burglars) one cannot develop: "This door is alarmed," because the direction of *alarm* as a verb has already been appropriated to denote a human feeling. Yet that warning sign has come into use, and the same disregard is shown in other places: "Our tweed suits are all vested." One need only think of "Our suits are all buttoned" to see the absurdity of ignoring "direction."

*Vesting* is in itself a subtle idea with both concrete and abstract, technical and workaday meanings ("a man who has invested his opinion with the status of a cause"). It should not be played with recklessly. Lately, one of its kin, *divest,* has been mistreated by turning it into a curious kind of absolute term. "The *Los Angeles Times* must divest the San Bernardino newspapers" suggests an unseemly act of stripping. *Must divest itself of* is the only tolerable phrasing. Yet between statements about antitrust rulings and objections to certain foreign investments—"This university must divest from South Africa"—an important verb has lost its bearings.

Speaking of bearings, attentive readers detect a breach of the novelistic "point of view" when the author in supplying details writes: "He had lost his cherished wife three months ago." It should be "three months earlier," for *ago* can only be said from the speaker's point of view; the novelist's own time is by definition not the same as his characters'. This difference should be observed generally. The character says: "I will call again tomorrow." The storyteller or reporter writes: "She would call again the next day," changing both the time indication and the tense of the verb.

The perception required to use verbs properly is that which distinguishes transitive from intransitive (see pages 31–34), coupled with the knowledge of what may be done when a verb is capable of both uses. Transitive "goes over" toward an object; intransitive stays within its subject. Take the overpopular verb *boggle,* which describes what a horse does when it it is startled and refuses to budge—an ideal illustration of the *in*transitive. Hence *the mind boggles* makes sense, whereas *boggles the mind* makes nonsense. One suspects that users of the latter phrase feel it as more explosive—it blows up the mind—rather than see it as merely halting. Even so, if the mule resists, then the same meaning cannot be got out of "it resists the mule."

Whole series of parallels are met with daily. A secretary of state says: "If the situation decontrols . . ." *Control* and *decontrol* express the very essence of transitiveness—a mind or hand *getting at* something else and holding or guiding it. No situation has such power; a situation is inactive, intransitive. An even more common neglect of direction is the use of *convert*. In colloquial speech one says: "He converted to oil," implying "his furnace" or "his house"—clear enough. But when one reads: "He converted to Catholicism," there is no object that is converted. Besides, the idea of a deliberate and mechanical switch is offensive. "He converted himself" is awkward and psychologically inaccurate, so the old established "he became converted to" (or "a convert to") is the only acceptable wording.

MODIFIERS MISMATED

With adjectives, flouting "direction" throws doubt on what they modify. In an earlier section we came across *a creative gap* in the schools, *creative difference* in movie making; in other places we find: *artistic vandalism, a cognitive deficiency,* and the like. These phrases tell us nothing or the wrong thing. The first two were intended to report: a gap (lack) *of creativeness* in schools, differences *about creative work* in movie making. Unless these ideas are fully articulated, guessing and ambiguity result. For suppose a film studio managed by partners who are quite unlike but congenial. Their differences might well spur original thoughts, creativity pouring like lava from a hot volcano over the product. Those would be rightly called *creative differences,* whereas the phrase in the article only meant to account for the parting of associates who could not agree about their work.

Turning to the other two examples, one might ask: if *mental deficiency* is all right, why not *cognitive deficiency?* Because the context shows the sense to be "deficiency in one instance of cognition"; or in more decent English, "lack of understanding"; whereas mental (or cognitive) deficiency means a permanent condition of the mind. Likewise, it is "vandalizing works of art" that was being discussed, not anything *artistic*. Well, but if the context held a clue, why not accept the shortcut? First, because the reader should not be made to stop, puzzled, retrace his steps, and work out the sense. And second, because the phrases as they stood would be clear and to the point in another context, as we saw about *creative differences*. Thus *artistic vandalism* might characterize a work of art that parodied another, well-known work. Such things have been done in our time, to great applause.

Some words of the same type have acquired a meaning not guessable from the root idea they contain. "He was assigned a *problematic* role" means *dubious, uncertain,* not "full of problems." The force of such words can only be learned from reading widely and noticing that the obvious does not fit the sense. Finally, where "direction" might have been clear in either of two directions, usage has often chosen one exclusively. That choice must be respected. "Your friends sang their praises to me" means, by custom, "they praised themselves." The writer wanted to say: "they praised you," and should have written: "sang *your* praises to me." The possessive must point toward the recipient of the praise, not the giver of it. The same fixity is to be observed in words whose meaning might have been attached to either of two parties but has settled on one. To be *embattled* does not mean besieged, forced to do battle; it means ready to do battle on one's own initiative. (See NOTE below.)

---

NOTE ALSO pages 29ff. and: Trouble affording us to view the dim outline of what is to come/ In the semifinal, the challenger blundered a piece in his play against . . ./ The jury is expected to begin deliberating her case on Friday/ It rankled him all the way home/ Fowler's Classic on Language Translates to Paper/ U.S. productivity is low and lags other nations/ They were shocked by the prosecutor's exposure (who was exposed by whom?)/ It was a case of where things lost perspective/ Herman Melville, aware of his own posterity, knew the value of his work.

---

## MEN, WOMEN, AND OTHER PEOPLE

As everybody knows, the effort to recognize and defend women's rights has deviated from the social and political spheres into that of language, where it has succeeded in confounding usage without advancing its own praiseworthy cause. Innovation has affected several forms of expression, doing injury to idiom, grammar, and logic. The best-known case is the attempt to substitute *person* for *-man* (as in *chairman*) and to ignore sex even when the facts are clear: not *Men* but *People Working,* declares the sign over a street excavation. To what was said on page 102 about *-man,* it might be added that the English Bible reinforces the linguistic truth that *man* means "human being" generally and "male" only in limited cases: "And God made man, male and female" (Genesis I:27). There is thus no point in disfiguring dozens of good words as if doing so would help make salaries equal, as they should be.

Next in question is the small word *he,* which (with its derivatives) does refer to males, but has by long convention meant *anyone* when used in general statements ("the reader in *his* armchair"). The lack of an impersonal pronoun in English is to be deplored; but it is hard to see how a less frequent use of the inconspicuous *he* could hasten social progress. The same deficiency long ago brought about the nearly universal use of the wrong plural after *everybody, anybody, anyone:* "Has everybody got their tickets?"/ "Did you see anyone go in? What were they like?" Inspired, no doubt, by this colloquial usage, a journal supplying linguistic abstracts tried to make *they* the universal pronoun, regardless of verb forms and of sense; "When the student looks at the facts, *they notices* that *they has been* misled." It seems a doubly strange effort, for the science of linguistics is supposed to be descriptive, not prescriptive; and its students know that language is impossible without a good many compromises such as *he = he and she = one = they*—all in their proper traditional places. For the writer, the main guideline applies to this difficulty too: What trouble lies ahead if we tamper and innovate here? (See NOTE on page 236.)

NOTE ALSO page 197 and: Lay ambush to her primrose path/ The door was substituted with a curtain/ The speaker regressed at length on his early experiences/ I have never imposed myself into the debate/ The names are those worthy for an award/ Bulgaria is a land of gratitude toward Russians/ They escaped by a hare's breath/ a man of dialogue, conviction, and culture/ They showed at once an affinity to each other/ The collection contains the music to 625 hymns/ Setting up a business now, it's got to be a risk/ The blade, in stainless steel, is more rigid/ When anyone coughs, I know they're no longer paying attention/ Her next clear impression was of a shattered William/ The circumstances demand statement of our views (U.S. Supreme Court)/ She stuck to the beliefs of cautious clinician/ And nor were they unaware of it/ As of yet no word has been received/ They chatted about as of where they would dine/ Neither knew as of when the promotions would be announced/ She plays flute, he piano/ They were both an anathema to the bosses/ The deputy reassigned the top aides to his departed chief.

---

DEGREES OF THE COLLOQUIAL

Advocates of the free-for-all in language make a great point of the vigor and fecundity of slang and of the good nature and democratic spirit of colloquial expression. There is much to be said in favor of "colorful language" and "racy speech." The past of American English shows plentiful examples of the enrichment of the vocabulary from those sources, and our literary tradition from Mark Twain to Hemingway has encouraged the attitude that leads to the advice: "Write pretty much as you would speak."

But the benefit of that teaching has long since been garnered. No one has written in eighteenth-century "periods" for some time, nor even in formal nineteenth-century prose. Meanwhile, common speech has changed too. As we have seen from the contents of earlier sections, the colloquial—what one hears all around—is not racy and colorful;

it is dull and heavy with pseudo-technical words and roundabout expressions. Some interlard this pedantry with routinely obscene modifiers, but the prevailing tone is pretentiousness. We are back in the eighteenth century, though with a different kind of pomposity and another set of "noble" words. Both the old and the new tendency embody the same urge to dress up commonplace thought in plush diction. In short, our workaday talk in business, journalism, and the professions is anything but down-to-earth and pleasantly slangy.

So let us cut the cackle about the glories of colloquialism in the abstract. Slang is always with us and everybody draws on it more or less: After adolescence, one hopes, it is used expressively at the right time and place, and not merely to keep up status in a clique. For slang at any given moment is not the same everywhere; and anywhere most of its terms last but a short time. Nothing dates faster or sounds stupider than stale slang. Even during its currency, much of it is unusable in writing, because the same term can mean good, bad, or indifferent, depending on tone, glance, or eyebrows. For example, *funky,* as defined by an expert, means: "very good or beautiful; solid; cheap; smelly; or generally, no good."

Far from injecting new blood and vigor into the upper layers of speech, slang today has managed to destroy or make doubtful more good words than it could make up for in a long time. Whole series —*fairy, pansy, faggot,* down to *gay*—have achieved nothing but to rob the language of irreplaceable, often beautiful, resources. Other words, such as *ball, bomb, blow, screw,* etc., have been left uncertain in slang and unexpectedly embarrassing in straight talk. Slang now seems to prey upon the vocabulary rather than nourish it, and even when not hostile or obscene (as the bulk of it is designed to be), it multiplies ambiguities. At the moment, *tacky* signifies cheap, ill-made, so that suddenly the sense of "not completely dry" requires one to say, "I mean . . ." and to give the three-word explanation.

In these conditions, what has to be guarded against is the failure to recognize the colloquial or slang term for what it is. The author of a business journal article should have known better than to write: "The $350 terminal is available for free to depositors." *For free* was originally a joke—"What do they sell it for?" "For free." In speech the stale joke may be repeated absentmindedly; it is neither racy nor colorful in economics. Keep saying, so as to avoid writing the "for":

"They give it away free"/ "Public schools are free"/ "Admission is free." (See pages 36ff. and 94.)

The line that divides slang from colloquialism can never be sharply drawn, but one can hazard the generality that the colloquial is well-established and therefore clear at sight; slang, thriving on novelty, needs interpretation. For slang when first launched expresses an attitude much more than a novel perception. "Get down to brass tacks" is a colloquial metaphor; whereas "cluck and grunt" for ham and eggs was invented to show off and puzzle a little, and it has to be explained. Accordingly, novelists who want to seem true by recording current talk, and who also want their works to survive somewhat longer than the season following publication, have the difficult task of guessing what pieces of slang will outlive the year. Oddly enough, at the same time as they choose slang, they will avoid using most colloquialisms, because these have very likely become clichés. If by good luck they pick a slang term with a future, it, too, will in that future qualify as a cliché.

The desire to be "of one's own time" is not the only one that tempts to slang and the colloquial. Some writers, no doubt, would not have hesitated to entitle the present chapter "Thumbs Down Update." The pairing of *up* and *down* might pass for wit, while the pause needed to work out the meaning of the combination might be supposed to create a smart yet chummy atmosphere. Its purpose, in turn, would be to jolly the reader along. For what reason? He or she is free to read or not to read and can stop at any time. So long as courtesy obtains, there is no need to coax and conciliate, especially by means of a folksiness that is pure pretense.

Too many books that tell the public "How to . . ." these days vulgarize their contents by adopting just such a tone. It seems to say: "Though I know more (or else I could not teach you), I do not on that account think of you as an inferior; let my jocular, slangy style suggest my grinning face and show you what a good fellow I am." In that stance lies the real insult. The case is different when an author has the good fortune to meet one of his readers; then colloquial speech and a measure of camaraderie may ensue naturally; it is not put on; the choice of words will be guided by relative age, common acquaintance, and other facts contributing to the sense of occasion. But on paper (as has been shown), feelings, true or false, are conveyed willy-

nilly through the quality of one's words. It follows that writers should
be simple-&-direct in their emotions too.

### TIME OUT FOR GOOD READING VII

Hilaire Belloc (1870–1953) was an English poet, historian, essayist, sailor, and
hiker, whose versatility with words gives pleasure even when his matter
happens not to interest the reader who comes across one of his books.

#### How to Be Respected at an Inn, Hotel or Pub

As you come into the place go straight for the smoking-room, and
begin talking of the local sport, and do not talk humbly and tenta-
tively as so many do, but in a loud authoritative tone. You shall insist
and lay down the law and fly into a passion if you are contradicted.
There is here an objection which will arise in the mind of every niggler
and boggler who has in the past very properly been covered with
ridicule and become the butt of the waiters and stable-yard, which is,
that if one is ignorant of the local sport, there is an end of business.
The objection is ridiculous. Do you suppose that the people whom you
hear talking around you are more learned than yourself in the matter?
And if they are do you suppose that they are acquainted with your
ignorance? Remember that most of them have read far less than you,
and that you can draw upon an experience of travel of which they can
know nothing; do but make the plunge, practising first in the villages
of the Midlands, I will warrant you that in a very little while bold
assertion of this kind will carry you through any tap-room or bar-
parlour in Britain.

I remember once in the holy and secluded village of Washington-
under-the-Downs, there came in upon us as we sat in the inn there
a man whom I recognized (though he did not know me) for a journalist, incapable of understanding the driving of a cow, let alone horses:
a prophet, a socialist, a man who knew the trend of things and so
forth: a man who had never been outside a town except upon a motor
bicycle, upon which snorting beast indeed had he come to this inn.
But if he was less than us in so many things he was greater than us
in this art of gaining respect in Inns and Hotels. For he sat down, and
when they had barely had time to say good day to him he gave us in

minutest detail a great run after a fox, a run that never took place. We were fifteen men in the room; none of us were anything like rich enough to hunt, and the lie went through them like an express. This fellow "found" (whatever that may mean) at Gumber Corner, ran right through the combe (which, by the way, is one of those bits of land which have been stolen bodily from the English people), cut down the Sutton Road, across the railway at Coates (and there he showed the cloven hoof, for your liar always takes his hounds across the railway), then all over Egdean, and killed in a field near Wisborough. All this he told, and there was not even a man there to ask him whether all those little dogs and horses swam the Rother or jumped it. He was treated like a god; they tried to make him stop but he would not. He was off to Worthing, where I have no doubt he told some further lies upon the growing of tomatoes under glass, which is the main sport of that district. Similarly, I have no doubt, such a man would talk about boats at King's Lynn, murder with violence at Croydon, duck shooting at Ely, and racing anywhere.

❖

In this essay the attentive reader will note a couple of solecisms, of which "less than us . . . greater than us" is the most surprising. If we assume, as there is good reason to do, that Belloc "knew better" and put those words down on purpose, with his eyes open, can we discover the stylistic purpose of avoiding *than we?* Does the bent grammar spoil clarity or sense? Does it contribute to—what? Finally, how good a writer must one be to be able to afford such faults?

# Take a Little Thought

## VIII

To adults the uttering and hearing of words is so familiar, so automatic, that the commonest response to them is either to seize on a meaning, no matter how ill-expressed, or to pay no attention to what is said—suppress it as background noise—and pursue one's own train of thought, confident that the other person agrees or doesn't count. Together, these events form what the learned call Communication. They also account for the ever-present "problem of communication."

But quite often a pressing need or some clash between expectation and fact will make consciousness spring to life, as when a circular from a laundry urges: "Don't kill your wife with heavy washing and ironing. Let us do it for you, at reasonable rates." At that point, words acquire a new existence, like physical objects, which in fact they are. Thus, in a pleasant suburb an efficient and very pious postman has a wife who bakes excellent cakes. These he sells on order to patrons along his route. In due course, the recipient of a first cake is startled to find on top of the package a printed and decorated card that reads: "Prepare to meet thy God."

This more vivid presence of words is due to their interconnections, and these in turn explain why it is said that without a fair command of language one cannot think straight. Another form of the dictum is: "I don't know what I think till I've written it down."

All these propositions are reversible: to write decently one must take thought, continuously. So far, the thought has been about the words in themselves—their tone, implications, and accepted meanings. But—still with words in mind—a second order of thought is needed to fit our words to our intentions, to draw that sketch so as to resemble the model in our mind's eye. Take the simplest pair of ideas—yes and no, positive and negative—and ponder: "No one, including his mother, had a good word to say for him."/ "Nobody was casting a glance at each other." The illogic of these remarks is plain once attention is drawn to it. *No one* cannot *include* anybody; *nobody* cannot contain any *each other(s)*.

These faults lie on the surface. Generally, thought has to dig below it. Except in British usage, where *peers* can be found listed in directories, the use of the term is a figure of speech for *equals*. What then are we to make of: "Half the class ranked well below its peers"? The sentence is a puzzle as it stands. We must be told *peers* in what—age, school grade, national average—since by the one measurement given they are *not* peers. But then it dawns on us that *peers* possibly means the remainder of the same class, or schoolmates, not peers at all.

Looking still deeper to test meanings, one must question "ameliorate their obvious faults." That effort entails knowing that *ameliorate* means "make better," and deciding whether a fault can be made better. The hasty mind may think: Why, yes, of course; getting rid of faults makes things better. True, but the remark doesn't say anything about getting rid or about the object being ameliorated; it refers only to the faults, and *they* cannot be "made better." One can only ameliorate things already good, or at least of neutral quality.

From words to grammar to the intended thought itself, the same kind of analysis will bring sense out of babble. Consider: "To the extent we have not scheduled a date which is convenient for you, we extend our apologies and will mail you the materials covered in the meeting." This was not meant to sound like a grudging apology; in fact, no apology is due for failing to suit everybody's convenience; but the grudging is there in "to the extent"—no farther than that! And one wonders how the writer could measure that extent, not knowing who would be inconvenienced. Lack of thought about the situation is made worse by straining for the diplomatic tone, by an unwillingness to say "If."

This reluctance to use the short words whose sense is clear to everybody accounts for much muddled thought. To use *if, then, when, next, but, now, while, soon, before, after(ward), often, seldom;* instead of their lumbering substitutes: *in the eventuality, at this time, in the years ahead (in the not distant future), to the extent that, prior to, under the present conditions, in the course of, in the expected contingency that, at a subsequent moment,* etc., would clear much prose of its mud and afford protection against lapses of sense. (See pages 12–20)

NON-SENSE ON THE FACE OF IT

The soft-focus expressions that have just been listed betray a preference for not concentrating on the fact or the point in matters of time and space and other relations. Such phrases are matched in looseness by a good many modern words and expressions that either misname or say the same thing twice over. By repetition, each contributes its mite toward thoughtlessness. For example, merchants and magazine publishers used to offer *premiums*—not the best word, but clear enough; now they hand out a *free gift.* What does that do to plain *gift?* Argument goes on about *ballistic missiles;* the name tells us that they are both *thrown* and *sent,* as if any projectile were not ballistic by the very fact of being "missiled." The two, some devotees of tautology would answer, are *co-equal, co-partners.* When a man kills six or seven people he is dubbed a *mass murderer.* Where does that leave Herod and others who have really compassed a massacre? Isn't a *multiple* murderer sufficiently heinous? As for "the architectural nature of the building," it can only be a matter for congratulations.

The permanent target before the thinking writer's eye, of course, is ambiguity: can these words, put together thus, possibly present two meanings? The reader takes one of the two, and like a train switched to the wrong line, has to back up and start again. But the difference between reading and traveling is that any word or phrase can be a switch to a dead end. "New Jersey plans extra holiday checks . . ." A bonus for its state employees? No: "for drunken drivers." *Check* is a particularly ambiguous word; money, restraint, survey, verification, are all possible interpretations of the bare sound, and situations are many in which what precedes the word gives no hint of the sense required by what follows.

Among phrases, one must be on guard when writing "there is no question." If the next words are: "that the police officer will be reinstated, said the commissioner," one can only speculate. Does it mean he will be or won't be? The riddle is insoluble; one must try to catch a hint from later paragraphs. The positive has to be written: "without question" (he will be); and the negative: "there is no thought of his being reinstated." Another pair of phrases, once clearly separate, have now lost their distinctive marks. "The play, written—to my knowledge—before she left for Paris . . ." This statement was very likely meant to be cautious—"so far as I know" is the point of the insert. But what it says is: "I know it for a fact." To my knowledge = *in* my knowledge. The expression for doubt is: "to the best of my knowledge."

Offhand one would not suppose that phrases with *or* would be similarly dangerous, yet in scientific and other instructional writing (including the directions that come with gadgetry) the ambiguous *or* is rife. "When you go fishing there, you go for chavender or chub." Are these two kinds of fish or two names for the one kind? *Or* has the peculiar honor of uniting with equal ease two opposite possibilities: it may mean identity or alternatives. A clear signal "also known as" is imperative when the nomenclature allows two names for one thing (chavender *is* chub). Sometimes an apt omission of the article will do the work: "The President lives in the Executive Mansion or White House." Put *the* in front of White House and you instantly create two residences.

MINDLESSNESS, INC.

Once the exercise of first and second thoughts has become a habit, it will naturally go on to question new or entrenched expressions of the sort the alert writer wants to keep out of his work. Take the common-place: "Being kind to others is what life is all about"/ "What School Libraries Are All About"/ "A train that reminds you of what civilized travel is all about." None of the subjects discussed is *about* anything. The dull trick of substituting *is all about* for *consists in* or its equivalent is a sure way to bedim thought. For life does *not* consist in being kind to others. As for the rest, what we need to be told is what libraries *are for,* and which features *characterize* civilized travel. The ready-made phrase blocked these more complex ideas.

Verbal automatisms are by definition mindless and the important ones must be brought to consciousness. *Half . . . half* is one of those. To induce the public to drink sake, one advertiser evokes the samurai, "a breed of men half noble half warrior." Meaning? Another warns: "The 1 oz. supply is limited"—and so it is, limited to one ounce. Watch *limited:* it is a euphemism for *small* and often justified; one says "My means are limited" to suggest that one has budgeted the present outlay. "My time is limited" is politer than "Make it brief!" But in most situations, human affairs being what they are, the limitedness is inherent and stating it says nothing.

The opposite verbal tic is the *more than* superlative: "more than a supermarket, an experience." Of all forms of boast, the indefinite is the most irritating. Why should one send a child to "more than a college," buy one's wife "more than a perfume"? Must the second child go to "not just an art school"? It is obvious that "an experience" is vouchsafed by an ordinary supermarket too; indeed, by any conscious act. In the other cases the mind is tempted to make up satirical sequels: more than a college, a bordello as well. More than a perfume, a nerve gas besides. Descriptions, favorable or unfavorable, are undone by *any* thoughtlessness: "It is considered the *most definitive* biography." Never split a *definitive!* Meanings sometimes change when epithets are inflected: "The mayor's archest rival" is no longer an archrival (already a superlative)—he turns into a Southern belle.

Professional people who invariably use the same phrasing for recurrent facts should make sure that their words do not generate tautologies, contradictions, or puns: A judge giving a decision in favor of workers wrongly dismissed tells "what led to their termination." A reporter, having been cautioned about attributing crimes, writes that the official "committed alleged perjury." And the doctor describes the case as "permanently terminal." (It is, incidentally, the disease only that may be said to be *terminal;* the patient is, unfortunately, *terminated.* )

Not an excuse, but possibly a reason for the frequency of mindlessness in all of us who read print, is the amount of nonsense that has come to be tolerated in the "literature" our society emits as it goes. Political nonsense is only a small part of it: all activities that invite public attention now tend to address it in verbiage from which thought is absent. College brochures, charity appeals, propaganda for the local zoo or distant wildlife, annual reports from high-technology firms, short biographies in proxy statements or announcements of art exhibitions, blurbs on books, descriptions of goods in reputable catalogues, fliers stuffed with the invoices in the package or the monthly canceled checks—all these, and overt advertising too, regularly assault the mind with empty or fantasizing propositions and accustom us to think unmeaning thoughts. Our talk then echoes or imitates the same product without control. Every minute the mind must strain to reject the spurious, the anti-idea. For example, of three consecutive headings in a department store catalogue, accept: "The country-fresh look"; tolerate: "The citified safari look"; and spit out; "The uninhibited cotton casuals."

SOME PERSONAL REMARKS

As for giving thought to single words, take first the one that needs most attention these days: *personal*. Since the first edition of this book (see pages 128–129), it has become the emptiest sound in the language and the most frequent epithet outside slang. No argument is needed to show its pointlessness. Examples from the file are enough:

1. Be sure to take your personal belongings.
She runs a p. bookshop in the country.
The artist has contributed a p. and expressive text.
The p. apartment: rooms with a viewpoint.
5. I got a p. handwritten note.
He observed the boys' p. development.
His p. income is very large.
My own p. record at billiards is . . .
We'll send a truck for your p. furniture and carpets.
10. Well known for his p. eccentricities . . .
The new infantry helmet is called Personal Armor System.
It coiled itself round the tentacles of his p. disappointments.
Soon everybody will have their p. computer.
On Friday he called his p. accountant.
15. He was found lying in his p. office.
My most p. affairs . . .
On a p. note, I will be traveling extensively.
You mean you still don't have a p. banker?
They pointed out the p. value of his being appointed.
20. Together they write a column on p. health.

Each kept a p. diary.
The woman with whom he had a private, personal relationship . . .
To write a p. biography, one must . . .
By phone or mail or p. visit to the bureau . . .
    25. A repetition of her p. sufferings . . .
The bodyguard he referred to as his p. security force . . .
He knew everybody, either personally or professionally or both.
As I have met you personally . . .

What may be the cause of this obsession with *personal?* Does it make up for a sense of helpless anonymity or cater to the fantasy of ownership? Or is it simply echo at work? Several of the quoted phrases are certainly due to this last cause: In nos. 7, 15, and 16, the needed modifier is *private*—private income, private office, private affairs. It is likely that *private* is avoided nowadays as somehow undemocratic; it suggests secrecy and elitism. Surely, we must keep the orphaned word for many uses—the private sector, a private (not *personal*) secretary, the private eye in crime fiction and just as surely not "a personal diary," but a plain diary for our *private* thoughts. On one of Bernard Shaw's famous printed postcards was a polite apology for being "unable any longer to receive visits at his private residence except from his intimate friends." An American of today would very likely write: *personal* friends at his *personal* residence, which would be a pity. Note example no. 27, where the proper contrast within the man's acquaintance should be that he knew them "either *socially* or professionally or both," for he was bound to know them *personally* if he knew them at all.

Next among causes comes the misdirection of the word *person.* One has to guess what nos. 2, 6, 11, and 25 can possibly mean. In writing *personal* on an envelope, the clear instruction is: for the person addressed, no one else. But what is a "personal bookshop"? The adjective cannot by itself indicate the various relations of things to a, some, or any person. She runs a bookshop *in person,* herself/ the development of the boys' person(alities)/ armor to defend the person (body) —a meaning that occurs again in 26: a bodyguard for the security of his person. But of course, *body* and *armor* already imply *person* and it is foolish to repeat the idea. The army could say *individual* armor, to distinguish it from tanks and battleships, but in these two and all the rest of the examples, the person is already represented by other words—e.g., in "take your belongings" there is a *you* who is a person and *belongings* can then refer only to a person. How can I "have met you" otherwise than "personally"?

That leaves the thoughtless use of the word to suggest a quality not openly avowed. "Personal banker" insinuates the idea of "one's very own"; its contrary is not an *impersonal* banker (which might be a true description) but "public banker"—Tom, Dick, and Harry's—which every banker inevitably is. The other examples follow the same kind of roundabout implication, which is also present in *personalized* hairbrush (= monogrammed) and which winds up in the merely intensive use of nos. 5, 8, 10, 12, and so on: "personal" eccentricities or disappointments seem more intimately eccentric and bitterly disappointing (so to speak) in being flanked by this all-purpose word.

When tempted to use it, first ask: Do I mean *private?* then: Is the sense *in person*—e.g., the main actor of this film will appear *in person* at the premiere? Finally, test your true meaning by raising the contrary idea—would *impersonal* be appropriate in the reverse case? If none of these apply, omit *personal.* One more thing: the established phrase *personal appearance* will turn ambiguous unless one knows that idiom makes it mean *grooming*—physical looks and dress well cared for. If used to mean "X will turn up" (put in an appearance), there is, once again, no need of *personal.*

MAKE SENSE

*Make sense* is appropriate as a subheading for two reasons, not just the obvious one of reinforcing the recommendation to think. The second reason is that the words *make sense,* as commonly used, do not make sense but its opposite. In ninety-nine places out of a hundred they should be stricken out.

Why? Someone proposes a plan, offers a suggestion, describes his wishes or his hopes, whereupon his close friends immediately say to his face "Make sense!" and his enemies behind his back "It doesn't make sense." They are against the idea; it won't work. How do they know? The plan in fact *makes sense* or they could not discuss it. If something does not make sense, no judgment can be passed upon it except that it is unintelligible. To gibberish the only possible response is not "it won't work" but "I don't understand." In other words, the plan, proposal, suggestion, hopes, and wishes make such clear sense that they arouse disapproval, opposition, apprehension. The friends fear the result, the enemies want to dash the hopes: "Commodore Peary's plan to go to the North Pole doesn't make sense; he'll catch his death of cold."

A remark made by the father of a young woman injured during the fans' storming of the goalposts after a football game urged that colleges should prohibit the students' assault on these posts: "It just doesn't make sense." It did to the students and his meaning was "it isn't a sensible way to celebrate." If we catch his meaning, why object to the usage? Because, first, it blurs an important distinction. To act sensibly and to make sense are widely different forms of human behavior. And second, because the argument advanced in "it makes sense" or "it doesn't make sense" is a thought-stopper; it begs the question by praising or damning a statement when acting upon it may or may not be desirable—one can only argue for or against. The summary judgment of senselessness is bad enough in conversation; in writing, it becomes a kind of chicanery, like the notorious "it stands to reason"; or the debater's claim that he is *realistic* and everybody else, by implication, a fool. (See NOTE on page 250.)

SECOND THOUGHTS ARE REALLY THE FIRST ONES

When we say "revise," it is likely that what we are referring to is in fact our first careful look at our written text. Perhaps we should say "vise," for in the actual writing we are thinking more of the object, the "model," as our parallel with drawing suggested on page 208, and not of the "pencil sketch" growing under our hands.

So until we are truly practiced writers, the recommendation to take thought applies to the words already on paper. It is not enough to go over them several times with enjoyment and approval, happy that the chore is over and that *believe* and *receive* have been spelled right, or that most plural subjects have been awarded plural verbs. At this point it is not mechanics that matter, or surface polish; it is substance itself. It must be looked at in a "know-nothing" spirit: "What is the fool trying to say?"—the fool being one's humble self.

It is noteworthy that when readers scan the writing of others for faults, the first thing they find (other than misprints and trifles) is mixed metaphors. "This field of research is so virginal that no human eye has ever set foot on it."/ "They believed the manager would be dismissed because of the negative atmosphere that engulfed the team last season." The first sentence offers clashing images; the second is incoherent and dim—atmospheres don't engulf, especially when negative. Either one of them makes the reader sit up and perhaps comment by laughter. But to revise one's own work thoroughly, one must see deeper into one's ideas than their expression in clashing images; one must think in the same carping way about abstract relations. That is one reason why one must be familiar with both the meaning and the scope of words: they can clash in their outriggers of sense without raising ludicrous images—or any images at all. "The narrative shown on your new bank statement provides sufficient [= gives enough] detail." If there is one thing that is not a *narrative*, it is a bank statement. "The governor will unveil his proposed mass transit plan"/ "To end up with she unveiled a chocolate soufflé." Neither of these

---

NOTE ALSO pages 128–129 and: make history (every event, big or little, does that)/ more than an answering service/ They tell you how to deport yourself/ I have personally been involved in a large number of criminal cases, as a prosecuting attorney, as a defendant, and as a federal judge/ Due to a printing error, the enclosed poster replaces the one previously printed/ The most important days of your life in relationship to your enjoyment and your wealth—all tax deductible/ examines Jack Dempsey and Jack Johnson in terms of the symbols which they represented/ Fasten seatbelt while seated (i.e., don't try it standing up in the aisle)/ We are known for our low prices, fully matched by the quality of our goods/ A tired and failed path to peace/ He returns the ball hopefully for a touchdown/ That kind of thing is shunned by the annals of the great/ Into that tragic morass sails Ronald Reagan . . ./ Chinese Press Tries to Mend Soiled Image/ Children under 12 with an adult made possible by Manufacturers Hanover Trust.

---

things is unveilable; the word remains concrete except for figurative uses close to the palpable—"unveiled his spirit to his followers" or the like. Similarly, "A Library of Ingenuity" will not do for a display of mechanical devices: *library* = books or their near relatives, and by no stretch of sense can it go with the abstraction *ingenuity.*

The next step in thought-full revision is to draw implications beyond what the words say. An art gallery that puts up the notice "Many of these paintings by fine artists" informs the public that some of the canvases are by daubers. The common street sign "Bus Stop— No Standing" overlooks the pedestrian's unwillingness to crouch or lie down while waiting for a bus; it sees only the motorist's urge to *park.* A play on words that is not perceived will produce misplaced humor; e.g., apropos of a housing scheme: "As for the midtown proposal, the *premises* are not valid anymore." Terms used close together must fit at all points or they will counteract each other: "A divergence of views as far as the immediate future is concerned." *Far* leads one way and *immediate* the other. *On* or *about* would have put it without any false lead. Or again, more subtly: "The Board is trying to contend that . . ." The board may be trying to *say,* or to *prove,* but it can only contend or not contend. In reverse, two close words should not duplicate *(peculiar idiosyncrasies)* and cause a moment's hesitation to see whether a shade of meaning is intended. Unnecessary variants always puzzle. In the following, which is which piece of writing?—"The passage was plagiarized from a well-known work in the field and occurs in a paper already accepted for publication. It covers only one page of the monograph." Other types of loose wording cover too much and again leave us wondering what is what. The dreary phrase "meaningful relationship," someone pointed out, could refer to the mutual attachment of a hunter and his dog or even to the union of hydrogen and oxygen in water. Is the fact a serious love affair? If so, it deserves a plainer, stronger term, such as—love affair. If it is friendship, collaboration, partnership, say it in those words.

COHERENCE FROM RIGHT CONSTRUCTION

In writing English, thought is always needed as to the placing not of words only, but of the longer parts of the sentence. A prime example of this truth is the statement on the medicine bottle: "Take one pill three times a day," which is a physical impossibility, whereas "Three times a day take one pill" is what the doctor really ordered. I do not suggest that the old phrasing be changed, for everybody corrects it in practice, but the example is worth remembering for the occasions where the placement principle matters.

The same kind of scrutiny must be brought to bear on meanings determined by grammar and syntax. The familiar sequence "just because . . . does not mean that . . ." is flawed by incoherence. Whatever "does not mean" must be a fact, a condition, a state of things resulting from a cause—e.g., illness. The cause itself ("just because he is ill") is not a result but a reason: "Just because he is ill he should be forgiven." In the false construction the thought has twisted in mid-flight and must be unwound. Less common but of the same species is this oddity: "Soon we were more at our ease than any other drink can make the high-strung." The "more at ease" calls for naming a standard—"than we expected," "than our visitors." We are offered instead a second uncompleted comparison, between drinks, and the original one is left dangling. This false linking across a chasm of thought is another form of the more usual wrong juxtaposition: "The girl was repeatedly kicked in the head by a man wearing heavy-soled shoes after going into a woman's rest room." (See pages 58–59.)

And of course, the so-called dangling participle ("unattached" would be a better term, as Follett points out in *Modern American Usage*) exhibits the same inattention: "Being that nobody finished to the goal, the race was canceled." *Being that* is a fatal way to begin *any* sentence; nothing acceptable can follow it; and what follows here is not thought out, for the race was not *canceled* if the contestants ran and failed to finish it. The race was declared null and void. Bad, because unattached, openings occur in two forms with *Based on.* One of these has a shadow of coherence in it: "Based on his past record, he can hope to persuade the voters." Some agent is at least *basing himself*—and the thought should be so worded. As it stands, its grammar reads: "he, based on his past, can hope"; and so far, *based* has not acquired the abstract sense of *relying, counting on.* But in the commonest usage, *based* does not even come close to linking ideas properly: "Based on prior experience, the losers are expected to file federal and state appeals."/ "Based on what *we* know, *it* is too soon to act." This last sentence shows the unwillingness to use short, straight words: "*From* what we know . . ." In the earlier example, *based* is ambiguous: who has the "prior experience"—the losers or the reporter who is guessing what they will do?

*Base*-minded writers evidently yearn for a single word that will enable them to introduce the source of their forecast or decision. There is no such word, for the good reason that each instance implies a slightly different idea—*from, on, with, because of.* We saw just now how *from* would satisfy us in front of *what we know;* in the political sentence, the word should be *on:* "On his past record, he can hope . . ." In the next, according to the meaning: "Experience shows that the losers . . ."; or, "Experience will doubtless lead the losers . . ." Unfortunately, faith in the power of any first thought to couple itself correctly with the next is as strong as it is unwarranted: "So what that some women earn more than their husbands?" To which the matching answer might ring out with equal coherence: "Three cheers that they do."

DOUBLE-TALK UNPREMEDITATED

Revision almost invariably shows that one began by setting down in good faith words that are capable of two meanings, as in the "based on experience" just discussed. The cause of this lapse lies in the very freedom that English permits. Without case endings and signs of gender (see page 235), words keep or lose their aim by position alone, and some words are less virtuous than others. *As,* for example, is easily seduced: "The control group were not on a whole-milk diet, as the report says." Does the report say they were (and I say they weren't)? Or does the *as* clause support the statement? This sort of doubt is obviously serious in science, law, and scholarship generally. The cure is to put the clause first: "As the report says, the group were not . . ." If the report is being disputed, then an adversative is needed: "*Though* the report says . . ."

Comparable confusion often occurs in relative clauses, with or without *that* or some other pronoun. Ambiguity comes when there is a pair of possible antecedents: "a beautiful part of the country that she has never seen." What has she not seen—the part or the country? "A number of properties with buildings and businesses which were lost through mismanagement . . ." State what was lost. The only remedy is to recast: "She has never seen the country, of which this is a beautiful part"/ "A number of properties, all lost . . ."; or, "properties, on which were buildings and businesses subsequently lost . . ."; or, a last possibility, "properties with buildings on them, in which businesses were later lost through mismanagement."

Yet another important source of ambiguity is the careless use of verbs, notably the indicative where the subjunctive should be, and the misplaced auxiliary *may*. In England, for a generation or more, writers have thoughtlessly accepted such sentences as: "It was important that he *asked* the question tactfully" where American usage (and clear thought) demand *that he ask* (= that he should ask). The English sentence is bad because there is a sense, not the intended one, in which it can be right: the question *was* asked tactfully and it was important to note the fact. But of course the desired meaning, which requires *that he should ask,* is of an action not yet accomplished. Verbs such as *urge, call for, suggest, concern, insist, demand,* and their nouns, will bring on ambiguity wherever the wobbly English practice is followed of using the past or present indicative in the sequel. "The courts insist that those procedures are followed." Are they followed or should they *be* followed? "It is essential that the patient has no fever"; i.e., if you use this drug, it's essential that he *have* no fever; or else: it is essential (to my diagnosis) that he *has* none, right now, as I look at him.

That in the U.S. the *be* (or *should be*) is still instinctive is shown by its frequent correct use in news items and quotations from officials: "It is not desirable that he *remain* . . ."/ "It was specified that the tenant *give* assurances." But the feeling for *may* and *might,* which is also a matter of time sequence, is noticeably weakening. "I thought you *may* need them" (this from a good novelist, not writing dialect). "It *may* have been an extended thing if it had not run into disaster" (from a congressman). "He says in a letter he *may* have been happier as a grocer" (from a biographer). In this last case the ambiguity is flagrant. As written, the words imply he was a grocer at one time; he thinks now that he may have been happier then. But the facts are that he merely thinks he *might* have been happier as a grocer had he chosen that calling. As for the congressman, speaking of an armed landing, his foggy thought was: It *might* have been a long struggle if it had not run at once into disaster.

## WORDS POINT: FOLLOW THE ARROW

The most general advice about revising is that one must follow where written words themselves lead, not where one would like them to go. Here are several cases of the need: "In some places the poor black youngsters are approaching the writing skills of their white peers." Since *peers* means *equals,* whatever the subject involved, it is obvious that *approaching* conflicts with *peers.* The youngsters are not equal in writing, so far. How are they peers? In age, probably, and that fact must be set down to make the report signify.

In the next case, equality is invoked in another way: "X is surely correct in presenting the reasons for . . . But he is equally incorrect in asserting that . . ." If correct on point one, can X be equally *in*correct on point two? The writer wanted his *equally* to hark back to *surely* (= just as surely incorrect), but nine readers out of ten will interpret the words as meaning *incorrect again.* If measurement is needed, better say: "To the same degree, he is incorrect . . ."

Finally, consider the epithets that express indignation at a murder during robbery, an assassination, or a terrorist attack: "a senseless crime," "a cowardly deed." Owing to the frequency of such events, the phrases come forth as by reflex. But a moment's thought shows that in a political killing, or to avoid capture, or in holding hostages, the motive may be shortsighted, vicious, revolting, but it is not senseless; and in assassinations and acts of terrorism where the doers sacrifice their lives, the deed may be cruel or treacherous, but cowardly it is not.

Keeping categories straight goes beyond matters of language; it affects individual belief and state policy. And as these instances show, confusion of subjects and stating false conclusions come first from words ill-chosen or ill-placed, some of which turn into clichés contrary to fact. (See NOTE on page 256.)

## WHY DISTINCTIONS MUST BE MAINTAINED

A language grows rich by distinguishing, through different words, between pairs of feelings or ideas or sensations that are close but in some respects unlike. For example, *wet* and *damp* distinguish degrees of the same sensory experience. Nobody questions the utility of telling

NOTE ALSO pages 136–141 and: They were fast friends, having been co-equal almost from birth in everything they did/ The specter of sharply rising interest rates, of choked-off investment, and of renewed recession . . ./ They contain statements such as "not noncaloric," to warn . . ./ Our extensive Treasury of Fine Homes . . ./ As a participant in the distribution program, we are pleased to send you . . ./ His immediate priority is to make sure that life is extinct/ The increase has been largely due to in-migration from Massachusetts/ Basically, this bird is on the wrong side of the ocean/ We don't realize how important it is that our memory functions quickly and effectively/ One crisis has tripped over another all over the world/ It is my concern that more young people are trained as scientists/ Includes "Stars and Stripes Forever," "La Marseillaise," and six more spirited works by others/ Joe's death is a tremendous shock—to himself, to the firm, to his family, and to the community as a whole.

---

these two apart; and when thinking of them for his purpose, the wide-awake writer will further ask himself whether he does not mean *moist* rather than *damp.* In the realms of feeling and of thought, distinctions have also been established by the hundreds. Not being physical, they seem more elusive, but persons who read good writing learn them automatically and find them indispensable. *Annoyed, irritated, vexed, gravelled, angry, furious, outraged* distinguish not only rising degrees of a familiar emotion but also different elements of it that are called forth by different situations. Among ideas, *persuade* and *convince, assure* and *ensure,* are distinguishing pairs, not interchangeable.

Obviously we must think in order to choose the right word; but in return, its being there to use enables us to think more accurately. All thought, like all writing, is discrimination—separating ideas and, by means of a word, assigning to each the feature that matters in the present case. It has been said that one difficulty with distinctions of thought is that they are usually lodged in very similar words—*ostensi-*

*ble* and *ostentatious, incredible* and *incredulous, precipitous* and *precipitate, perspicuous* and *perspicacious.* But that is what we should expect when closeness of idea is at the source and when the distinguishing has come about slowly, after some writers and speakers had discovered the need for it. In the beginning, *disinterested* and *uninterested* were used indiscriminately; later, the perception that there were two kinds of "lack of interest" led to a differentiation we have latterly had the honor of sabotaging.

Nor is it true that verbal similarity is the cause of blurred distinctions. Every commonplace idiom resembles some other in sound or form, yet most native speakers keep them apart without effort: they put up *at* a wayside inn, where they put up *with* the local bore; they may *feel chilly* in the country, but when they *feel a chill,* they know the difference. No; the failure to distinguish properly and the consequent destruction of crystallized differences in thought and feeling come from ignorance, usually the result of inattention, often compounded with pretentiousness. Why use *perspicacious* or *euphuistic* (thinking it has to do with *euphemism*) when one does not know their meaning? All distinctions have to be learned, even the obvious ones; few, if any, are intelligible at sight; they are usually shown in some small part of the word—which is no excuse for overlooking it. If a writer or speaker confused a *draft board* with a *drafting board,* would anyone maintain that the trifling *-ing* should not stand in the way of spontaneous utterance? The two cautions not to be forgotten are: No two words in the language mean exactly the same thing; and: Do not guess at the meaning of a word from its looks.

A distinction which is being regrettably manhandled is that between *strategy* and *tactics.* Literary critics, always in search of flossy new terms to express they know not what, started a while ago to write of the author's *strategies* in a poem or play. The plural is a blunder to begin with: there is only one strategy—one general plan—for each piece of work, as there is for a battle or campaign. What is done at each line or section in a literary effort (in battle, each sector or period during the fight) is *tactics.* This last word is the one that journalists picked up earlier as a gaudy synonym for *move* or *step;* and since these simpler words are what was really called for, writers felt the need to make their great find singular—*tactic.* So here we have two words of different number for a very precise reason, which ignorance inverts and misuses. Critics and reporters, moreover, show us that they have gone on to make the terms synonymous: "To get the job you want, you must think over your interview strategies"/ "The tactic of wearing out her patience by indecisions [*sic*] did not pay off."/ "Shakespeare's strategies in the last two acts are controversial."

The value of distinctions is such that the painstaking writer will look for those not yet noted or not apparent on the surface and will observe them scrupulously in his own prose. The distinctions we now have grew in no other way. Here is one for adoption: we read of "drug abuse" among teenagers, soldiers, young criminals, and others. *Abuse* properly means "excessive use"; if so, perhaps all the peoples of the Western world are chargeable with *drug abuse:* we doctor ourselves with drugs for every mood or indisposition. Drug *addiction* is the word for those who regularly rely on narcotics for pleasure or for enduring the tedium of life. Because distinctions are a natural product of the human mind, the reader of a passage in which the right ones are employed will feel the resulting clarity and *distinctness,* even though he himself has not consciously marked the differences conveyed. It is this consciousness that he must develop and there is no royal road to it, only attention to the words in which perceptive minds have, as it were, registered their observation of unlikeness.

A GROSS FAILURE AND ITS SEQUEL: "GENDER"

As with every other misuse of verbal resources, neglect of distinctions leads to trouble later on, whether the failure is individual or collective. Consider the sudden vogue of *gender* as a word to denote what is properly *sex*. This very sentence has now a startling effect, because of the confusion that overtook *sex* in the 1920s. It was then that the three-letter word was made to stand for *sexuality* (sexual impulse, sexual act). It flourished in "sex appeal," from which came in turn "to have sex" and "the joy of sex," "oral sex"—in English: making love and the pleasure of it.

Before this verbal sex debauch, the word *sex* denoted the physical and other characteristics of either half of humankind, as well as other species. *Sex* in its root meaning says nothing more than "cut"—the whole human creature being thought of as divided in two. People accordingly used to speak of "the fair sex," meaning women, and even "the sex," indicating its preeminence. In that original sense of the word, everybody "has sex," day and night, indefeasibly, and *unisex* is non-sense.

Now see what followed. When the feminist movement renewed its struggle in recent decades, *sex* had to be resorted to in something like its forgotten guise. *Sexism* has nothing to do with copulation—just the reverse; it means making of sex a cause of pride, contempt, injustice. "Sexual politics" does not signify promotion or power obtained through sexual favors. At meetings of learned societies, "Sexual Poetics" and "The Role of Sex in Victorian Fiction" deal with social attitudes, not bodily ecstasy. In short, *sex* and *sexual* have in half a century become thoroughly ambiguous—whence the desperate recourse to *gender* in hopes of clearing up the mess.

"My gender travels with me," declared the first woman judge appointed to the New York State Supreme Court. The *gender gap* now seen and heard of daily presumably means the unequal treatment of women in employment. "These remarks," cautioned a public official, "should not be taken as an attack on your gender." The White House is said to be "Facing the Gender Gap with Conflicting Advice." But if it is also true that "Susan Anthony's political strategy was to create and sustain a Republican gender gap," it becomes difficult to assign a precise meaning to the phrase. Leaving out the increasingly mindless use of *gap,* one is tempted to conclude that *gender* = female sex; that is, only women have *gender.* One writer assumes such a fact when he refers to "the harsh truth that men are deficient versions of the basic gender."

Where does that leave *sex?* A headline announces: " 'A Matter of Sex,' Story of a Bank Strike" (by eight women employees seeking their rights). Does that archaic use of *sex* convey the idea? The word is surely ready for discard. In its last stronghold, science, I have found one clear case of its demise: a paper on a biological topic recently given before a scientific academy speaks of "species in which adults are able to change gender." *Sex* has become a dirty word.

But the annexation of *gender,* which has always belonged to the grammar books, is not a happy one, even if it were for a clear purpose. It creates difficulties as it goes. If *gender* is to be solely the attribute of women, and *sex* that of men (since only men are accused of sexist behavior), then the redefined "war of the sexes" becomes "gender *versus* sex" and some new terms will be needed for the sexual function in its traditional form—all this, if we are consistent. If we are not, the whole range of distinct subjects, from descriptive biology to love to social equality, will be in perpetual confusion. We have the proof in the utterly misleading title "A Matter of Sex," quoted above.

Nor is this all. If *gender* continues to be used in grammar, it will most readily suggest "feminine" or at least an inherent trait in nouns and other words that must agree with nouns, instead of denoting arbitrary *forms* which often disagree with fact and which vary from language to language. In German the (female) maiden is neuter, the moon masculine, and the sun feminine; in French the moon is feminine and the sun masculine, while in English both are neuter. And Latin and Greek genders vary similarly irrespective of sex *and* fact: a male poet in Latin is *poeta* and a sailor *nauta,* words of feminine-gender form. In short, gender has nothing to do with sex. Gender is syntactic, sex is notional; one is grammar, the other nature. In the many languages that make use of gender, it may indicate a variety of differences other than sex—human and not human, animate and inanimate, for example. In Bedauyo, an African language, a woman's breast is masculine, a man's feminine—because it is smaller.

Not all confusions are as far-reaching as this present one, fortunately. Yet even the limited are annoying. Take the important subject of money. Some years ago, *financial* and *fiscal* began to be used interchangeably. Hospital directors would speak of their "fiscal difficulties," probably because their income and expenses were computed within the "fiscal year." The distinction thus destroyed robs us of a handy way to tell apart the money matters of the government *(fiscal)* from those of the country *(financial).* The nation may be in fiscal but not financial trouble. The Federal Reserve, in fiddling with the money supply, uses *financial* means to end a recession; the Congress, in raising or lowering taxes, uses *fiscal* measures. Think how *economically* information could be conveyed if the difference were preserved! (See NOTE on page 261.)

INITIALS ARE RUDE TO READERS

Since ideas can be expressed by other means than words, the question arises, how far and how often to mix words fully written out with one or more systems of abbreviations or symbols. The first rule of courtesy

NOTE ALSO: Other distinctions worth grasping firmly: advance and advancement/ persuade and convince (the former is the advocacy, the latter its result; hence, never "I convinced him to buy the house," but "I persuaded him," "my arguments convinced him")/ sensuous and sensual/ visiting and visitation/ power (verb) and empower (hence, not "so dull as to empower a yawn")/ resource and recourse/ feasible and possible/ historic and historical/ defenseless and indefensible/ and the bad confusion of oversee, oversight, overlook (the mistake, the valley), look over (the trinkets, the hedge)/ and finally, the unintended rudeness in the would-be polite "my pleasure." The form "it is my pleasure to" means "I choose to" and it is patronizing. Kings and queens might use it, as they do: "I am pleased to dub you knight." English judges serve "at Her Majesty's pleasure" —i.e., as long as she chooses. The courteous forms for everybody else are: I have the pleasure of . . . ; I take pleasure in . . . ; I have just had the pleasure of meeting her.

suggests itself at once: use only those initials or symbols that have become conventional. That defining word, which denotes agreement beforehand, is applicable in two forms, the universal and the special. Usage has established the meaning of such abbreviations as *i.e., e.g., p.,* and a number of others; they must be learned by anyone who wants to be fully literate, for they will be found in ordinary print. These signs are "universal" within the English language and some of them in other languages as well. The several trades and professions have made conventional other sets of abbreviations and symbols. These are similarly current and indispensable for reading the professional journals. At the edges, any two sets may overlap. The general public has learned *mph* for miles per hour, *g* for gram, *km* for kilometer, $H_2O$ for water, QED for "which was to be proved," the plus, minus, and equal signs from algebra, and so forth.

The number of these inarticulate triggers of thought, to which we respond without noticing that they are not words, is very large. Latterly, groups and individuals have tried to add to it, for their convenience and at the expense of the public's. It has seemed clever and promotional to name causes and organizations by initials, some of these being called acronyms when they form a recognizable but irrelevant word—SHAPE, NOW, CARE. A recent one, AIDS, denoting a syndrome that kills, would be callously ghoulish if those who make up such "words" stopped to think and feel.

The mania then overtook writers dealing with any subject in which some degree of repetition was necessary, and they now freely substitute for intelligible names a set of initials made up *ad hoc* and used only in the particular book or article. In modern biographies one may find oneself reading about the different opinions of HJ1 and HJ2 or the passionate affair between GC and EW. Do you read TAD, *The Armchair Detective,* or TAD, *The Anglican Digest?* Perhaps both, in which case be careful when the subscription renewal notice comes around. In books about different institutions of a like kind—say, philanthropic organizations—the reader is bewildered by clusters resembling ciphers in crime fiction: the RBF being an offshoot of the GEB, which became the RFB, and the Executive Committee of the Board of the CEIP turning into the ECCEIP, matched by the EC's of the other B's of the aforesaid RBF and RFB. (These are actual examples.) After much less than a chapter—after six paragraphs of this sort—the most willing reader is exhausted. For one thing, these initials do not, like words, make familiar ideograms readable at a glance; and for another, they overlap confusingly. If the reader pushes on, it is likely he will attend only to the general drift, unconcerned with the particulars.

The conventional abbreviations and a growing list of the institutional initials are recorded in both regular and specialized dictionaries, but it is clear that none of these can hope to be complete, let alone up to date. And too often, the reader who consults such a work will remain unsatisfied: the set of initials is there but their decipherment does not fit. He looks up (let us say) BLT, encountered in a release from the DOD Commission on the Marines (COM) and turns up only: "Bacon, lettuce, and tomato sandwich"; the Bureau of Labor Statistics masquerades as the Bachelor of Library Science, and the NC's range from nitrocellulose, nurse corps, and North Carolina to New Caledonia, Navy Cross, New Church, and No Charge. One sometimes wishes that man, having invented the alphabet, would go on to produce words.

A group of resisters has formed in Washington to repress the further growth of initials in government work, where the uncontrolled production has begun to generate grave errors. But it is not enough to cry out and make fun. A remedy must be found, and it is quite simple. The currency of acronyms and their unspeakable cousins incites to the formation of long names for every new organization, process, or fugitive idea. Heaven only knows what the Red Cross would have been called if recently founded, or the Salvation Army. So the first step is to promote as a new chic short names—single words preferred. They are memorable from the word go: Prudential, Boy Scouts, Winter Olympics, Green Berets, instantly evoke images and associated ideas. Who can name correctly the words behind SHEAF and SALT, UNESCO and NATO (National Association of Taxi Owners), and what images do they raise?

With short words—this is step number two—repetition in a text is much less cumbersome; nobody minds writing or reading at close intervals: the Senate, the White House, Princeton (University), the Rotary Club, etc. With longer names that cannot be changed now, the third step is taken: forbid yourself the use of initials. Leave them to Euclid, whose only topic is angle BEF, but who at least provides a diagram for easy reference. The good writer, faced with a sesquipedalian institutional designation, has no need to repeat it at every turn. Once it has been given, he can say: the Fund, the Board, its executive committee, the directors, this body, they, etc. He must of course take care not to cross the trails of two organizations and produce ambiguity. But for this purpose, too, brevity will work: "Meanwhile, the *Merridew people* started a new program." The reader will much more readily catch cross-references from abridged names or synonyms than from a forest of initials.

Indeed, part of the craft of writing consists in knowing what readers will carry easily in their heads after one mention. To remember and to strain to remember are vastly different acts of mind—as is shown by one's impatience with the overdetailing storyteller or the writer who does not know what to skip.

SIGNS TOO OFTEN SLOVENLY

A desirable side effect of the proposed remedy is that it reaffirms the primacy of language. Ideally, good prose should be all words, an aim that has been honored in the modern tendency to reduce punctuation to the minimum. Do not, therefore, regress to the inarticulate by succumbing to either of two bad habits of recent growth. One is seen in "From 1914–1918 war raged in Europe." That is, strictly speaking, unreadable, for one does not normally verbalize hyphens into the word *to*. What one silently voices on looking at a tombstone is: "Henry Fielding, seventeen nine, seventeen fifty-four" —nothing between the dates. Likewise with the hyphen: "the war of nineteen fourteen eighteen"—from which it follows that the illiteracy above is read: "From nineteen fourteen eighteen war raged in Europe."

If anybody thinks that the hyphen should regularly replace *to*, then we must begin to write: "the boys stood back–back, comparing height"; "she is going out–shop"; and possibly, "–be or not –be."

The second malpractice with signs makes use of the slash or virgule (/) to avoid deciding on *or, and, with:* "the reader/writer"; "a husband/wife team"; "the rate for parent/child is 10% less." It is not merely a matter of looks. Ambiguity lies in wait behind the apparent shortcut: "For the same price as the bed/breakfast option the guest has a lunch/dinner one." How many comforts are offered here and at what price? Can one take two meals and no bed? Within a single sentence the slash means or may mean *and* and *or* in the sense of *either but not both,* and *option* is made intolerably ambiguous. In *Finnish Design/Past,* the suppression of *in the* betrays the poseur, and gives *past* the connotation of *over and done with,* instead of the desired contrast with *new* or *latest.*

There is a use for the slash, notably in books of reference or instruction. It is exemplified in these very pages, where quoted phrases or sentences follow one another to illustrate a point. The slash replaces the period (or semicolon) that would be required and thus reduces cluttered punctuation. Elsewhere, it replaces the two sets of quotation marks. Incidentally, the recourse to *and/or,* which was always unnecessary and often confusing, seems to have lessened a little (though I find a lecture entitled "Philosophy and/as/of Literature") and it is certain that the matching *if/when* was short-lived. With these killed or maimed, let us make an effort to get rid of this slash/virgule menace.

WOLVES IN WORDS' CLOTHING

A curious fact about the use of signs in prose is the latter-day tendency that has run counter to the one just noted. Some fifty or sixty years ago, typographers began a war of extermination on the hyphen and the dieresis. Readers had to adjust to such false visual leads as *coop* (eration) and *nono*(bjective). The theory was that words for single ideas must be written without mark or break. Some writers—notably John Dos Passos—found the notion irresistibly modern and began to write *picturegallery* and *sidewalkcafe.* Since the genius of the English language is to use nouns freely as descriptive modifiers of other nouns, one could expect an endless series of agglutinated terms—*dancehall, showerbath, armycot, millendremnant,* to say nothing of *onnoaccount* and other negatives—English à la Eskimo.

Perhaps the depth of irresponsibility in linguistic innovation is to be found in a recently published biographical dictionary of poets and dramatists—presumably a work of scholarship—in which author and publisher have permitted themselves to print *BeaumontnFletcher, FletchernMassinger,* and the like to designate collaborators. Besides the discourtesy to the dead authors and the present readers, the point to note is the egocentric shortsightedness of these inventive minds. They do not see that they are setting an example which the habit of parallelism, so useful to language, invites us to extend to *Whiskeynsoda, lifendeath,* etc., thereby eliminating the word *and,* as well as the civilized practice of spacing words and names no matter how often they are thought of together.

Good sense has generally prevailed against system, yet the reader of print has had to grow accustomed to cryptic compounds, nonwords, and the disregard of commas and apostrophes. The aping of Joyce's amalgams has become general, as we saw in the tacking on of *-thon* and *-tron* to any handy word. In the daily paper and not alone in technical journals, one comes across *monodispense, macrodimension, subtopia,* and other unmeaning monsters. In novels, a new affectation is to leave adjectives in series without commas: "Her slim pale medieval hands." In business names, the apostrophe is taboo: the Farmers Cooperative, the Bankers Trust, etc. Suppose a Sailors Relief Society soliciting funds, would it explain the ways in which it comes to the *sailors relief* or would it yield to custom and punctuate right?

If omitting customary signs is uncivil, the opposite—using unfamiliar ones—is equally so. Readers would justifiably protest if a story read: "The captain then ordered the . . . – – – . . . to be given." Morse is not yet required for the high school diploma or bachelor's degree. In English, no vowels bear accents and none should intrude in common print. It is a pity that a desire for pseudo-accuracy prevented the assimilation through respelling of *cliché, naïve, negligee, bête noire, schwärmerei, chiaroscuro, mañana,* and the rest. In Shakespeare's time and even later, we would have had *cleeshay* (as we have *sashay*), *nave, svermery,* or some such approximations showing full adoption into the language.

But lately we have done worse in the way of pedantic display. Encyclopedias and other reference books now carry articles in which mention is made of Muḥammad and the Qur'ān. The dot under the *h,* though useless to us, is no obstruction, but that other word concealing the well-known Koran, while meant as a courtesy to Islam, is an insult to anyone's intelligence. For the affectation of correctness is wasted on the English reader; it only makes him wonder how to pronounce the fake Arabic. It is twice a fake, because it is not in Arabic characters and because in English a *qu* with a following consonant and an apostrophe between *r* and *a* are meaningless—like the mark over the *a.*

This example forms part of a larger issue. Over and over again, we are expected to learn foreign words and names of which the pronunciation is at variance with the spelling. We had to say Khrushch*off* when it read Khrushch*ev, Jung* Kaishek when it read *Chiang;* now it is W*a*l*ensa* for W*a*l*esa, Mewosh* for *Milosz, Lednitsky* for *Lednicki, Auda* for (Hungarian) *Ade,* and so on. We have to insert a *y* in Dostoevsky and we are told that if we say *Omar Khayyám* by the light of nature and our own alphabet, we utter in the second word something which in Persian is obscene. The entire theory of modern transliteration is highbrow absurdity. The Chinese have shown it to be so when they bade us change *Mao Tse-tung* to *Mao Zedong* and translettered their other leaders' names in such a way that we can utter sounds approximately right.

For the word *transliteration* means supplying in one language the letter that will in effect correspond to the role of the original. To spell Qur'ān in a *Britannica* or an *Americana* corresponds to nothing whatever, since *Qur'* does not signal anything intelligible in our speech. What are we to make of *Qaddafi?* Is it *Kwa* or *Ka?* The regular scheme, no *q* without a *u,* no *qu* without a vowel following, must be clung to as a guide we cannot spare. When the letters in the foreign tongue determine our spelling because those letters look like ours, we have neither a word of ours nor one of theirs. Although educated readers have learned to say *off* when they see *ov,* that is about as far as higher education can take us.

If it is objected that spelling for our convenience would be provincial, self-centered, discourteous, the answer is that, on the contrary, respect for others' ways is shown by good attempts at matching their pronunciation, and this is made impossible by using spellings that look as if designed to make people say the wrong thing. In addition, putting accents that only specialists can interpret is sheer scholar's blindness. With French accents almost the only ones familiar (in a vague way), what is a reader to make of *Kâmpóng Saôm?* Is he not less provincial, more "global," if he is guided by the alternative *Kompong Som?* Indeed, it would be even better if *Saôm* were to be given as *Soam.*

More generally still, names established in the language should be left alone, in speech and writing both. We rightly say *Parriss* and *Bur-linn* instead of fooling around with *Paree* and *Bare-leen,* where the *r*'s and *l*'s as well as the vowels would be travesties of the real thing. That goes for the wild distortions of an earlier day—*Venice, Florence, Leghorn, Austria,* the *Dutch,* the *French,* the *Germans,* the *Spanish* and their *sherry,* which disregarded the natives' jealous claim to *Venezia, Firenze, Livorno, Oesterreich, Jerez,* and the rest. In their turn, the French (not *les Français*) are entitled to their *Londres* for *London* and "Aytazunee," which don't sound much like *United States.* Likewise, we should continue to say *Mohammed* (the former *Mahomet* having succumbed to an earlier pedantry); *Koran;* "*Charlemayne*" (*-magne* is not in our power); Don *Quix*ote and Don *Joo*en as spelled; *Cicero* and not *Kickero*—in short, follow usage instead of trying to be more meticulose than our ancestors. (See NOTE on page 268.)

NOTE ALSO pages 26, 119, 193–196, and: "Timbuctu, spelled Timbuctoo in Britain"/ "In Manhattan, the central business district (CBD)"/ "Owner/drivers of these cars should know"/ "Consent and involvement in the design of family life/sex education programs"/ "Attitude, Preparation, Innovation, Enthusiasm, factors which I call the A-PIE concept"/ "The Conference on baptism, the Eucharist, and Ministry (BEM), on peace and politics (PP), and the dialogue with the Orthodox Russian Church (LORD) were scheduled for the same week"/ "From ASH a decade ago, things have now gone on to GASP, to PUFF and even to CIGARS"/ "If you wish for a full list of these books, just send a SASE" (bookshop ad).

A company that makes motor vehicles has the non-word Flxible among its product names and has seduced the press into reproducing the affront. It should be changed and properly *ee*sed into print./ "It is being earnestly argued in Greece that Greeks are not Greeks but should everywhere be called Hellenes. . . . If 'Greece' were expurged from the lexicon . . . how would Byron sound . . . 'the isles of the Hellenes, the isles of the Hellenes . . .' Would it be said of Shakespeare that he had 'small Latin and less of the Hellenic language?' "

CHOOSINESS, NOT NEEDLESS FUSS

We come back to our starting point: of all the words, non-words, and imitation words that flit before our eyes or invade consciousness through the ear, which shall we choose to convey our thoughts, in print or letter form or conversation? Writers could adopt without a change the motto "Eternal vigilance is the price of liberty," because they are sure to find ease in their work in exact proportion as they are watchful about words. But it does not follow that in writing or any other art one cannot overdo critical care. Prose is good only if it sounds easy, and when the subject prevents its seeming spontaneous, it should at least be natural.

That is the reason why in letter writing and conversation, where the colloquial is both proper and desirable, one must play a double game —avoid the jargon and creeping malaprops of the moment and at the same time not sound like a book, or even like an article. Practice develops the sense of where care ends and fussiness begins. Not long ago, a columnist who settles questions of life, love, and etiquette was asked by "Accuracy in Speech": "Does a person 'make a bed' or 'dress a bed'?" This sort of worry is pathetic; a little reflection would cure it: "The bed was unmade," not "undressed." No one is going to suppose that "make a bed" means constructing it.

Similarly, do not fuss about the placing of modifiers when the sense is unmistakable. "A Big Welcome Hug" is as good as "A Big Hug of Welcome"; "the wallop packed by a wet bag of cement" is as accurate as "by a bag of wet cement" and it has the advantage of better rhythm. In the past, such imaginary errors as using nouns to modify adjectives were warned against and the false rules survive. A moment's thought, again, will settle the issue. English is a mass of terms in which one noun qualifies another: *wood work, army officer, king fisher, land rover, copper plate, granite face*—hence *music critic* and *drama school* are legitimate too. Indeed, they are more exact than *musical* and *dramatic* would be in those places. Has anyone ever proposed (or accepted) the title of *dancing critic?*

Being overscrupulous will not ensure a prose style at once pleasant to read and adaptable to all usual purposes. The real difficulty is to distinguish among the commonest expressions those that carry meaning readily, precisely, and gracefully. A great many terms now current have been disallowed in this book, singly and by types—some, because they were vague or ambiguous, which is to say *in* expressive; others, because they are now used without regard to the fact that they express more or less than the user is aware of. How is this sense of the force of a word arrived at? Consulting a dictionary sometimes helps to remove a misconception; but not unless a doubt comes first and sends one to the dictionary. There is really but one way to tighten one's grip on language and that is by reading.

It is best to read not only widely but a wide variety of things— books, magazines, newsletters, catalogues, annual reports, advertising fliers. But all must be read, not just absentmindedly swept over by the eyelashes. The point is to extract meaning and note where it fails and why, as well as observe the bearing and relations of words when they are adroitly used. Reading of this quality has become uncommon; illiteracy is back, and not solely among the uneducated. Here is one of many writers for the press who have had cause to complain of readers highbrow enough to care about difficult subjects but unable to follow a plain text: "I received a host of letters. . . . I do wish, however, that my respondents had read what I said with the attention they devoted to taking me to task for supposedly saying something else. I did *not* say that I prefer to sit in the rear of the auditorium, but rather that *half* the audience (actually more than half if one includes the balconies) sits in the rear half of the hall. This seemed to me such an obvious statement, requiring no more than grade-school arithmetic for its proof, that I was taken aback at its misinterpretation. Yet *every one* of the letters I received upbraided me for my supposed preference!"

Such readers are clearly not capable of choosing how they speak or write; everything with them resembles a badly conditioned reflex. Whoever wants to write reasonably well is, on the contrary, self-aware and ready to accept any new word or turn of phrase when it fulfills certain conditions he has set his mind on. It is then a matter of ear, association, foresight as to drawbacks and advantages. He is not alarmed or indignant at others' casual errors, but he is adamant against nonsense and absurdity. He knows, for example, that English is not endangered when the plumber, surveying the effects of a leak in the ceiling, says: "I think it has slown." But there is danger when *sex* and *gender* are used with four or five indeterminate meanings.

THE ACCEPTABLE NEW: A SHORT LIST

By way of example, I reconstruct below the reasons that have led me to accept some innovations of recent date. They and others I find *not* acceptable are discussed from the individual (not arbitrary) point of view here recommended. Let me first state my conditions of acceptance: (1) that the newness should no longer jar—i.e., some "usage" has already taken place; (2) that the term be clearly wanted—not just abstractly needed—by reason of a recurrent lack; (3) that the sound and shape conform to the spirit of the language, permitting easy pronunciation and ready derivatives; (4) that no confusion arise with words already in use. These conditions exclude all new Graeco-Latin mongrels and portmanteaus of the Jabberwocky kind.

Now for those few words. Until recently, for obscure reasons, *humans* was considered an illicit form, fit only for comic effect. But being an exact parallel to *animals,* both of them adjectives turned into nouns with crystal-clear meanings, the word gives no cause for further objection. It is doubtful, though, whether *a human* will gain admittance as readily: *a human being* sounds natural and the other incomplete.

Comments about books in the "briefly noted" column seem to be the source of the phrase "a good read." It has a vaguely improper sound at first, but it can claim acceptable form—*a good sleep, walk, buy, swim.* If we do not say *a good eat,* it is because we have the words *meal* and *dish,* whose counterpart is missing in those other phrases. True, we also have *a good book,* but as I understand the meaning of *a good read,* it does not go so far as to label the *book* good. It intends to be somewhat patronizing: "you will enjoy the reading but soon forget all about it." What must be avoided, then, is to say *a wonderful read* when we mean *a wonderful book.*

Turn now to two Latinate words, *data* and *trivia.* The first is now often used with a singular verb, the true singular *datum* being rarely thought of or written. Writers in scientific and other journals use *the data* to mean "the entire set of facts" much as *the agenda* means all the items on the program. If the latter acceptably takes a singular verb, why not the former? Indeed, there seems no reason to deny *data* whatever number fits the thought—the *data is* or *are.* (See page 25.)

*Media* is another Latinism we could have done without. In its attempt to "cover" it is never clear: does it include newspapers or not? One reads: "the press as well as the media"; and next to it is an unrelated use: "the work is a multimedia experiment involving mylar sheets . . ." Besides, what is the proper form of the verb—the media *are* or *is?* To answer question with question: why not boycott the word? *Broadcast(ers)(ing) (news)* will cover all of *media* that is usually meant, namely, television and radio; and when printed sources are also being referred to, it is surprising how well *news* by itself and in the plural will serve: "They tell us in the news . . ."/ "The news that month were chiefly concerned with . . ."/ "I just don't believe those news people . . ." By the way, to refer to both newspapers and weekly journals of opinion, the handy expression is *the public prints.*

That leaves only the artistic effort unprovided for. Here reflection suggests two courses—either a name for a particular mixture, as happened with the first "multimedia" genre, opera; or, since the new genres of today are not yet fixed, skip the empty label and simply name the several ingredients, as a reviewer or describer invariably does anyway. French gives a model for a particular pairing: *son-et-lumière;* for us, *light-and-sound.*

With *trivia* the question is also of number and of meaning. *Trifles* was handy and clear before the love-hate for Latin forced it aside to make room for this substitute, which bothers those who know some Latin. For *trivium,* the singular, has a use and a lofty meaning (= half of the medieval curriculum) and its modern deviation brings uncertainty: *trivia is* or *are?* By now, owing to *trivial,* "trifles" lacks the connotation of "common, everyday things," so we must legitimize *trivia,* but in the plural only: a mixture of numerous little things is the very point of the word.

Some words that have long been wanted for frequent use are found at last, often in a form that is cumbrous or learned. Such is *recapitulation,* and its fate could have been foretold—radical amputation. I find nothing wrong with *recap:* it could have been made fresh in that form if someone had thought of the "heads" of a subject being gone over. It clearly differs from *review* and *repeat* and *reiterate,* and it disposes of an ungainly six-syllable word. But do not infer that the guillotine can be set to work ad lib. Shortenings such as *out of sync* will not do: work out the reasons why not.

REVIEW FOLLOWED BY NON-ACCEPTANCE

In a famous dictum by Nero Wolfe, that careful writer Rex Stout disallowed *contact* as an all-purpose verb with the abstract meaning of "get in communication with." Many other writers agree with Stout, citing its awkward sound (especially in the past tense) and the vividness of its concrete meaning in *contact sports* and *electrical contact.* How does a letter or phone call *contact* a person three thousand miles away? If the answer is: "Wouldn't you be willing to say you *got in touch*"? Yes, and that is part of the point: we have this perfectly good phrase and it does *not* say: "I am going to touch Jones." Hence the interloper *contact* is not needed; its sound and what it suggests are unsuitable; and it adds to the number of words that try to "cover" several distinct actions by a general term.

Among general terms, the verb *fund* and verbal noun *funding* have changed in meaning, but cannot be turned back or used in the former sense. They used to mean: provide a fund the income of which would serve a designated purpose. Now it means only subsidize a project. The private foundations and the government have brought on the change by their handouts, which are expressly not to be used as a fund in the old sense. So far, so good; let us all apply for *funding* to our hearts' content. But two extensions might well be disallowed; in an organization that has an income or endowment, the verb *appropriate* suffices at budget time—no need to say "we are funding postage and stationery at $9,000." And in a foundation that decides to stop subsidizing a program, let us keep at bay the emergent *defunding*. It is too liable to confusion—one trustee wanting to *defund* and another rising to *defend*.

What about words of the *pickpocket* pattern? Recent newspaper stories and posters in vehicles warn against *pickpocketing*. Surely, *pocket picking* is the more sensible term. There is such a thing as a *picklock;* would *picklocking* really serve our resentment of *lock picking?* And are we to call the other minor arts *breaknecking, thinktanking, spoilsporting,* and lose sight of the active verb in their designation? We see here the ill effect of the tendency toward the single, generalizing word. It seems convenient to say: "He was pickpocketed while talking on the corner with his friend." But there is no hardship in: "His pocket was picked while, etc." It gives a more vivid view of the deed, it is more agreeable in sound, and it does not falsely suggest a complete "processing" of the victim.

TWO INSOLUBLES

Among people who discuss points of style a perpetual review goes on about two difficulties of English: the *who(m)* question and the *everybody* dilemma. On the first, anarchy reigns, with perversity as consort. Writers who hear nothing wrong in "the aunt who he was staying with" go out of their way to write: "the friend whom she thought was trustworthy." This switching of forms might conceivably become good usage if it were not contradicted by the persistence of the un-switched forms in the usual places. Nor is this all. While many good usagers regularly say: "Who do you wish to speak to?" they will also write: "This is addressed to whomever is in charge," where it should be *whoever.* One can only continue to labor under the burden of having learned the true parallel forms—*who* for subject, *whom* for object, with the single exception *than whom,* which is accounted for by the force of the disjunctive (like: *it's me*).

The trouble with *everybody, anybody,* is: what follows? "Has everybody got *their* tickets?" The plural is a visceral response to the noise and number of the crowd milling outside the entrance. Very well, let's decree *everybody* plural. Then you must say: *"Have* everybody got . . ."* and you will feel like a fool doing it. Besides, how can you impose the plural number on every*one,* any*one,* which bring on the same predicament? The plural has been wished on *none,* of course, but somehow there the *one* is hidden; and when we say *no one* the singular is the only possibility.

If in spite of many casual precedents in the great writers one sticks to the singular for *everybody, everyone,* etc., the further question nowadays is how to by-pass the issue of *he* and *she.* On that score, one point is certain; *he/she* will not do. Enlightened feminists will note that the device would invariably give first place to a *he* no longer neutralized by convention but turned masculine by the trailing *she.* As for reversing the order, *she/he,* besides the worsened sound, incurs the same objection in reverse. In any case, such pairs are disallowed as contrary to the ways of prose and also ambiguous, since the slash may mean *and, or, with, against* ("the landlord/tenant tradition"). Fortunately, the *everybody* often occurs in a context that suggests the appropriate sequel. For instance: "Everybody here has given much of his or her time . . ." It would hardly occur to the speaker to use only one pronoun; the writer can follow suit. But in "Everybody likes his own way in small matters," the convention that he = everybody on earth obtains and cannot be bettered. (See pages 73 and 102.)

Amid these reflections on the links between words and ideas, feelings, and facts; on preferences for sound or suggestiveness; and on choices between old and new, one purpose remains imperative—to be as simple and direct as possible. This aim means: asking what is before the mind's eye—the object one is trying to copy in words—and then stripping away everything that blocks the view. For a final, trivial, yet indicative example, one might take the heading of a regular column in the theater section of a large metropolitan daily. It reads: "Availability of Tickets." Clear enough, but roundabout. And it bears on its front the mark of the modern: abstraction. Compare it with: "Tickets Available," which is the meaning in simple-&-direct.

---

Instead of a NOTE ALSO for this final section, a unique catalogue of contrasted ideas will serve readers and writers as usefully as any list of failures—or even better, for tone and rhythm are present too. Consider also the connotations. Some are obvious, others subtle, still others strange, but clearly there is a reason for each opposing thought. The passage comes from the famous Scene in Hell in Shaw's *Man and Superman.* The devil has just complained that Don Juan has insulted the nice respectable people who have chosen to reside in the nether world as the more enjoyable of the two.

DON JUAN: . . . Your friends are the dullest dogs I know. They are not beautiful: they are only decorated. They are not clean: they are only shaved and starched. They are not dignified: they are only fashionably dressed. They are not educated: they are only college passmen. They are not religious: they are only pew renters. They are not moral: they are only conventional. They are not virtuous: they are only cowardly. They are not even vicious: they are only "frail." They are not artistic: they are only lascivious. They are not prosperous: they are only rich. They are not loyal, they are only servile; not dutiful, only sheepish; not public spirited, only patriotic; not courageous, only quarrelsome; not determined, only obstinate; not masterful, only domineering; not self-controlled, only obtuse; not self-respecting, only vain; not kind, only sentimental; not social, only gregarious; not considerate, only polite; not intelligent, only opinionated; not progressive, only factious; not imaginative, only superstitious; not just, only vindictive; not generous, only propitiatory; not disciplined, only cowed; and not truthful at all —liars every one of them, to the very backbone of their souls.

## TIME OUT FOR GOOD READING VIII

Red Smith (who hated his baptismal names, Waltcr Wellesley) was born a writer rather than an athlete. He edited his school yearbook and got his self-education in the outdoor life as a hiker and fisherman. He learned his literary craft on several newspapers, first as copy editor and later as sports writer, till he won national renown through a syndicated column. Originating in Philadelphia or New York papers, the column was finally a feature of *The New York Times,* which Red Smith joined ten years before his death in 1982.

### Writing Less—and Better?

Up to now, the pieces under my byline have been run on Sunday, Monday, Wednesday and Friday. Starting this week, it will be Sunday, Monday and Thursday—three columns instead of four. We shall have to wait and see whether the quality improves.

Visiting our freshman daughter (freshwoman or freshperson would be preferred by feminists though heaven knows she was fresh), we sat chatting with perhaps a dozen of her classmates. Somehow my job got into the discussion. A lovely blonde was appalled.

"A theme a day!" she murmured.

The figure was not altogether accurate. At the time it was six themes a week. It had been seven and when it dropped to six that looked like roller coaster's end. However, it finally went to five, to three and back to four, where it has remained for years.

First time I ever encountered John S. Knight, the publisher, we were bellying up to Marje Everett's bar at Arlington Park. He did not acknowledge the introduction. Instead, he said: "Nobody can write six good columns a week. Why don't you write three? Want me to fix it up?"

"Look, Mr. Knight," I said, "Suppose I wrote three stinkers. I wouldn't have the rest of the week to recover." One of the beauties of this job is that there's always tomorrow. Tomorrow things will be better.

Now that the quota is back to three, will things be better day after tomorrow?

# Hints Toward Improving Sentences Quoted

Page 14     Nos. 2, 4, and 20 contain words that overshoot the mark; they add nothing to the meaning and at the same time suggest irrelevant ideas. No. 2, for instance, would be clearer and stronger if it ran: "Living here will bring you many great comforts and much pleasure." In no. 4, try *expect* for *anticipate* and use the obvious word for *replication.* In 20, *elegancies* and *efficiencies* should be replaced by concrete terms and the idiom *wax eloquent* restored.

In 5, 7, 8, 10, 11, and 14, the jargon and vogue words to be replaced are: *moment of truth, credibility gap, controversial and controverted, genocide* (= massacre of a whole people), *unrealistic, wishful thinking, non-operational,* and *quantum jump* (see pages 216–217).

In 4 and 11, look carefully at *as of right now* and *personal disinterest* and translate the phrases into straight talk.

Nos. 12, 16, and 17 contain malaprops—words used with the wrong meaning: *apostolic, familiarity,* and *degraded.*

No. 19: The word order here is incoherent. Ask yourself: surgery of what . . . for what? and connect the elements that go together logically.

Page 20     No. 1: Start out: "He wanted . . ." and then try to figure out what he did want.

No. 2: ". . . are asked not to talk . . ." and go on from there.

No. 3: If you don't use *quality* (or *nature* or any other noun) you can come to the point directly.

No. 4: Replace the *-tion* words and other abstract nouns with better ones and query the difference between *unity* and *absence of,* etc.

No. 5: How much would be lost if the writer had said: "A change of character follows events that one comes to see as requiring a review of one's feelings, motives, and choices"?

Nos. B 1–5 are up to you!

Page 27    Nos. 1–20: By now you should have begun to learn how one goes about rewriting. In this group, let me merely point to *some* of the wordings that should make you pause and revise: *positioned, imprinter, extremest/ durable/ previewed for/ area man, citian/ Mycenaeology/ loosed, grip/ coagulate/ inertion/ obliviated/ despoilation/ literally, one at a time/ freshness insurance/ space-age.*

Page 34    Nos. 1 to 30 contain malaprops or misdirections of verbs; here are a few of the less obvious ones: *quixotic/ peroration/ travesties/ smattering/ divert/ quantity/ inestimable/ rankled/ belabor/ beguiling/ pending* (and squint hard at *due to*).

Page 41    In Nos. 1, 2, 5, 7, 8, 9, 12, 17, 19, 20, there is an adjective or a verb that says something other than what the writer intended. In no. 3 the contrast is drawn for you: what does it consist in? No. 10 offers you an image: what do you think of it? Can any part of it be salvaged and made into sense? No. 11 is ambiguous on first reading, because of *of;* on a second reading it is clear that *of* is not possible; what then?

Page 56    Nos. 1, 2, 3, 6, 13, 18, 19, each lack a very short word —*to* or *the.* Put it in and see decent English emerge from misplaced headline style. Nos. 4, 5, 16, 17, 19, and 20 show a clutter of modifiers preceding nouns; rewrite so as to articulate the ideas. Nos. 7, 11, 13, 14, violate idiom, just as 9, 10, and 12 stumble over the adverb-and-infinitive difficulty. Again, in no. 20, one little word could be cut with advantage.

Page 65    In this set the words to watch are *with, as, of, in, from, including, on,* and *it.* Make sure of two things about them: do they link the right portions of the sentence; are they the right link—strong enough—for the job? Also to be found in these sentences are ill-chosen or misplaced modifiers—e.g., *aging, in eight parts, who is two, recommended, called, invisible.* The rest is incoherence.

Page 71    As you read through this collection, you should find yourself stopped by (and jibbing at) such phrasings as: *discovered . . . , offered them/ don't have good . . . credaholics/ an, shall we say/ never saw but was made/ that the students . . . that the college . . . that had prepared/ frames of reference . . . in terms of/ wounded . . . by a policeman/ causing it to its source/ locality, that is for rent/ buys . . . with money in a secret drawer.* Flaws in the other sentences should be obvious and easy to remove.

Page 78    Nos. 1, 2, 4, 6, 7, 8, 10, 13, 15, 16, 18, 19, and 20 are all spoiled by failures of agreement in number, person, or case. Correcting them should require very little effort. In no. 3, the *which* in the parenthesis is ambiguous: what does it refer to—not the prisoners, surely? The sentence must be broken up and a new one made for the "quarrel" idea. No. 5 shows the effect of automatic association: *. . . father, who art in heaven* was put in as a solid block, the writer not noticing that the speaker was talking about himself, not addressing God. No. 9 commits the *one . . . he* fault. In no. 11 *and nor* is absurd. No. 12 is merely awkward; some other way of separating *his* from *Hank* can be found if the relation between the men—brother, cousin, classmate—is invoked. No. 13 suggests that the writer's birth happened twelve times a year. The pretentiousness of *Is a point,* etc. and *aggregate* is matched by the lumpy sequel pivoting on *be admitted,* which should be "is acknowledged" or "recognized." No. 17 would be more idiomatic with *there was,* despite the two bills.

Page 83    In this set, verb tenses are a main object of scrutiny. Consider *may* (three times)/ *would have . . . to have/ if he knows I am* (twice)/ *if he did/ he lived/ would have*

*proposed/ they went/ didn't come yet . . . she did/ if I was
. . . I have never/ she plays/ would of.* Nos. 6, 10, 13, and
18 pose different questions. In 6, would not *my being* be
clearer and more elegant? In 10, the *States's* is surely
foolish. In 13, the idea itself raises doubts as to the intended meaning. In 18, *do* instead of *have* at the end kills
the emphasis.

Page 96    What is called for here is judging, not improving. But
about the middle of the series, from no. 7 on, the false tone
is compounded with misusage: *plenary, abhorrent, circumvented, localized, vintage,* are malaprops; *pendula,
space-age, unhurried, dictates,* are affectations—and there
are a few others to get rid of.

Page 103    Silly, pretentious names for things, metaphors that fail
to strike, circumlocutions in words that are long also,
modifiers in the wrong place or the wrong sense, and lack
of common sense—these singly or in combination make
the score of statements groanworthy.

Page 113    The first three sentences rely on our willingness to jump
over gaps in expression. No. 4 is both rude and contrary
to fact: it is *not* usual for a speech to be graceful and
intelligent. No. 6 assumes that the customer is an idiot
and no. 11 that Professor V. is deranged most of the time.
No. 12 sounds like a bad imitation of Damon Runyon.
No. 15 is only awkward. In 17 and 18, *inestimable* and
*degradation* are miscast—as they were in two earlier sentences. No. 20 is not lacking in clarity, but the amount it
shows could be increased.

Page 126    Stop to reflect on such expressions as: *more than de-
fended/ who isn't . . . isn't/ and . . . for them both/ disguise
. . . proved to be a habit* (an unintended pun, besides)*/
neither . . . or/ if anything/ can't be too hot/ but with/ Due
to . . . sales tax/ but it must not/ more than offset by
. . . know nothing/ often . . . everywhere/ if capsizable/ and
its place/ meat product/ almost antiquated/ for whatever
may be found.*

Page 135    The root meanings to keep a firm grip on in this set of
sentences include the ones that follow, but the list is not
complete: *represent/ check/ exclusive/ break down, sake/*

*positive/ person/ brief/ complete/ wrong/ suspend/ have to/ own/ never/ same/ person.*

Page 141    Decide for yourself what realm of existence or imagination the main figurative word belongs to and then see whether the following or preceding term(s) fall within the same realm. If not, the metaphor is incoherent: *architecture/ flame/ color/ living/ books/ wrap/ catalysis front* (military)*/ whine/ impact/ peninsula/ fulcrum/ abrade/ cushion/ forgery/ linking/ falling/ key/ nudity.*

Page 147    Epithets and other qualifiers cannot all be used alike; their implications must be considered. A girl's "lunchtime stroll" implies her habit of strolling at that time and thus precludes speaking of "her lunchtime murder" unless she killed somebody every day. In a similar way, a modifier that fits the thought when positive will turn inappropriate in the negative. One may say: "the facts were immediately reported," but the journalists' cant phrase "No further details were immediately available" sounds silly because there is no reason to think that full information about anything can obtained at once. If this idea seems strange, because the phrasing is so familiar, transpose the situation. A party goes into a half-empty restaurant: they are served immediately. But if this should not happen and they tell their friends later, "We were not served immediately," the remark clearly implies that they counted on immediate service. In any incident reported as news, there can be no expectation that details will be ready for disclosure immediately. It would be like the foolishness of asking for "an excellent cup of coffee"; excellence and immediacy are qualities observed after the fact; they can never be presupposed.

Page 161    Besides the judgments called for in the outline of demands, notice such wordings as: *gusto/ conflict/ due to/ book of the words/ alleging/ in the circumstances.*

Page 176    This exercise gives no opportunity for hints; as for advice, it is contained in this entire book.

Page 201    In no. 2, why say something twice? In no. 3, why the weak little word at the end? No. 5 is marred by a hyphen. No. 7 is redundant by three letters in one word. No. 15:

*Styli?* Really! No. 17: "future examinations"—what about them? No. 22: "some brevity" is how much? No. 24: *brownly* is an odd adverb and it does not fit; as for the rest, *deformity* describes the sentence too. No. 26: Wouldn't "more or less of a Beagle" be factually sounder? No. 27: Do we distinguish *straight* from *crooked* jackets? No. 29 has one blunder in each line. No. 30: Tautology again, with an annoying lack of punctuation. No. 31: What advice was given about using . . . *a of a* . . .? No. 35: Bad echoes throughout. No. 38: Jargon reigns in writing by commissions; what, by the way, is factually wrong in the cant phrase "You can't prove a negative"? No. 40: Adjectives have one or more distinct meanings, not any old meaning in the neighborhood of those accepted by usage. No. 41: Ponder "prior appointment." No. 42: Imagery must be visualized and controlled. No. 44: Verb tenses and parts need exact adjustment. No. 47: The sentence tries to make a point about spelling. Does the allusion to Hamlet help the reader? No. 48: That little word *for* and that long one *vultural* need attention. No. 49: "A stitch of furniture" is probably what gives the room its upholstered effect. No. 50: This observation calls for a *Who's Who.*

# Index
## words, *Topics,* and AUTHORS

This index was prepared, like that of the previous edition, by Virginia Xanthos Faggi.